Key Concepts in
Tourist Studies

Recent volumes include:

Key Concepts in Urban Studies
Mark Gottdiener and Leslie Budd

Key Concepts in Sport Studies
Stephen Wagg, Belinda Wheaton,
Carlton Brick and Jayne Caudwell

Key Concepts in Community Studies
Tony Blackshaw

Key Concepts in Ethnography
Karen O'Reilly

Key Concepts in Public Relations
Bob Franklin, Mike Hogan, Quentin
Langley, Nick Mosdell and Elliot Pill

The SAGE Key Concepts series provides students with accessible and authoritative knowledge of the essential topics in a variety of disciplines. Cross-referenced throughout, the format encourages critical evaluation through understanding. Written by experienced and respected academics, the books are indispensable study aids and guides to comprehension.

MELANIE SMITH, NICOLA MACLEOD and
MARGARET HART ROBERTSON

Key Concepts in
Tourist Studies

Los Angeles | London | New Delhi
Singapore | Washington DC

First published 2010

SAGE Publications Ltd
1 Oliver's Yard
55 City Road
London EC1Y 1SP

SAGE Publications Inc.
2455 Teller Road
Thousand Oaks, California 91320

SAGE Publications India Pvt Ltd
B 1/I 1 Mohan Cooperative Industrial Area
Mathura Road
New Delhi 110 044

SAGE Publications Asia-Pacific Pte Ltd
33 Pekin Street #02-01
Far East Square
Singapore 048763

Library of Congress Control Number: 2009930951

British Library Cataloguing in Publication data

A catalogue record for this book is available from the British Library

ISBN 978-1-4129-2104-6
ISBN 978-1-4129-2105-3 (pbk)

Typeset by C&M Digitals (P) Ltd, Chennai, India
Printed in India at Replika Press Pvt. Ltd
Printed on paper from sustainable resources

contents

key concepts in tourist studies

acknowledgements

We would like to dedicate this book to all of the tourism academics and scholars who have inspired us over the years. Although these are almost too numerous to mention, they include in particular:

Cara Aitchison, Dimitrios Buhalis, Peter Burns, Graeme Evans, John Fletcher, Derek Hall, Michael Hall, Keith Hollinshead, Howard Hughes, Greg Richards, Mike Robinson, Chris Rojek, Valene Smith, John Tribe, John Urry, Brian Wheeller and Heather Zeppel.

Thank you all for continually moving the field of tourism studies forward and for keeping us all on our toes!

Introduction: Why do we need another book on tourist studies?

The field of tourist studies has come of age with new and highly specialised texts being produced on a regular basis. Where once, in the early days of the discipline, the field was dominated by generic tourism planning and management handbooks, we now have texts covering such diverse tourism related topics as sex tourism, tea tourism, battle-field tourism, Olympic tourism, marine tourism and extreme tourism, to name just a few. How does *Key Concepts in Tourist Studies* fit into this growing literature?

The objective of this book is to present what the authors feel are the key concepts within our discipline in a concise and user-friendly manner. Each of the 40 concepts begins with a simple definition and provides a succinct and well-referenced overview of the topic with illustrative examples drawn from a wide international field. The concepts end with suggestions for further reading, should the user wish to pursue a particular topic in more detail. Useful web resources are provided where appropriate. Throughout, there is cross-referencing between the Key Concepts (given in the text in bold) as tourism studies is a multi-disciplinary field and none of our key concepts is an island.

We hope that this book will be used in a variety of ways. Students of tourism studies/management and those of associated disciplines such as leisure management, events management, countryside management or geography will find it a useful reference text to consult when they need to check up on particular topics (perhaps when beginning an essay or preparing for a tutorial). But the book can also usefully be read from start to finish as a good introduction to the field of study. We have tried to keep our Key Concepts as current as possible, including new topics such as e-Tourism, the Experience Economy, and Health and Wellness Tourism. We have also ensured that the references we cite and the further readings that we suggest are up to date.

We, the authors, have many years of experience in teaching tourism at both undergraduate and postgraduate level in the UK and further afield (e.g. Spain and Hungary) and have approached the writing of this book with our students, past and present, in mind. Tourism is an increasingly global industry which touches more and more people and places as it continues its expansion. The study of this industry touches on a number of other fields of academic study, such as cultural theory, planning, geography, economics, environmental studies, anthropology, marketing, politics and many more. To become conversant with such a wide range of disciplines and their literature is not possible for a student (or indeed for a university lecturer!) but our academic backgrounds and research interests have brought us in touch with a range of subject fields which have allowed us to explore the interdisciplinary nature of tourist studies and, hopefully, contextualise it in a useful way in this book.

One of the common questions for a book of this nature is how were the Key Concepts chosen, and how is it possible to reflect the diversity of a field like tourist studies in only 40 concepts? Our choices were reflected on at great length, including discussions with our publisher and taking into consideration the views of our colleagues and reviewers. Of course, no such book could hope to be fully comprehensive. The choices will also inevitably be contentious for many other academics, and maybe students too. Why did we choose to exclude concepts and topics which seem to be important for others?

Our choices take into consideration a range of factors, including the past, present and future of tourist studies. Some of the concepts are quite well-established now within the academic literature, such as Authenticity, Planning Tourism, Sustainable Tourism and the Tourist Gaze. However, they may be new and unfamiliar to students, or the literature may be so vast or complex that it is difficult to synthesise. Also, as the nature of tourism and society changes rapidly, many of the concepts need to be revisited regularly (e.g. Authenticity in the light of the Experience Economy; the Tourist Gaze in relation to globalization; Sustainable Tourism in connection with climate change; Planning Tourism at a time of Crisis Management, etc.).

Some of the concepts relate to the disciplinary frameworks which can help us to understand tourist studies better, for example Anthropology, Sociology, Economics and Geography. Of course, we could have added to this list Political Economy, Cultural Studies, or Environmental Studies, among others. However, we decided instead to allude to these disciplinary frameworks in the context of other concepts (e.g. Ethical Tourism, Cultural Tourism, Ecotourism).

Many of the concepts are what we might describe as typologies of tourism. This was a deliberate decision, as it is often the case that a student needs a concise summary of a typology of tourism when choosing an appropriate and interesting essay or dissertation subject. Lecturers may also require such material for course outlines and introductory lectures. Therefore, we refer to many typologies of tourism, such as Arts, Business, Cultural, Eco, Festivals and Events, Film and TV, Gastronomic, Health and Wellness, Heritage, Literary, Spiritual and Religious, Rural, Sports and Adventure, and Urban. Many of these are also categorised generically under Special Interest Tourism. Of course, we could have included Space Tourism and other even newer typologies, but it is assumed that tourism will continue to move forward and products will constantly be relabelled and repackaged. For example, Geotourism (discussed under Geography of Tourism) seems to be a combination of Eco and Cultural Tourism rather than a truly new form of tourism.

Some of the concepts refer to types or market segments and not just typologies, for example Backpacking, Ethical Tourism, Gay Tourism, Mature Tourism, Post-Tourism and Sex Tourism. It is often difficult to pin down these 'market segments' and define typical activities and motivations, as they are either so diverse (e.g. Backpacking, Mature Tourism) or covert (e.g. Sex Tourism, Gay Tourism). It is also sometimes difficult to define what is meant by an 'ethical' or a 'post' tourist. Therefore, these issues are discussed in some depth to help clarify these concepts.

Controversies and sensitivities abound in tourist studies and we have referred to many concepts which are the subject of ongoing and unresolved debate. These include Dark Tourism, Identity, Neo-colonialism, and Self and Other. Although these have been the subject of academic discussion for many years, the structure and politics of the world change constantly and so new issues need to be negotiated on an ongoing basis. For example, many countries are now in an era of transition (e.g. post-socialist countries), and are thus seeking new identities, often through tourism. Indigenous and tribal groups are slowly gaining some ground in asserting their true identities through tourism and countering the process of 'othering'. Decisions are still being made about how to deal with the legacies of imperialism and colonialism around the world. Dark tourist sites are being created all the time, one of the latest being Ground Zero in New York. Interpretation of dark heritage also changes constantly as time and space create a distance between events, their victims and their perpetrators.

A few of the concepts are especially topical right now, such as Crisis Management, Destination Management, e-Tourism, the Experience

Economy, Mobility and Regeneration. In several years, other issues may become more prevalent or the terminology will change. However, the impact of tourism on the planet and its people is likely to be an enduring subject (we chose to discuss the impacts of tourism under Planning Tourism). Natural disasters are likely to increase and cause more and more crises for destinations. Terrorism, however, may become less of a threat depending on political negotiations. Mobility will no doubt increase, unless climate change and fuel depletion radically affect the transport industry. Tourism destinations will always need a form of Destination Management, but may also stagnate, decline and regenerate in the meantime. Tourism has arguably always been about experiences, therefore the Experience Economy will continue to be a major theme, however it is labelled.

This all means that whatever concepts we choose to focus on, they may largely be variations of already existing issues in tourism, perhaps just repackaged or relabelled today or in the future. The past, present and future of tourist studies are clearly inextricably connected. We hope that our work reflects this, while presenting some fresh views of concepts which may be incredibly familiar or somewhat new. Whatever your view of our choices, we hope you find this work useful, interesting and thought-provoking.

Melanie Smith, Corvinus University, Budapest, Hungary
Nicola MacLeod, University of Greenwich, London, UK
Margaret Hart Robertson, University of Las Palmas de Gran Canaria, Spain

key concepts in tourist studies

Anthropology of Tourism

> **Anthropology of tourism is concerned with the social and cultural nature of tourism and the behaviour of tourists.**

The anthropology of tourism offers an insight into the socio-cultural dimensions of tourism, such as the behaviours of cultures and societies. International tourists in the second half of the twentieth century started to visit those locations in which many anthropologists had carried out their fieldwork. The interaction between tourists and local people provided a new source of anthropological enquiry (Holden, 2005). Therefore, traditionally in tourism studies, anthropology tended to deal with the impacts of tourism on the lifestyles, traditions and cultures of local people, residents or 'hosts'. Over the past few decades, anthropologists have started to shift their focus from largely negative ethnographic critiques of the cultural impacts of tourism to a more balanced discussion of travel and tourism as a social and cultural phenomenon.

The anthropology of tourism has strong connections to sociology, development studies and behavioural psychology. Anthropology and **sociology of tourism** are two sides of the same coin. Both study the qualitative aspects of the experience of tourism, the former at the individual level of perceptions and aspirations, and the latter at the level of social community analysis. Both anthropology and sociology study identity, differentiation and sense of place. In addition, they focus on the tourist's motivations, attitudes, reactions, relations, interaction with the locals and socio-economic and cultural impact on a resort and its people. As reflected in other Key Concepts (e.g. **self and other, identity**), the anthropology and sociology of tourism look at questions of acculturation, authenticity, identity construction and consumption theory as applied to the tourism industry and activities. Perhaps where anthropology, sociology and economics show potential overlap is in marketing studies, branding, image and consumer psychology. However, the economic focus is on the industrial perspective of scale economies and profit margins, whereas the anthropological/sociological focus is on the social and cultural changes and impacts produced, for example by globalisation. However, anthropology has its own specific characteristics, and tends to be more focused than sociology, which often examines general social phenomena rather than specific ones relating to individual communities or tribes.

Nuñez's 'Tourism, Tradition, and Acculturation: Weekendismo in a Mexican Village' (1963) is often credited as the earliest tourism-related article in American anthropological literature, and Valene Smith's seminal work, *Hosts and Guests* (1977/1989), was to mark the course for the anthropology of tourism to follow in the future, together with Margaret Mead's valuable work in the field of visual anthropology. In 1983, the academic journal *Annals of Tourism Research* devoted an entire issue to anthropological submissions. The work of anthropologists such as Nelson Graburn (1977) focused on tourism as a personal transformative experience, and Dennison Nash (1977) discussed tourism as a form of modern imperialism. Influential too has been the work of Victor Turner on rites of passage (1969), that is, rites that accompany the passage of a person from one social status to another in the course of his or her life. Tourism is seen as a ritual or sacred journey, and its traditional associations with pilgrimage have also been discussed. Turner (1978) describes how the ritual process involves three key stages: the first is the 'separation' stage from the routine of everyday life; the second is entry into a state of 'liminality', where the structures and order of everyday life cease to exist; and the third involves a state of 'communitas', where the normal structures of social differentiation disappear and people are brought together.

Selwyn (1996) identified three main strands within the anthropology of tourism:

- social and cultural change
- semiology of tourism
- tourism's political economy.

Social and cultural change includes the process of acculturation. Anthropologists have been studying acculturation for decades, and it is recognised that tourism is only one of many factors that can lead to permanent cultural change. It is an inevitable fact of tourism that cultural changes occur primarily to the indigenous society's traditions, customs and values, rather than to those of the tourist. This is particularly prominent in the case of tribal or **indigenous tourism**. There are fears that host culture and identity may be assimilated into the more dominant or pervasive culture of the tourist. The homogenisation of culture is often exacerbated by tourists whose behavioural patterns are sometimes copied by local residents. Although tourism may be intermittent and seasonal in some destinations, the constant levels of visitation over time can have a considerable impact on the social and cultural fabric of the host society. Mathieson and Wall (1992) differentiate between acculturation and cultural drift, stating that cultural drift is a phenotypic change to the hosts' behaviour which takes place only when they are in contact with tourists, but which may revert back to normal once the tourists leave. Genotypic behaviour is a more permanent phenomenon whereby cultural changes are handed down from one generation to another. This is most likely to occur where tourism is non-seasonal, its influence is strongly pervasive, or local people are favourably disposed towards its development.

The semiology of tourism relates to signs and symbols. Dean MacCannell was one of the first to make an explicit application of semiotics to the study of tourism. MacCannell (1976) argues that signifiers are the first contact that a tourist has with a site, even though they are merely a representation of the site. This can include travel media, guidebooks and other information sources. The creation of myths, dreams and fantasies is also an important part of semiotics. Myth and fantasy have always been central to the tourist experience. As stated by Rojek (1997: 52), 'Mention of the mythical is unavoidable in discussions of travel and tourism', and by Tresidder (1999: 147), 'tourism at its most simplistic level is concerned with the production and consumption of dreams'. Iconic images, such as the Mona Lisa or the Taj Mahal, are common in tourism marketing. However, the reality may be somewhat disappointing compared to the representation.

The political economy of tourism studies can refer to tourism as a new form of imperialism (see **neo-colonialism).** It can relate to the power relationships in tourism, such as host–guest relations, but also core–periphery and dependency theory. Mowforth and Munt (1998) describe how Western capitalist countries have grown as a result of expropriating surpluses from developing countries, which are largely dependent on export-orientated industries. The notion of core–periphery relationships is used within dependency theory to highlight this unequal, often exploitative relationship. Economists have focused traditionally on core–periphery theory and the growth–dependency relationships between host nations and their Western 'benefactors', but this is also a subject of interest for anthropologists. It is especially significant in neo-colonial countries and developing countries which are dependent on tourism. It is also important to consider who owns culture and in what ways it is appropriated by non-indigenous agencies.

Anthropology of tourism uses qualitative and intense participatory processes to be able to understand what makes a community work, and an individual within that community fit, through extended life histories, participant observations and personal interviews, plus content analysis. Ethnography has become an established methodology in the anthropology of tourism studies. Sociology of tourism does the same on a less subjective and more generalised level, through social and statistical surveys of populations and the reasons for their choices of movement within a determined structure.

See also: authenticity, identity, indigenous tourism, neo-colonialism, self and other, sociology of tourism, tourist gaze

FURTHER READING

Apart from Valene Smith's classic, *Hosts and Guests: The Anthropology of Tourism* (1977 and the updated version 1989), the work of Dennison Nash, Nelson Graburn, Tom Selwyn and Peter Burns, to name but a few, has been valuable towards the consolidation of the field of study.

RECOMMENDED BOOKS

Burns, P. (1999) *An Introduction to Tourism and Anthropology*. London: Routledge.
Nash, D. (1996) *Anthropology of Tourism*. Oxford: Pergamon.
Nash, D. (2006) *The Study of Tourism: Anthropological and Sociological Beginnings*. Oxford: Elsevier.
Smith, V.L. (1989) *Hosts and Guests: The Anthropology of Tourism*. Oxford: Blackwell.

key concepts in tourist studies

Arts Tourism

Arts tourism refers to travel which is motivated by an interest in the performing and visual arts including opera, ballet, music and arts festivals.

Arts tourism is a sub-set of **cultural tourism** and **heritage tourism** and is also closely related to **special interest tourism.** The arts have long been a key motivator for travel with the early Grand Tourists, from the sixteenth century onwards, being keen to experience the theatres, opera houses, concert halls and festivals that Europe had to offer. The buildings were as much a draw as the performances that went on within them and many of these venues still form the basis for arts tourism itineraries today. Including a visit to an arts venue is a popular holiday activity and, typically, arts tourism is generally thought to refer to tourists' visits to the following types of venues:

Type of venue	Examples
Art galleries	Uffizi, Florence; Prado, Madrid
Opera houses	La Scala, Milan; Sydney Opera House
Theatre	Broadway, New York; Royal Shakespeare Company, Stratford-upon-Avon
Ballet	Sadlers' Wells, London; Bolshoi Ballet, Moscow
Classical music	Vienna Konzerthaus; Symphony Hall, Boston
Arts festivals	Edinburgh Festival; Venice Carnival

Wider definitions have, however, recently been suggested which also encompass popular entertainment, contemporary music/pop festivals and ethnic arts (Hughes, 2000; Smith, 2003). As with all aspects of culture, there are definitional problems when looking at arts tourism and its relationship to both popular culture and the wider cultural tourism sector. Should popular seaside entertainment (enjoyed by many as part of their holiday experience) be included? Are pop festivals (a major motivator for youth travel) a rightful part of the arts tourism sector? Could the many art galleries which house historic art collections perhaps be considered to be part of the heritage tourism sector rather than arts tourism attractions? Despite this lack of clarity, arts tourism is certainly seen as an attractive option for many tourists, for the industries that have developed a range of arts tourism products and for regions and cities that either promote their existing arts scene or have pursued arts-led tourism development and urban regeneration strategies (Evans, 2001).

The demand for arts tourism has increased in tandem with a greater maturing of the tourism market. This maturation process has included a greater interest in individualised special interest holidays and the search for deeper experiences, meaning and identity through tourism activities, all of which suggest a greater interest in artistic encounters. It is also true to say that the supply of arts tourism sites and experiences has grown in recent years, with many new arts festivals and flagship arts venues such the Tate Modern in London and the Guggenheim Museum in Bilbao proving themselves to be very popular tourist attractions. The Tate Modern was the fourth most popular free visitor attraction in England in 2007 with over 5 million visitors (VisitBritain, 2008). Increasing numbers of short-break tour operators sell weekend accommodation and theatre ticket packages in major cities, and specialist arts tourism operators provide packages which offer personalised itineraries and additional benefits such as back-stage tours and talks with directors. Some of these companies, such as Prospect Tours, which has been in business for over 25 years, have specialised to the point of offering single-artform packages to discerning and high-spending arts tourists often travelling in very small groups (Prospect Tours, 2009).

However, despite these examples, recent research carried out by ATLAS (Association for Tourism and Leisure Education) in 2007 suggested that arts tourism is significantly less popular than heritage tourism, with over 65 per cent of tourists surveyed stating that they had visited a museum, 52 per cent a historic site but only 24 per cent stating that they had been to an art gallery, 12 per cent to the theatre and 5 per cent to a classical music event (ATLAS, 2007). This may be explained by the fact that heritage sites are usually highly place-specific and are considered to be part of the process of getting to know a destination, while arts performances are often more global in scope. Visitors may consider that historic sites offer them more spontaneity and freedom than a performing arts venue and there is often a language barrier associated with the arts. Of course, heritage and the arts are not mutually exclusive activities and it is often the case that visitors will enjoy historic sites during the day and experience the arts in the evening (Hughes, 2000: 70).

As we can see from above, arts tourists are not necessarily a homogeneous group with shared interests and behaviours. Instead, they are disparate types of visitors who range from those who have a very focused interest in particular art forms to those who are visiting an arts venue in a more casual manner. Hughes has addressed this disparity with his classification of the arts tourist by their levels of motivation and interest. According to Hughes (2000), the *arts core* tourist is one who has chosen to travel in order to see a particular arts performance and the *arts peripheral* tourist is one who will be travelling for some other purpose but will experience an arts performance as part of their trip. The *arts core* tourist can then be further classified as either a 'primary' arts-related tourist (they have made the decision to attend a performance before they leave home) or a 'multi-primary' arts-related tourist (where attending a performance is equally important as their other reasons for being in the destination). Similarly, the *arts peripheral* tourist can be further examined in terms of whether they are an 'incidental' arts-related tourist (a visitor whose interest in a performance is a secondary reason for their visit) or an 'accidental' arts-related tourist (someone who makes their decision to see a performance after they have arrived at their destination and for whom the arts are not part of their initial decision to visit). Such classifications help those involved in the arts tourism sector to understand the complex motivations and decision-making processes of the arts tourist, and this knowledge can aid arts tourism organisations to develop appropriate products and target their marketing efforts.

Arts tourism undoubtedly brings benefits to individual venues and destinations. Additional revenue can be generated through ticket sales and the higher spending that is generally associated with all culturally motivated tourists; moreover, as arts events often take place in the evening, they can encourage more overnight stays. A vibrant arts scene enhances the image of a destination, making it a more attractive place to visit, live and work and arts venues play a leading role in urban regeneration strategies. However, there are some tensions within the arts tourism sector. Those working in the arts often have very different priorities from the wider tourism industry and often the lead times for performances and exhibitions provided by the arts sector are inadequate to allow them to be included in arts tourism holiday packages (Smith, 2003). Finally, there are often anxieties about the impact that an association with tourism can have on the arts – that it may lead to trivialisation, inauthenticity and other negative impacts on the art form itself. Hughes researched the impact that tourism has had on the output of London's Theatreland, where the dominance of tourists in audiences has led to an over-supply of musicals to the detriment of more serious theatre (Hughes, 1998).

Arts tourism, as defined above, will continue to attract relatively small but high-spending groups of visitors and will be seen as a prestigious route to tourism promotion and development in many regions and destinations. However, numerous other forms of artistic experience are enjoyed by participants and enhance the visitor experience:

> the high arts ... often tend to attract audiences who are motivated partly by prestige value or social status of attending such a performance ... Compare this with the genuine and spontaneous delight that spectators and participants often take in a festival, carnival or rock concert and it is not difficult to see why certain arts events are more popular with tourists. (Smith, 2003: 139)

A wider definition of the range of arts performances that are appreciated by tourists and which contribute to the visitor economy may better reflect the scope and impact of contemporary arts tourism. There will always be a market for opera tours, theatre breaks and visits to international arts cities such as Rome, Paris and Florence, but the popular art forms, including rock festivals and light entertainment, are enjoyed by a much wider audience and deserve to be recognised as important contributors to the arts tourism sector.

See also: cultural tourism, festivals and events, heritage tourism, regeneration, special interest tourism

FURTHER READING

This is a rather under-researched area and Howard Hughes' book, *Arts, Entertainment and Tourism,* published in 2000, remains the most thorough and recent examination of this sector. The wider associated cultural tourism field is well covered in Melanie Smith's *Issues in Cultural Tourism Studies* and in the work of Greg Richards, for example *Cultural Tourism: Global and Local Perspectives.*

RECOMMENDED BOOKS

Hughes, H. (2000) *Arts, Entertainment and Tourism*. Oxford: Butterworth-Heinemann.
Richards, G. (ed.) (2007) *Cultural Tourism: Global and Local Perspectives*. New York: Haworth.
Smith, M.K. (2003) *Issues in Cultural Tourism Studies*. London: Routledge.

Authenticity

> **Authenticity in tourism can be defined as the value that tourists and hosts place on the development and consumption of what are perceived to be genuine cultural events, products and experiences.**

Discussions of authenticity are common in the literature of tourism studies and have been central to explorations of the social and cultural impacts of tourism since the American anthropologist Dean MacCannell first published his influential text *The Tourist* in 1976. The increasing influence of the tourism industry, the greater ease of travel and ever-widening range of visited places has increased the urgency of debates on the impacts of tourism on the authenticity of cultures. These debates focus on the ways in which tourism has impacted on the authenticity of:

- the tourists' experience of places and culture
- the culture of the hosts themselves
- the nature of the host–guest relationship
- the production of cultural objects and events consumed (but not necessarily exclusively) by tourists.

The assumption is that tourism and the presence of tourists results in a loss of genuine real culture, to be replaced by trivial, commodified events, products and experiences that debase both the producer and the consumer. Of course, what is 'authentic', 'real' or 'genuine' is difficult to

authenticity

13

define as these are relative terms that are not shared among the world's cultures. Consequently, three different perspectives on authenticity and its relevance to tourism have emerged within the literature of tourism studies, namely:

1 'objective authenticity' – an externally verified truth
2 'constructive authenticity' – an emergent form of authenticity
3 'existential authenticity' – an approach to the genuine that takes into account the individual's own experience (Cohen, 1988; Jamal and Hill, 2002; Wang, 1999).

(1) Objective authenticity assumes that genuine touristic experience and products exist, can be verified as such, but are perhaps less easy to find in contemporary society. Importance is placed on objects made from what we consider to be authentic materials and by indigenous craftspeople or on events and rituals that we perceive as being traditional expressions of genuine cultures. This view of authenticity concentrates on original objects that provide genuine touristic experiences for those who recognise the authenticating signs. Cohen cites the work of Trilling (1972), who traces the provenance of the word 'authenticity' in this context to the world of museums where experts authenticate objects using a range of strict criteria (Cohen, 1988: 374). Objects displayed in museums and, importantly, the information provided on these objects, are generally perceived by the visitor to be genuine and meticulously researched. Of course, the objectivity and authority of the museum and museum curator are now no longer taken at face value and museums are seen as products of the societies that support them: a selective treasure house reflecting past and contemporary power relations (Bennett, 1995; Macdonald and Fyfe, 1996). However, the idea that objective facts can be known about objects or historical events is still central to the work of scientists, anthropologists and archaeologists.

In *The Tourist* (1976), Dean MacCannell suggests that authenticity is a characteristic of pre-modern or primitive societies and that modern tourists are on a pilgrimage to seek that lost innocence. Our contemporary lives have alienated us from the genuine experiences and relationships experienced by our ancestors. Therefore, instead of simply living our own lives, we are increasingly consuming experiences and products that are based on other lives and times and created by the **heritage tourism** industries. Thus:

[t]he modernisation of work relations, history and nature detaches these from their traditional roots and transforms them into cultural productions and experiences ... Modern Man is losing his attachments to the work bench, the neighborhood, the town, the family, which he once called 'his own' but, at the same time, he is developing an interest in the 'real life' of others. (MacCannell, 1976: 91)

Authenticity is essentially a modern concern of the industrialised West (Cohen, 1988: 373). The Romantic Movement of the eighteenth century mourned the triumph of science and the loss of innocence brought about by the industrial revolution and saw nature and the pre-modern as a source of genuine, unadulterated culture. MacCannell (1976) suggests that 'primitive' remote communities have no concept of authenticity and consequently have not yet developed a system of 'front and back stage' to protect their privacy. Once visitors begin to arrive, communities engage in 'staged authenticity', setting up contrived events to satisfy their guests' desires for authentic cultural manifestations. Meanwhile, back-stage, real life continues unadulterated. Back-stage regions thus become holy grails for adventurous independent travellers but, MacCannell suggests, as outsiders, they will never gain entry. Conversely, the work of Boorstin (1964) suggests that tourists are on a deliberate search for 'pseudo-events' and superficial experiences and that they are responsible for the inauthenticity of the tourism industry.

(2) Constructive authenticity argues that reality is not an elusive entity but, instead, a constructed phenomenon. Reality is created in our own minds, which are influenced by our personal worldviews and external social, cultural and political factors. This suggests that ideas of what is authentic are not static but emerge over time and are relative and negotiated. Constructive authenticity is not only formed within the individual's mind but is also created and shared within communities. In their work entitled *The Invention of Tradition* (1983), Hobsbawm and Ranger explore how seemingly ancient traditions are created for contemporary purposes (including tourism) and very quickly become accepted as part of a community's or nation's history. The British Coronation ceremony, the Romantic imagery of Wales and the Scottish Highlands and the symbols of nationhood (for example, flags and national anthems) have all been deliberately, and relatively recently, created to encourage patriotism,

authenticity

15

loyalty or even subservience and yet are considered to be authentic from both the community and the visitor perspective (Hobsbawm and Ranger, 1983).

The tourism industry and its associated media are involved in the business of constructing authenticity as part of the product presented to visitors. Such versions of reality become accepted by tourists as part of the package of holiday experiences, and the power of the industry, the media and other stakeholders in creating attractive versions of reality is considerable. Indeed, John Urry talks of the post-tourist (Urry, 1990/2002) who actively enjoys the artifice of staged authenticity while being aware that this is a game to be played (see **post-tourism**).

(3) Existential authenticity suggests that the individual creates a sense of truth within him or herself (Hughes, 1995; Wang, 1999). The demands of everyday life have led to concerns that we are losing sight of our true selves – the simpler, more playful, natural selves that are repressed by work and responsibilities. The rituals of tourism include relaxation, freedom from constraint and a simpler, more pared-down routine based on sensual enjoyment. Therefore, tourism itself can be seen not as a corrupting and commodifying influence but as a way of being that is genuine and natural. Tourists involved in active participation rather than observation are more likely to experience this sense of existential authenticity. Ooi (2002) notes that there is more chance of this happening if cultural mediators, such as tour guides, absent themselves and allow the tourists to feel they are both part of the local community and experiencing culture bodily. Having a sense of performing within a culture and creatively adjusting the body to the shape of a dance, for example, will create a sense of existential authenticity (Daniel, 1996).

There may be few opportunities and places within our daily lives to experience such existential authenticity and so those environments which do offer such liberation have become increasingly prized. Tourism activities that involve a close association with the countryside such as camping or hiking are therefore popular because they allow individuals to test themselves and rediscover their essential selves. These tourists are seeking authenticity within themselves rather than in the places or objects that they encounter. Wang (1999) suggests that existential authenticity can also be experienced within close family relationships which become more genuine and binding in tourism's playful environments. Other relationships can be equally genuine, however – the experience of being with a like-minded group is akin to a pilgrimage or rite of passage, with the places and events being of secondary importance.

Authenticity is, therefore, a complex and socially constructed concept that is problematic and highly emotive when applied to tourism. It has been suggested that the post-tourist is unconcerned with authenticity which has become an outmoded concept (Urry, 1990/2002). However, the wide range of **ecotourism** and special interest tourism products and businesses that base themselves on authentic, genuine experiences suggest that the concept is still attractive to consumers.

See also: heritage tourism, post-tourism, tourist gaze

FURTHER READING

Dean MacCannell's seminal text *The Tourist* (1976) is a useful starting point for studies of authenticity as is Eric Cohen's work (1988) and that of Boorstin (1964). More recent works include that of Wang (1999) and Jamal and Hill (2002) who provide comprehensive overviews of the issues outlined above.

RECOMMENDED BOOKS AND ARTICLES

Boorstin, D. (1964) *The Image: A Guide to Pseudo Events in America*. New York: Harper & Row.

Cohen, C. (1988) 'Authenticity and commoditisation in tourism', *Annals of Tourism Research*, 15: 371–86.

Jamal, T. and Hill, S. (2002) 'The home and the world: (post)touristic spaces of (in)authenticity', in G. Dann (ed.), *The Tourist as Metaphor of the Social World*. Wallingford: CABI. pp. 77–107.

MacCannnell, D. (1976) *The Tourist: A New Theory of the Leisure Class*. London: MacMillan.

Wang, N. (1999) 'Rethinking authenticity in tourism experience', *Annals of Tourism Research*, 26 (2): 349–70.

authenticity

Backpacking

> **Backpacking is independent travel undertaken by individuals or small groups, which tends to be flexible, low budget and with light baggage.**

Backpacking is the very essence of independent travel, offering an unlimited level of flexibility and use of alternative means of transport and accommodation to the types used by the conventional 'tourist'. In many ways, the backpacker has been mythified as the 'anti-tourist', although it has been seen that where the backpackers first 'explore' as uncharted, exotic destinations, they spearhead package or timeshare tourism, Goa being a prime example. Originally identified with the Hippies and the drug culture of the sixties and seventies, and thus, following a large part of the Silk Trade Route, backpackers are now moving more as a result of budget travel and IT. Backpackers are the epitome of the 'uninstitutionalised' traveller as envisaged by Cohen (2003), and the 'allocentric' explorer as envisaged by Plog (1974) (see **self and other**). A quick surf around the websites for backpackers on the internet will reveal certain aspects held to be common to all: they are intrepid travellers who want to go light and low-cost, and who wish to see the world and experience everything while they have the chance. This can include students on 'gap years' before or after attending university, retired people, or even executives taking a break from a stressful working life.

Much of the recent literature in the field of backpacker tourism (e.g. Richards and Wilson, 2004 and Hannam and Ateljevic, 2007) has been based on research which answers questions such as the following:

- Why do people become backpackers?
- Which destinations do they choose?
- How do they travel?
- What do they experience on their travels?
- How has the backpacker experience changed over time?
- What impact does backpacking have on later life?

Although backpacking has traditionally been dominated by young people and students, it is increasingly attracting middle-aged tourists, who perhaps reach a mid-life crisis and can give their life some new perspective and meaning through backpacking. Richards and Wilson (2004) explore the idea of backpacking as a form of nomadic experience which is a response to the alienation of modern society. For example, some of the authors in Hannam and Ateljevic (2007) comment on the ability of middle-aged women to find new freedom and express their various identities through backpacking. Backpacking is also thought of as a form of self-development. Richards and Wilson (2006) suggest that long-distance youth travel of this kind is primarily based on a collection of unique experiences, building on self-identity narratives, and enjoying an element of risk and adventure.

These recent publications also explore in some detail the relationship between backpackers and the enclaves they create in destinations. Richards and Wilson (2004) suggest that the 'global nomad' manages better than most tourists to transcend physical and cultural barriers with ease. However, although the aim of backpackers is usually to experience 'real' and 'authentic' places and people, they often end up seeking the company of other backpackers and creating geographical and social enclaves where few locals can be found. Richards and Wilson (2006) describe enclaves as places which have been created by backpackers and travellers since the 1960s. These are locations where they can take a rest from the harsh reality of travelling and 'refuel'. This might include taking a hot shower, eating familiar (Western) food, using the internet, or watching the latest movies. It is also a place where they can relate their stories to other travellers and confirm their status as an 'adventurer'. Examples include the Khao San Road in Bangkok, which is now avoided by many backpackers as it has become too enclavic.

Increased mobility of information, thanks to the internet and IT in general, reduced prices of transport (with student or discounted rail passes figuring highly as motivating forces) and networks of decent alternative accommodation (hostels, campsites, community and volunteer tourism) have allowed for this sector, previously considered to be of minor importance, to grow exponentially in the twenty-first century. Backpacking usually consists of a longer period of time spent travelling than organised tourism, and tends to take in more than one site, with the travel along the road forming a major part of the experience, in contrast to package tourism where the travel is seen as the necessary means to an end, rather than as an end in itself. Backpackers, as a result, are well-prepared and well-informed about the route to be taken, usually depending heavily on the 'word of mouth' of other backpackers as to where and what to visit and do along the way. Backpackers often like to think of themselves as independent and flexible; however, they tend to follow quite well-trodden paths because they take the advice of other backpackers or they rely extensively on the 'backpackers' bible', the *Lonely Planet Guide*.

Although backpackers are envisaged as more set on interacting with other peoples and cultures, Cohen (2003) has written extensively, showing that, in fact, they are seeking to meet up with people like themselves, and spend much more time interacting with other backpackers than with the locals. In another article, Cohen (2008) shows how backpackers can be rejected by the locals – in this case in Thailand – above all by those sectors interested in upgrading the product on offer.

Backpacking is now divided into various sections, such as 'gap-packing' and 'flashpacking'. The former, 'gap-packing', refers to the gap year taken between secondary school studies and further education, on an ever-increasing basis, by young school-leavers. 'Flashpacking' is completely different. 'Flashpackers' are Bobous, bohemian but bourgeois, mixing a wanderer's lifestyle with the bourgeois trappings of modern existence, such as the iPod, the digital camera, and the PDA. Anthropologists and professional photographers, such as those contracted by *National Geographic*, are backpackers, but of a completely different ilk from the gap-packer or ordinary backpacker. They travel to live and to observe other people in distant places, and to register these observations for other people to learn and profit from their studies. Flashpackers may travel in style but 'slum' it in the local site of observation. Flashpacking has allowed for photographers, such as Sebastião Salgado, to achieve the photographic registers in Africa that he required to alert the world to the desperate situation being faced by the African continent.

There are still some contentious issues surrounding backpacking as a form of **neo-colonial** tourism, where the power dynamics are in favour of relatively wealthy, middle-class travellers, even if they happen to be extremely young. Host–guest relations can still be fraught despite the fact that backpacking is often presented as a more **ethical** or **sustainable** form of tourism. In reality, the behaviour of backpackers, especially large groups (e.g. many Israeli backpackers travel in groups on post-military service trips) may not differ radically from that of package tourists. One only has to think of the backpacker rave parties on the beaches of Goa and full-moon parties in Thailand to find evidence of this. Nevertheless, the Western dominance in backpacking is starting to change as young Chinese start to take up this Western habit (Richards and Wilson, 2004).

FURTHER READING

The work carried out by Erik Cohen (2003; 2008) has been particularly influential here. More recently, publications have emerged specifically on this subject, for example Richards and Wilson (2004) and Hannam and Ateljevic (2007).

RECOMMENDED BOOKS AND ARTICLES

Cohen, E. (2003) 'Backpacking, diversity and change', *Journal of Tourism and Cultural Change*, 1 (2): 95–110.
Cohen, E. (2008) 'Death of a backpacker: incidental but not random', *Journal of Tourism and Cultural Change*, 6 (3): 202–28.
Hannam, K. and Ateljevic, I. (eds) (2007) *Backpacker Tourism: Concepts and Profiles.* Clevedon: Channel View.
Richards and Wilson (2004) *The Global Nomad: Backpacker Travel in Theory and Practice.* Clevedon: Channel View.

Business Tourism

> *Business tourism involves the travel and accommodation of people who are travelling for reasons of employment or professional interest. This includes meetings, seminars, conferences, exhibitions, trade shows and corporate hospitality.*

Rogers (2003) suggests that although business and conference tourism is a modern phenomenon mostly developing over the past fifty years, the notion of travelling for meetings, politics, commerce or trade is an ancient practice dating back to the Romans or even earlier. In its contemporary incarnation, business tourism has been growing exponentially over the past ten or fifteen years, with huge investments in conference facilities being made since the 1990s. Over the past ten years, it was estimated that there has been a 53 per cent increase in business tourism, and the spending of business tourists in the UK, for example, exceeded that of leisure tourists by the early 2000s, and constituted up to a third of all tourist spending (Business Tourism Partnership, 2005).

Davidson and Cope (2002: 3) describe business travel as 'all trips whose purpose is linked with the traveller's employment or business interests', and IMEX (2006) defines business tourism as 'the provision of facilities and services to the millions of delegates who annually attend meetings, congresses, exhibitions, business events, incentive travel and corporate hospitality'. However, there are some debates about the term 'business tourism', as many researchers and practitioners see business and tourism as diametrically opposed (i.e. tourism was traditionally seen as a leisure activity which represented a *break* from work). These days, it is sometimes hard to differentiate between working time and leisure time, and thus the combination of the two has become more widespread. For example, many business hotels provide golf courses or spas for their guests, and many leisure hotels have conference facilities and internet access. Davidson and Cope (2002) differentiate between business travel and business tourism, suggesting that business tourism is a more occasional feature of work and often takes place in groups (e.g. corporate hospitality, trade shows, conferences and incentive trips). Swarbrooke and Horner (2001) suggest that business travel tends to take people from one place to another, but it does not always include tourism (e.g. when it is for one-day meetings, conferences or seminars). However, most researchers and practitioners agree that the terms are by no means clear-cut.

key concepts in tourist studies

Business travel and tourism can include the following main activities:

- Individual business travel (i.e. travel to carry out work in an alternative location).
- Meetings (e.g. conferences, workshops, seminars, annual general meetings, product launches).
- Exhibitions (e.g. trade shows, trade fairs and consumer shows).
- Incentive trips (e.g. trips which are offered to employees as a reward for good work or performance).
- Corporate hospitality (e.g. lavish entertainment offered to high-profile clients and VIPs to create goodwill and build rapport).

(after Davidson and Cope, 2002)

However, Swarbrooke and Horner (2001) identify up to 15 categories of business travel and tourism, adding training courses, short-term migration for employment, student and teacher exchanges, taking goods to markets or to customers, military service away from one's own base, charity and aidwork, diplomatic service, even commuting to work. They further divide these categories into sub-sets, indicating the complexity of the field. The management of business tourism is also quite complex, as it involves a number of different sectors, including not only transport and accommodation providers, but also specialist intermediaries such as business travel agents, exhibition companies, event management companies, catering services, etc.

The acronym MICE is also used frequently in the field of business travel and tourism and stands for 'Meetings, Incentives, Conferences, Exhibitions', but is not always a favoured term for many professionals (Davidson and Cope, 2002). Ladkin (2006) suggests that each sub-section of MICE has very different characteristics, and that the industry needs to recognise this. Although the sub-sections may have similar accommodation needs or technological requirements, they need to be managed in a different way and by different agencies. For example, conference tourism tends to include leisure elements and social programmes, and incentive trips can be almost entirely leisure-orientated, especially if they are offered as a reward to employees. On the other hand, some business meetings may require little more than catering.

The Business Tourism Partnership (2005) suggests that the principal characteristics of business tourism include the fact that it is of higher quality and higher yield than other forms of tourism. It can also be more sustainable, partly because it is non-seasonal and can create year-round employment opportunities. Business tourism can also be a catalyst for regeneration, as it can help to stimulate inward investment and may improve infrastructure. Many business travellers also tend to return to destinations which they enjoyed, with families or friends for leisure vacations.

This means that business tourism is a highly lucrative and attractive sector for most destinations, but it is also incredibly competitive, and the need for top-quality facilities and services is paramount. Business tourism is increasing globally, although European cities and destinations struggle to compete with North American and Australian ones, which can offer better facilities. For example, the MPI (2006) noted that Europe is failing to capitalise fully on increased interest from Asian travellers because many countries do not have adequate services and infrastructure for that burgeoning market. This is especially true of Central and Eastern Europe, and a global study by the Economic Intelligence Unit (EIU, 2004) showed that the only European cities that made it into the top twenty were Vienna, Zurich, Geneva, Copenhagen and Stockholm. The EIU (2004) carried out an assessment of some of the world's best and worst business and conference destinations. Five broad categories were selected: stability, healthcare, culture and environment, infrastructure and cost. Some of the most important issues were availability of good hotels, quality food and drink, efficient public transport and taxi services, distance to the airport and climate, as well as per diem costs. This meant that only Canadian, American and Australian cities made it into the top ten. However, it has been noted more recently that American destinations are now losing out to European ones in the business market because of the threat of terrorism and stringent security measures (USA Today, 2006). In addition, studies undertaken by the International Congress and Convention Association (ICCA, 2007) showed in their Country and City Rankings for number of meetings organised that the top five countries were the USA, Germany, Spain, the UK and France, and the top five cities were Vienna, Berlin, Singapore, Paris and Barcelona.

The main growth markets in the future in terms of business tourism are likely to come from Asia, especially China and India. The number of female travellers and those in older age groups is also expected to rise (EIBTM, 2004). Ladkin (2006) also notes that destinations need to accommodate disabled business travellers. Business travel and tourism must be receptive to a number of external factors. For example, global climate change will affect the extent and nature of business travel in the future, inevitably becoming more expensive as fuel costs rise. Companies may need to be more selective about which trips are essential, and which could be dealt with using new technology instead (e.g. tele-conferencing). Global terrorism has already had a major impact on international travel, and businesses will choose their destinations carefully to maximise the safety of their employees. Growing competition and increasingly demanding consumers will mean that service quality will also be a major issue for business tourism destinations and operators. This is a real challenge for both existing and emergent destinations.

See also: *special interest tourism*

FURTHER READING

Two of the best textbooks on this subject are Swarbrooke and Horner (2001) and Davidson and Cope (2002) However, many new books are emerging which focus on one aspect of Business Tourism such as conferences, e.g. Rogers (2003). This is a fast-growing and dynamic sector of tourism, and these books may become quickly out of date. Reference should therefore be made to more up-to-date statistics, such as those of the International Congress and Convention Association (www.icca world.com).

RECOMMENDED BOOKS

Davidson, R. and Cope, B. (2002) *Business Travel: Conferences, Incentive Travel, Exhibitions, Corporate Hospitality and Corporate Travel.* New Jersey: Prentice-Hall.

Rogers, T. (2003) *Conferences and Conventions: A Global Industry.* Oxford: Butterworth-Heinemann.

Swarbrooke, J. and Horner, S. (2001) *Business Travel and Tourism.* Oxford: Butterworth-Heinemann.

Crisis Management

> *Crisis management in the tourism industry could be defined as the way in which tourism destinations and the tourism industry respond to sudden disasters or catastrophes, which can be natural or man-made.*

Crisis management in the tourism industry has become something of a necessity in recent years due to the growing number of natural and political disasters at numerous destinations. As stated by Faulkner (2001: 135), 'Tourism destinations in every corner of the globe face the virtual certainty of experiencing a disaster of one form or another at some point in their history'. Although crisis management has been an established research field in business and management sciences for nearly 40 years, it was not until the early to late 1990s that tourism researchers and practitioners started to discuss the concept in public forums and to produce guidelines for industry practice. Tourism is now the second largest industry in the world after oil (WTTC, 2008a), but it is also one of the most vulnerable to crises, which can impact significantly on the reputation and image of destinations for many years.

Crises can occur at organisational, industry, destination, national or international level. Many localised, one-off incidents (e.g. a bomb or kidnapping) can still affect the destination, or even the whole country, for many years to come. Some disasters, such as hurricanes or tidal waves, affect whole regions. Some local or national events can affect the whole tourism industry for a long time after (e.g. 11 September in New York in 2001). Many diseases, especially airborne ones like SARS, bird flu or foot-and-mouth disease can easily be transferred across borders, and are not confined to one region or country (e.g. SARS spread from China to Canada in 2003 because of international travel, and swine flu from Mexico to other countries in 2009).

Many tourism academics and researchers over the past few years have attempted to categorise crises. Faulkner (2001) distinguished between crises and disasters, suggesting that many destination managers cannot prepare for the catastrophic effects of a disaster over which they have very little control. They can, however, help to avert a crisis through careful planning and management.

Aktas and Gunlu (2005) show how disasters and management failures can become crises:

A triggering event: Crises are a result of an unexpected event or flow of events evolving in a short period and with potential to cause significant change, challenging the existing structure or survival of the crisis-struck tourist destination.

Threat and damage: The crisis-triggering event is so significant in its impact that it causes panic and loss of control among those directly affected and would pose a threat to the effective functioning of the destination, with some short-term damage experienced instantly.

Need for action: In order to overcome long-term effects, crises require urgent and expert action through cooperation of key authorities and the industry stakeholders.

The likelihood of crises has increased because of the impacts of climate change and the growth of global terrorism. Economic recessions and political instability also have a major impact on the tourism industry, and these factors are generally unpredictable. The challenge for the tourism industry is, therefore, not only to deal with crises if and when they happen, but to be prepared for them at any time and to react appropriately. This might include developing crisis management plans for every eventuality and training staff accordingly.

Crises which can affect the tourism industry could include the following:

- terrorism
- disease
- food poisoning
- transport disasters
- political unrest (e.g. riots)
- natural disasters (e.g. earthquakes, hurricanes, fires, volcanoes)
- crime
- kidnapping
- war.

Some of the worst natural disasters in recent years include Hurricane Katrina in the USA in 2005, the earthquake in Pakistan in 2005, and the Indian Ocean tsunami in 2004/2005. Global terrorism has increased significantly since September 11 – for example, the Bali bombings in 2002 and 2005, the Kenya bombing in 2002, and the London bombings in 2005. Such incidents are an ongoing feature in some destinations, for example Egypt and Israel. Health crises can also badly affect tourism: the foot-and-mouth disease outbreak in the UK in 2001, the spread of SARS in 2002/2003, bird flu in Asia in 2005, swine flu in Mexico in 2009, and the ongoing HIV pandemic in Africa. Even outbreaks of food poisoning (e.g. ongoing incidents in the Dominican Republic) can adversely affect the destination's reputation, even if only one or two hotels are affected. Major transport disasters, such as plane crashes, are thankfully relatively rare but can have a significant impact on travel. For example, nearly 1000 people lost their lives when a ferry sank between Sweden and Estonia in 1994. September 11 was, of course, devastating for the airline industry for many months, even years afterwards. It is generally agreed that political threats, including terrorism, wars, civil unrest or long-term conflicts (e.g. Israel, Northern Ireland) tend to cause more severe and lasting damage to tourist destinations than other forms of crisis (Aktas and Gunlu, 2005). The kidnapping of tourists is a common political act, for example in Egypt, Kashmir, even Turkey (e.g. German tourists were kidnapped near Mount Ararat in 2008). South Africa has suffered losses in tourist numbers in recent years because of escalating crime and there have been fears about security for the 2010 World Cup football championship.

The impacts of crises can be many and varied, and they sometimes last for many years or can be short-lived. This mainly depends on the type of media which is used to convey the news to the world and the public. Journalistic sensationalism and bias are rife in most countries, and it is common for exaggerations of the truth to be transmitted, causing panic and chaos.

Typical Impacts of a Crisis

- businesses go bankrupt
- major job losses
- tourists lose money/holiday
- extensive damage to sites or destination attractions
- significant environmental damage
- local people and/or tourists hurt or killed
- tourists scared or deterred from visiting destination
- image damaged long-term.

Management failures tend to be common, so global guidelines have been prepared (e.g. PATA, 2003). One of the problems with preparing for crises is that the probability of a disaster or attack can be very low, but the impacts can be exceptionally high. A crisis management plan is similar to an insurance policy – it is expensive and rarely necessary, but it is foolhardy not to have one. A response to a crisis (if it happens) is needed quickly and urgently. There is no time to prepare a plan in the aftermath of a disaster. PATA (2003) suggest that destinations should follow a process whereby they detect early warning signals and learn how to reduce the impact of a crisis if it happens. Staff should be trained in knowing how to deal with a crisis and respond. For example, PR, managing the media and reassurance of the public, is particularly important, and responses should be quick and positive. The recovery period may also be a difficult one, and staff may need support and reassurance before returning to work.

Overall, the impacts and subsequent management of a crisis will depend on the suddenness and severity of the crisis. However, most destinations and practitioners now recognise the importance of immediate reactions, the careful management of media, the involvement of all stakeholders, and the benefits of learning long-term lessons from other destinations which have suffered crises. There are now numerous guidelines and publications available to practitioners, therefore the management of crises in tourism is improving all the time.

See also: *tourism planning*

FURTHER READING

Many new books have been written on this subject in recent years, including Glaesser (2006) and books of edited case studies such as Laws et al. (2006) and Proff and Hosie (2009). Relevant journal articles can also be found in most mainstream Tourism journals. Reference should also be made to some of the industry-orientated publications which offer practical guidelines, such as PATA (2003) *Crisis – It won't happen to us!* (www.pata.org/patasite/fileadmin/docs/general/CrisisJune07.pdf).

RECOMMENDED BOOKS

Glaesser, D. (2006) *Crisis Management in the Tourism Industry*. Oxford: Butterworth-Heinemann.

Laws, E., Prideaux, B. and Chon, K. (eds) (2006) *Crisis Management in Tourism*. Wallingford: CABI.

Proff, C. and Hosie, P. (eds) (2009) *Crisis Management in the Tourism Industry: Beating the Odds?* Aldershot: Ashgate.

crisis management

> *Cultural tourism could be defined as tourism that focuses on cultural attractions, activities and practices as major motivating factors for travel. It can include a number of sub-sectors, such as Heritage Tourism, Arts Tourism, and Indigenous Tourism.*

Cultural tourism has traditionally been difficult to define because of diverse and changing definitions of culture. The cultural theorist Raymond Williams (1976) once described culture as one of the most complex words in the English language, going on to define it as referring to both 'the arts and learning' and 'a whole way of life' of people. This means that culture is about the past and traditions (e.g. history and heritage), creative expression (e.g. works of art, performances), and also about peoples' ways of living, their customs and their habits. Many tourists are just as interested in the culture of different peoples around the world as they are in historic sites, monuments, museums and galleries.

Richards (1996) proposes two definitions of cultural tourism for his research for ATLAS (the Association for Tourism and Leisure Education and Research). These are:

> **Technical definition**: 'All movements of persons to specific cultural attractions, such as museums, heritage sites, artistic performances and festivals outside their normal place of residence.'
> **Conceptual definition:** 'The movement of persons to cultural manifestations away from their normal place of residence, with the intention to gather new information and experiences to satisfy their cultural needs.'

However, these definitions do not take into consideration culture as a way of life of people, but Richards' later definition (2001a: 7) is more comprehensive, suggesting that cultural tourism covers

> not just the consumption of the cultural products of the past, but also of contemporary culture or the 'way of life' of a people or region. Cultural tourism can therefore be seen as covering both 'heritage tourism' (related to artefacts of the past) and 'arts tourism' (related to contemporary cultural production).

Richards also argues that cultural tourism does not only represent passive consumption, that is, only looking at historic sites, museum collections, paintings or theatre performances. Many tourists are increasingly becoming interested in 'creative tourism', which involves participation in cultural activities (e.g. painting, photography, crafts, dancing, cookery). There has also been a growth in emphasis on the **experience economy**. Smith (2009: 23) therefore suggests the following definition of cultural tourism:

> Passive, active and interactive engagement with culture(s) and communities, whereby the visitor gains new experiences of an educational, creative, and/or entertaining nature.

This definition reflects the shift towards more active and interactive forms of cultural tourism, as well as suggesting that education and entertainment are not mutually exclusive, and that tourists engage with many different cultures and communities at the same time.

Most cultural tourists have a specific interest in the location and **authenticity** of the cultural experience. Smith (2003) differentiates, for example, between the so-called **post-tourism** and cultural tourism, concluding that cultural tourists are more interested in genuine interactions with local communities and their traditions. Cultural tourism may be described as 'travel' whereby the cultural tourist sees him- or herself as an adventurer or explorer. This is particularly the case in the context of **indigenous** and ethnic tourism, where tourists want to visit local people in their natural habitat, which can sometimes be quite remote (e.g. in a jungle, desert or small village). Richards' (1996) research also suggests that cultural tourists tend to be better educated than the average tourist and to be more sensitive to the impacts of tourism on local people, environments and cultures.

Cultural tourism is often cited as a growth industry and a sector of tourism which is becoming more diverse. It is therefore necessary to consider some sub-sectors or sub-segments of the product and the market. Hughes (1996) differentiates between 'universal', 'wide', 'narrow' and 'sectorized' cultural tourism. These definitions correspond broadly to perceiving culture as a whole way of life; to engaging with specific ethnic or indigenous groups; to experiencing the 'artistic and intellectual' activities of a society; and to visiting specific heritage attractions or arts venues.

According to some authors, culture can be *one* motivating factor for many so-called cultural tourists, but not necessarily the primary one.

McKercher and du Cros (2002) suggest five types of cultural tourists: (1) the *purposeful* cultural tourist, for whom culture is a primary motivator and who seeks a deep cultural experience; (2) the *sightseeing* cultural tourist, who travels for cultural reasons but seeks a shallower experience; (3) the *serendipitous* cultural tourist, who is not primarily motivated by culture, but who gets into a deep cultural experience by chance; (4) the *casual* cultural tourist, for whom culture is a weak motivating factor and who seeks a shallow experience; (5) the *incidental* cultural tourist, for whom culture is not a stated motive, but who does visit cultural attractions.

However, because of its diversity and complexity, cultural tourism can perhaps best be divided into a number of sub-sectors or typologies. These might include **heritage tourism**, **arts tourism**, creative tourism and **indigenous tourism**. The kinds of environments visited might be urban or rural, naturally occurring or man-made. Each of these areas tends to have its own specific issues, relating to both critical studies and practical management. Below is a summary of key issues:

Heritage tourism focuses on both tangible sites and intangible traditions. Typical attractions might include historical monuments, historic towns and World Heritage Sites, as well as the history and lifestyles of indigenous communities. The interpretation and representation of heritage can be complex and contested, with issues relating to ownership being paramount. Many heritage sites also suffer from over-visitation, so conservation and visitor management are also key themes within this sub-sector of cultural tourism. The concept of intangible heritage is becoming more significant, and UNESCO (among other heritage bodies) has recognised this fact. UNESCO has, therefore, developed a Convention which helps to protect intangible cultural heritage, including language, stories, art styles, music, dance, religious beliefs – in other words, those aspects of culture not directly embodied in material things (UNESCO, 2009).

Arts tourism focuses on both visual and performing arts, as well as cultural **festivals and events**. This may include visits to galleries or museums, theatres and concerts, as well as more experiential forms of tourism relating to the arts and crafts of local people, or their performances of dance and music. Increasingly, cultural festivals – particularly carnivals – are attracting large numbers of visitors. There are some concerns that tourism can dilute or 'trivialise' the arts through commercialisation. Many ethnic and indigenous art forms are certainly becoming more popular on a global scale, and so care needs to be taken that they are not over-commercialised or exploited.

Creative tourism consists of more active participation in cultural tourism activities, whereby tourists create something on an individual or collective basis. Holidays are increasingly being developed around artistic and creative practices, such as painting, pottery, photography or dance. In some cases, the activities will be undertaken by groups of tourists in isolation from local communities, but in others, the host–guest interaction will constitute a major part of the experience. UNESCO (2006) has recently been at the forefront of the so-called creative tourism movement, advocating that it should include more access to culture or history and involve doing something experientially, with an authentic engagement in the real cultural life of a place and its people.

Urban cultural **tourism** focuses on activities that take place within towns or cities. Many of these may relate to heritage or the arts, especially in historic or cultural cities. However, former industrial cities are increasingly being regenerated, and are offering new attractions in the form of large leisure and entertainment complexes, new cultural or creative quarters and 'mega-events' (see **regeneration**).

Rural cultural **tourism** tends to take place in countryside areas where the natural landscape may be a major attraction. Some activities focus on environmental and agricultural developments (e.g. eco-museums or agro-tourism), **gastronomic** and wine tourism, or cultural landscapes (e.g. those associated with **literary** or **film tourism**). Increasingly, many **health and wellness** or holistic centres are being constructed in rural areas, many of which include cultural and creative activities as well as spiritual ones (e.g. yoga, meditation).

Ethnic or **indigenous** cultural **tourism** attracts those tourists who are keen to visit local people in their homes and to partake of their traditions and cultural practices. The main motivating factor will be the genuine and spontaneous interaction between tourists and locals (although this can often be 'staged' without tourists realising). This is a form of tourism that needs to be managed sensitively, as many indigenous peoples have been treated harshly by colonial administrators and successive governments, who have deprived them of land and tried to dilute or eradicate their traditional lifestyles. Activities may include trekking or participation in cultural or creative practices (e.g. crafts production or dance). Although the environmental and socio-cultural impacts can be significant, cultural tourism can also help to raise the political profile of indigenous groups and contribute to the renewal of traditions and cultural pride.

Popular or contemporary cultural tourism focuses on some of the popular pursuits that many tourists are likely anyway to enjoy in their leisure time (e.g. shopping, sports, television, cinema). It represents an extension of these interests by supplying new attractions where tourists can enjoy several of these activities simultaneously (e.g. entertainment complexes, shopping malls, theme parks, film and TV studios or trails). However, these activities are more often said to belong to the category of **post-tourism** rather than to cultural tourism.

In conclusion, it is clear that debates about cultural tourism are changing all the time as tourism itself grows and diversifies, and critical and post-modern studies challenge definitions of culture. However, sub-dividing typologies and profiles can help to understand the nature and scope of cultural tourism.

See also: arts tourism, festivals and events tourism, heritage tourism, indigenous tourism

FURTHER READING

Smith's *Issues in Cultural Tourism Studies* and *Issues in Global Cultural Tourism* offer a comprehensive analysis of both the politics and the management of cultural tourism. Some interesting case studies can also be found in Smith and Robinson's *Cultural Tourism in a Changing World: Politics, Participation and (Re)presentation;* in Leslie and Sigala's *International Cultural Tourism: Management, Implications and Cases;* and in Richards' *Cultural Tourism: Global and Local Perspectives*.

RECOMMENDED BOOKS

Leslie, D. and Sigala, M. (eds) (2005) *International Cultural Tourism: Management, Implications and Cases*. Oxford: Butterworth-Heinemann.
Richards, G. (ed.) (2007) *Cultural Tourism: Global and Local Perspectives*. New York: Haworth.
Smith, M.K. (2003) *Issues in Cultural Tourism Studies*. London: Routledge.
Smith, M.K. (2009) *Issues in Global Cultural Tourism*. London: Routledge.
Smith, M.K. and Robinson, M. (eds) (2006) *Cultural Tourism in a Changing World: Politics, Participation and (Re)presentation*. Clevedon: Channel

key concepts in tourist studies

Dark Tourism

Dark tourism consists of tourist visits to sites associated with death, disaster, warfare, genocide and human suffering. These sites also include memorials to the dead and burial grounds.

As the name suggests, 'dark tourism' refers to tourist activity that is prompted by an interest in the more sombre aspects of the human experience. Lennon and Foley have popularised the term with their research in this area (2000), although other authors have written on the phenomenon in recent years, variously referring to this form of tourism as 'thanatourism' (Seaton, 1996), 'Black Spots' tourism (Rojek, 1993), the 'heritage of atrocity' (Tunbridge and Ashworth, 1996) and 'sensation sites' (Rojek, 1997). The places that come under these writers' scrutiny include cemeteries, battlegrounds, sites of the deaths of celebrities, places where disasters occurred, prisons, torture chambers, genocide sites and memorials. Famous examples include the Père Lachaise cemetery in Paris where Oscar Wilde and Jim Morrison are buried, Ground Zero, former site of the World Trade Center in New York, the spot where President Kennedy was assassinated in Dallas, and death camps such as Auschwitz in Poland, all of which draw tourists in varying numbers.

Dark tourism, as defined by Foley and Lennon, refers in particular to sites associated with *recent* death, disaster and atrocity (i.e. within living memory) and they chart their analysis within theories of post-modernity. Choosing the sinking of the *Titanic* in 1912 as their starting point, the authors believe that dark tourism is a product of post-modern culture with its global communications networks, anxieties about modernity, and its emphasis on commodification. Firstly, 'global communication technologies play a major part in creating the initial interest' (Lennon and Foley, 2000: 11). Then it seems to the authors that dark tourism sites themselves 'appear to introduce anxiety and doubt about the project of modernity' (ibid.), for example the use of rational planning techniques to bring about the Jewish holocaust and the failure of technology when the unsinkable *Titanic* sank, suggest that modernity may not be leading society towards a glorious future. Finally, the consumption inherent in post-modern culture is reflected in the potential of dark tourism sites to combine education with 'elements of commodification and a commercial ethic which ... accepts that visitation is an opportunity to develop a tourism product' (ibid.).

Other authors consider that this form of tourism has a considerably longer history and encompasses a much wider set of sites than Foley and Lennon would suggest. A brief summary of the work of these key authors is provided below.

Rojek, 1993   *Black spots tourism*
In coining the term 'black spot', Chris Rojek suggests a dual meaning associated with the darker side of visitor attractions. Firstly, the actual 'black spot' refers to a site which marks a death or deaths (for example, cemeteries and monuments to the dead). Secondly, the term can also mean disaster sites and the places where famous people have died. In both these cases, tourists visit the sites and leave messages: these may take the form of notes or graffiti or they may be more complex rituals such as role-playing. Rojek cites the example of the James Dean Fan Club who trace the route of his last journey each year on the anniversary of his death in Cholame, California.

Rojek, 1997   *Sensation sites*
Following on from his 1993 work on black spots, Rojek has refined his definition to include a category of tourist sites that he refers to as 'sensation sites'. These are the sites of major contemporary disasters that are associated with violent death, abduction or siege. Examples which Rojek cites in the later work include Lockerbie where the PanAm flight 103 exploded in 1988, or the Zeebrugge ferry disaster of 1987. We could also include more contemporary examples such as the 2001 Ground Zero site of the World Trade Center towers in New York, or Soham in the UK where two young girls were murdered in 2002. What differentiates these particular sites from black spots as defined above is that these sensation sites encourage people to travel both physically and in the mind to the site. Onsite observation or televisual viewing interrupt the everyday routines of the viewers and allow a much higher level of participation in the event than would be experienced in visiting a cemetery or war memorial. There is a sense of collective

(Continued)

(Continued)

experience, made possible by the media's coverage of such events, which may serve to affirm identity and a sense of community through shared engagement in the event.

Seaton, 1996   *Thanatourism*

Seaton suggests that rather than being a modern phenomenon, thanatourism is a tradition that goes back to the Middle Ages and refers to travel that is motivated by a desire to be in the presence of (often violent) death. Early examples include pilgrimages made to sites of the martyrdom or interment of saints. The motivation to visit may be intensified by the levels of fame of any associated persons. Thanatourism is behavioural in that it relates to travellers' motivations rather than to any specific features of the destination. It also includes a continuum of intensity with the most intense form of thanatourism existing where people are motivated solely by a fascination with generalised death, and the most diffuse form taking place where the dead are known to the visitor (for example, where a traveller visits a war memorial to remember a dead relative). Thanatourism does not include any judgemental evaluation as Seaton believes that this type of activity is so widespread and has such a long history that it must be a fascination that we all share.

Tunbridge   *Heritage of atrocity*
and   In their work on dissonant heritage, Tunbridge and
Ashworth,   Ashworth explore examples of heritage sites that
1996   embody discord or lack or agreement in the histories told and the forms of interpretation used. One of the areas of potential dissonance examined is that of the 'heritage of atrocity' – sites of human trauma which are turned into heritage attractions. The authors have identified seven different types of atrocity around which such sites are founded. They are:

- atrocity arising from natural or accidental disasters that have been aggravated by human intervention or neglect (e.g. the European potato blight of the 1840s which led to famine in Ireland)

(Continued)

(Continued)

- 'broad-group' atrocity – perpetrated by one broad category of people upon another (e.g. the slave trade)
- atrocity in war (e.g. the wartime abuse of civilians)
- massacre (e.g. the My Lai massacre of Vietnamese citizens by US troops in 1968)
- genocide – the destruction of large numbers of an ethnic group (e.g. the Jewish Holocaust of 1933–45)
- persecution and judicial processes – a category of atrocity which may be much less serious than the examples cited above – it relates to the discrimination of cultural or linguistic groups or to judicial processes which we may now see as 'atrocious' (e.g. apartheid in South Africa).

In all of the above categories, heritage sites have been developed which attract visitors but provide interpretive challenges about whose heritage is being displayed and how to deal with the conflicting perspectives of atrocity victims and perpetrators.

Although the authors above have very different perspectives on the phenomenon of 'dark tourism', it is agreed that this form of tourism, whether ancient or post-modern, can be critiqued for its commodification and trivialisation of death and disaster, turning suffering into a leisure experience for contemporary tourists. There are also concerns about the **authenticity** of some sites – for example, visitor attractions which explore dark tourism themes but which have no geographical link to the actual site of the dark event may seem to offer a less than authentic experience. Tunbridge and Ashworth (1996) highlight the potential for dissonance or discord in such sites, especially where the views of both victims and perpetrators are not given equal prominence.

Other researchers have extended the work of those described above by suggesting that death-related tourism sites are not uniformly 'dark' but instead demonstrate varying shades of the macabre (Stone, 2006;

Strange and Kempa, 2003). They relate this spectrum of darkness not only to the providers of such sites but also to the motivations of the tourists themselves. Those sites which are the 'darkest' are those orientated towards visitors motivated by education and commemoration, are perceived as authentic, relate to recent events and have minimal visitor facilities. 'Lighter' sites are aimed at those with a commercial entertainment focus, are perceived as inauthentic, relate to events from the distant past and operate within a well-developed tourism infrastructure.

It is true that an interest in death is a very human preoccupation, and in a sanitised society where death is privatised, perhaps it is useful for tourism sites to offer us an opportunity to contemplate the realities of life and its end. Whether it is appropriate for this contemplation to take place within a commercial leisure environment is one of the key debates within the field of dark tourism.

See also: *authenticity, post-tourism*

FURTHER READING

The reader will gain a fairly rounded insight into the recent development of this academic field of study by reading the sources listed below. Although it has been criticised for its narrow time-frame, Lennon and Foley's *Dark Tourism* is, nonetheless, an interesting collection of case studies and is a useful contribution to the literature. Also of interest is the University of Central Lancashire's website, the Dark Tourism Forum, launched in 2005. This useful website provides case studies, articles and an interesting attempt to understand the motivations of dark tourists by encouraging visitors to complete a 'diary of a dark tourist'.

RECOMMENDED BOOKS AND ARTICLES

Lennon, J. and Foley, M. (2000) *Dark Tourism: The Attraction of Death and Disaster.* London: Thomson.

Rojek, C. (1993) *Ways of Escape: Modern Transformations in Leisure and Travel.* London: Macmillan.

Seaton, A.V. (1996) 'Guided by the dark: from thanatopsis to thanatourism', *International Journal of Heritage Studies*, 2 (4): 234–44.

Tunbridge, J.E. and Ashworth, G.J. (1996) *Dissonant Heritage: The Management of the Past as a Resource in Conflict.* London: John Wiley & Sons.

Destination Management

> *Destination management refers to the processes of tourism planning, managing and coordination that take place in tourist destinations, usually carried out by a destination management organisation.*

Destinations are where much of the visitor's experience of a holiday takes place. It is usually the location where visitors stay and where they carry out many of their sightseeing activities. Simply put, a destination may be a seaside resort, an urban centre or a wilderness area, but destinations vary in terms of geographical and governmental scale and are therefore difficult to define. S.L.J. Smith (1995: 199) presents a set of criteria that may assist in identifying tourism destinations. These criteria include the need for a set of characteristics that provide a sense of identity; an adequate tourism infra-structure; a region that supports more than one community or attraction; the presence of existing attractions or the potential to develop popular attractions; the capacity to support a tourism planning and marketing organisation and, finally, easy accessibility to a large population base.

The destination is vital to the tourism industry as Davidson and Maitland point out:

> Destinations are a focus for attention since they stimulate and motivate visits, and are the location in which the major part of the tourist product is produced. As a result, much of the tourism industry is located in destinations, and most of its impacts are experienced in them. (Davidson and Maitland, 1997: 3)

Thus, the tourism destination is host to visitors, the local community and a tourism infrastructure, and the interplay between these can result in a series of impacts, both positive and negative. It is the potential for such impacts which necessitates the careful management of destinations.

Looking more closely at the characteristics of destinations, we can see that they tend to involve a number of core components which are sometimes referred to as the '4As' (Page et al., 2001: 245), namely:

- attractions: either natural, cultural or events
- amenities: hotels, restaurants, shops, tour guides
- access: transport infrastructure
- ancillary services: visitor information, banking, etc.

The diversity of these core components indicates that there is a range of stakeholders involved in a destination and, consequently, destination management is required to ensure that all interests are met, whether they be the needs of the host community, of the tourism industry, of the public sector or of the tourists themselves. Intervention is also required to ensure consistent standards of quality, the management of impacts and that the destination remains competitive.

The management of destinations is increasingly undertaken by a Destination Management Organisation who, like destinations themselves, can function on varying levels from the national, through the regional and down to the urban or municipal level. Specific examples of DMOs include Tourism Australia (a national organisation), Ibiza Travel (a regional organisation) and Brighton and Hove Visitor and Convention Bureau (a city-based organisation). Destination management organisations can also vary in terms of their structure, as they can be either government tourism departments, private sector organisations or joint public–private partnerships. A recent global survey of DMOs carried out by the World Tourism Organisation found that at the national level, DMOs were much more likely to be either a national government department or agency accountable to national government; at the regional level, they tended to be either a regional/local government department or accountable agency; but at the city level, it was more likely that a DMO would be a public–private partnership. Clearly, each of these structures brings a very different organisational philosophy to the management of destinations and it is interesting to note that the DMOs surveyed by the WTO strongly agreed that the best way to promote and manage destinations was through a public–private partnership (WTO, 2004b).

According to Ritchie and Crouch (2003), a DMO has nine core tasks that it must carry out to manage and promote a destination successfully. These tasks can be defined as internal or external activities. The internal tasks relate to the structures of organizations, administration, budgeting, community relations and publications, whereas the external tasks include visitor services and management, marketing, research and capital management.

In terms of internal tasks required by a DMO, many are purely administrative but the most characteristic is the responsibility for members and for community relations. DMO members are those who have been identified as stakeholders in the local tourism industry and who, in return for an annual fee, can benefit from the assistance of the DMO. These benefits can include networking and training opportunities. As well as working with members, the DMO must also liaise with the wider community, raising the profile of the work of the DMO and educating the public on the importance of tourism within their local community. Such awareness-raising can take the form of inviting residents to become 'a tourist for the day' and discover local amenities.

The external managerial tasks identified by Ritchie and Crouch (2003) are where much of a DMO's efforts are targeted mainly on the areas of marketing, visitor management and resource stewardship.

Marketing is an essential activity for any destination that wishes to remain competitive, and although marketing in tourism terms is often seen to be simply about promotion, successful destination marketing involves a number of key elements that include the identification of key markets, measuring destination awareness and image, developing a clear brand, establishing the destination's position within key markets, developing logos and promotional and advertising efforts, developing new experiences and identifying pricing (Ritchie and Crouch, 2003: 189). Readers interested in the details of destination marketing should consult Pike's (2008) *Destination Marketing*.

Visitor management is also key to the management of a destination. This involves managing the visitor experience before, during and after the visit (Shackley, 2004). Before the visit, it is important to provide visitor information and a bookings service through call-centres, visitor information centres and, increasingly, through the use of the internet (see **e-tourism**). Once at the destination, the visitor experience needs to be managed through the provision of appropriate signage, interpretation and pricing strategies designed to facilitate the flow of visitors through the destination. The visitor management approach that is taken will depend on the nature of the destination itself – sensitive, historic or natural environments that attract large numbers of visitors may wish to adopt an approach that limits visitor numbers in high season by differential pricing strategies, restricting access by private transport, using timed entry tickets and providing visitor interpretation that explains how visitor behaviour can impact on the destination. Increasingly, destination smart cards such as the Venice Card or the Budapest Card are being used as an important visitor management tool, allowing visitors to pre-pay for attractions, public transport and parking, and facilitating the management of visitor flow and the maintenance of relationships with visitors, post-visit.

Resource stewardship represents the responsibility that a DMO has for the built, natural and cultural environment. As identified above, much of the impact brought about by tourism is experienced in the destination itself, whether it be pollution, erosion and the depletion of species in natural environments, damage to historic buildings and overloaded infrastructures in urban centres, or the impacts on religion, value systems, arts and crafts in the socio-cultural landscape. Measures taken by destinations to address these issues include environmental impact assessments (EIAs), the creation of specific carrying capacities for destinations, setting limits of acceptable change within the environment (LACs) and zoning (see **sustainable tourism** for further discussion on these measures).

As tourism continues to grow on a global scale, it is increasingly important that destinations are managed to protect the resources on which tourism depends, to manage the needs and expectations of a diverse range of stakeholders and to ensure a good visitor experience.

See also: *e-tourism, sustainable tourism, urban tourism*

FURTHER READING

Further reading in the field of destination management could be usefully pursued within Papatheodorou's 2007 text, *Managing Tourism Destinations*. The World Tourism Organisation's *Practical Guide to Destination Management* is, as it suggests in the title, a good, practical resource.

RECOMMENDED BOOKS AND ARTICLES

Papatheodorou, A. (ed.) (2007) *Managing Tourism Destinations*. Cheltenham: Edward Elgar.
Pike, S. (2008) *Destination Marketing*. London: Butterworth-Heinemann.
Ritchie, J.R.B. and Crouch, G.I. (2003) *The Competitive Destination*. Wallingford: CABI.
WTO (2004) *World Tourism Organisation Survey of Destination Management Organisations*. Madrid: UNWTO.

destination management

Economics
of Tourism

The economics of tourism refers to the contribution that tourism makes to global, national and local economies. This can include income, employment and exports.

The World Travel and Tourism Council (WTTC, 2008a) estimates that tourism's contribution to global economic activity and employment is expected to continue increasing over the coming ten years. Travel and tourism contribute to a number of economic areas, these being:

Gross Domestic Product: In 2008, this was somewhere around 10 per cent on average in receiving countries.
Employment: In 2008, around one in every eleven jobs was in tourism.
Exports: In 2008, export earnings from international visitors and tourism goods generated around 11 per cent of total exports.

These statistics are expected to continue growing until at least 2018, and thus tourism will play a major role in the world economy for a number of years to come.

The branch of economics which focuses on the whole economy is termed 'macroeconomics'. Studies of macroeconomics in tourism tend to concentrate on economic growth, balance of payments, employment and expenditure. For most governments, tourism seems an attractive option because of its significant contribution to all of these areas. However, this should be weighed up against the environmental and social costs. Governments are attracted by the potential to earn foreign currency (especially traditionally strong currencies like the American dollar, the euro or the British pound), which can make a positive contribution to balance of payments, that is, the balance of a country's trade and financial transactions with the rest of the world over a specific period – usually a year. Tourism can contribute to Gross Domestic Product (GDP), namely the total market value of the goods and services produced by a country's economy during a specific period of time. Employment can be created at a number of levels, although jobs would ideally be full-time and non-seasonal. Tourism can also help to attract inward investment (e.g. from foreign companies), and income multiplier effects, the idea that an initial spending rise can lead to an even greater increase in national income.

However, there are some complications both with the approaches taken by national governments to economic development and with the research methods that are used to calculate the macroeconomic benefits of tourism. Developing countries and those with relatively few industries (e.g. small islands) tend to find tourism economically very attractive. This can lead to a high dependency on tourism. The GDP contribution of tourism in countries with a high dependency can be as much as 50 per cent or more (e.g. the Caribbean or South Pacific islands), which can be risky if any factors suddenly jeopardise the country's tourism industry (such as a natural disaster or terrorism). It can also cause social and cultural problems if expertise is imported from outside the country, as people feel they are subject to an imperial regime and to foreign control (a sensitive issue, particularly in post-colonial countries). Many governments, therefore, try to limit the amount of foreign investment and labour which is allowed in a country.

Dependent countries also need to strengthen other economic sectors and to link these more closely to the tourism industry. Instead of importing goods from outside the country, for example, which leads to economic leakages, the country can try to produce more of its own goods (by developing farming or fishing methods, for example, which generate larger supplies). The type of tourism will also influence the extent of economic leakage; for example, all-inclusive packages are generally not good for destinations as most of the revenue returns to the foreign tour operator or hotel chain. Small islands such as those in the Caribbean and the South Pacific can also agree to strengthen cooperation among themselves in terms of the supply of goods and labour, rather than importing them from outside the region.

Many countries now compile Tourism Satellite Accounts (TSA), as it is difficult to isolate spending on tourism from other national expenditure. TSAs are being used increasingly widely and are emerging as the recommended way of measuring the economic significance of a nation's tourism. The methodology has the approval of the World Tourism Organisation (WTO), the UN, OECD and EUROSTAT. TSAs tend to use tourism surveys to assign tourism values to broader economic activities. This includes visitor expenditure data from surveys and industry data from national economic accounts (Tribe, 2005). TSAs provide accurate measures of the size of tourism sectors, the nature of demand for tourism, the nature of supply in tourism sectors, and the direct contribution of tourism to GDP and employment. A satellite account reorganises the national system of accounts to identify the contribution of tourism to a national economy. The advantage of the satellite accounting approach is that it uses existing economic data and embeds tourism in an accepted system of accounts. The disadvantage is that the information necessary to extract tourism activity from national economic accounts is often not complete or is inconsistently collected. Also, satellite methods are much more difficult to apply below the national level or for sub-categories of tourism activity.

A report by the WTTC (2008b) clearly states the most common international approach to TSA data collection. This includes, on the demand side, the primary measure of travel and tourism (T&T) activity as the share of each final demand component of total GDP that arises from travel and tourism expenditures. On the supply side, tourism GDP is calculated as the sum of the demand components making up 'tourism consumption' (personal T&T spending, foreign visitor T&T spending, business T&T spending and individual government T&T spending) minus the imported component of this. 'Tourism economy GDP' is calculated as 'total tourism demand' ('tourism consumption' plus collective government T&T spending, T&T capital formation and T&T non-visitor exports) minus its import component. To determine the value-added concepts that contribute to the travel and tourism share of GDP, the WTTC (2008b) uses an input–output approach relating the output of each industry to the components of tourism demand.

It is recognised that there are still gaps in data and that this approach does not provide a comprehensive input–output model that compares travel and tourism to other industries. Although TSA methodology is being improved all the time, the accounts often measure only the direct impact of tourism, so multiplier analysis tends to be used to measure indirect and induced impacts. Tourism balance tends to be measured by the receipts from overseas visitors to a country (e.g. for accommodation, food, shopping, transport, entertainment, etc.) minus the expenditure of that country's own residents abroad. It is, of course, difficult to collect all receipts and to be accurate in such calculations. Tourism multiplier effects can be calculated using different methods, and it is a complex process. They can measure income, employment, sales and output. They measure the different rounds of spending in an economy and the way in which money circulates. For example, tourists may pay money directly into a local hotel, shop or restaurant, money which is then used to pay overheads or workers' salaries. Workers then use the money to buy local goods for themselves, and it is then used for something else, etc. Economists tend to talk about these rounds of spending as direct, indirect and induced. The same terminology can be used for employment, as many people are directly employed in the tourism industry, whereas others may be employed in supporting industries (e.g. construction). Ideally, money would circulate indefinitely around an economy, but eventually it leaks out to another country because of imported goods or labour. It is always best for a country to try to build a tourism industry without too much foreign investment, management and labour, otherwise leakages are high and economic benefits are minimal.

Microeconomics in tourism is concerned with the behaviour of companies, consumers and the determination of market prices. Tourism is mainly dominated by multinational companies who compete with each other for customers. The market is notoriously polarized with a number of very large chain airlines, hotels and operators at one end, and a number of small, niche operators at the other. The macroeconomic environment will have a considerable impact on the success of their businesses (e.g. global recession may cause the collapse of some companies). Tour operators and hotels compete quite aggressively, both in the high street and on the internet. There is a considerable degree of price elasticity, which means that operators can respond to competition and consumer demand in a flexible way. However, it can also make them vulnerable to bankruptcy and hostile takeovers. Many other factors affect the demand for tourism, including the amount of people's disposable income, the priority that they accord travel in their life, their responses to marketing and advertising, and changing fashions and trends. Price is a major determining factor in people's travel behaviour and patterns, and so we have seen the growth (and decline) of a number of budget airlines in recent years. Although tourism has become relatively cheap in recent years, especially air travel, the impacts of global warming, climate change and economic recession are forcing an increase in fuel costs and taxes. Natural disasters and increased terrorism have also had a devastating economic impact on many destinations.

Ideally, the economic benefits of tourism should trickle down to the poorest segments of society, and not just remain in government coffers or foreign investors' pockets. The income generated from tourism is not always reinvested in tourism development, environmental or local community programmes, and so the socio-economic benefits are not maximised. This largely depends on the government's attitude and the priority that they give to tourism. It is common to believe that tourism will somehow take care of itself ('build it and they will come', as the catchphrase goes). However, many governments with this attitude have found themselves in economic jeopardy if a crisis happens which affects the tourism industry (e.g. recession, terrorism, environmental disaster, war).

Many factors affect the economics of tourism, including the size of the country, the strength of the economy, the level of tourism development (e.g. mass or niche), the volume and intensity of visitor expenditure and seasonality. Many destinations cannot attract year-round tourism or support permanent full-time employment because of the climate (e.g. cold, dark winters, hurricane or rainy seasons, intense heatwaves, etc.). Tourism development is also frequently concentrated in one part of a country and some regions are relatively under-developed in comparison. Measures need to be taken to diversify tourism and spread the economic benefits where possible. On the other hand, there are certain locations which are too environmentally or culturally fragile to sustain tourism development, and so economic benefits should not always be prioritised. Overall, the environmental and social impacts of tourism are inextricably linked to the economic ones. This needs to be recognised by governments and private developers alike.

FURTHER READING

The most comprehensive book on the subject of the economics of tourism is Tribe's *The Economics of Recreation, Leisure and Tourism*. Reference can also be made to books about the impacts of tourism, which always include economic impacts, for example Puczkó and Rátz's *The Impacts of Tourism: An Introduction*, and Mason's *Tourism Impacts, Planning and Management*. The websites of the World Tourism Organisation (WTO) and World Travel and Tourism Council (WTTC) also provide useful economic statistics and research reports on different countries and destinations.

RECOMMENDED BOOKS

Mason, P. (2003) *Tourism Impacts, Planning and Management*. Oxford: Butterworth-Heinemann.

Puczkó, L. and Rátz, T. (2002) *The Impacts of Tourism: An Introduction*. Hämeenlinna: Häme Polytechnic.

Tribe, J. (2005) *The Economics of Recreation, Leisure and Tourism*. Oxford: Butterworth-Heinemann.

Ecotourism

Ecotourism takes place in unspoiled natural areas and is a form of tourism that strives to conserve the environment, enhance the lives of local communities and educate the visitor.

Ecotourism as a concept is strongly associated with **sustainable tourism** and **ethical tourism** and shares many features with adventure tourism. The term 'ecotourism' describes forms of tourism that take place in unspoiled environments with an emphasis on learning about the natural and cultural resources of the area. One of the most-quoted definitions of ecotourism was coined in 1987 by Hector Ceballos-Lascurain, a Mexican tourism consultant, as travel 'to relatively undisturbed or uncontaminated natural areas with the specific object of studying, admiring and enjoying the scenery and its wild plants and animals, as well as any existing cultural aspects (both past and present) found in these areas' (Ceballos-Lascurain cited in Page and Dowling, 2002: 57). Thus, the term ecotourism embraces a wide range of tourist activities, including mountain and jungle-trekking, visits to unique ecosystems such as rainforests or coral reefs and visits to see wildlife such as mountain gorillas, dolphins and whales, as well as safari tours. Ecotourism is a global phenomenon but there are regions of the world which are becoming favoured as ecotourism destinations, for example Australia, Costa Rica, Belize, New Zealand, Peru and the Antarctic. These areas have become popular because of their unique environments and wildlife.

Ecotourism emerged as a special interest tourism sector in the mid-1980s in response to a growing interest in environmental issues. It is currently the fastest growing segment of the tourism industry and, according to the International Ecotourism Society, it is growing globally at three times the speed of other tourism sectors (TIES, 2006). However, despite this recent growth, this form of tourism is not a new phenomenon as the earliest explorers were motivated by an interest in undiscovered animal and plant species and environments. Since the 1980s, industry, consumer and academic interest in ecotourism has flourished, and in 2001 David Fennell found over 80 different definitions of the terms in both academic and industry sources (Fennell, 2001). However, despite the proliferation of definitions and approaches to ecotourism, authors are generally agreed that there are five core principles underlying the concept (Page and Dowling, 2002).

Five principles of ecotourism

Nature-based

Ecotourism depends on a natural setting which may also contain some associated cultural features. The conservation of the natural environment is key to the development of ecotourism.

Ecologically sustainable

All forms of ecotourism should be ecologically sustainable and take place in a natural setting, although in practice this varies from activity to activity.

Environmentally educative

Environmental education and interpretation are key distinguishing features of ecotourism, and ecotourists expect to be educated about conservation issues.

Locally beneficial

Ecotourism projects should involve local communities to both benefit the community and environment and to improve the quality of the tourist experience.

Satisfying for tourists

Visitor satisfaction with the ecotourism experience and visitor safety are vital for the future sustainability of the ecotourism industry.

All ecotourism developments should incorporate these five principles, but in practice the emphasis varies depending on whether the development can be defined as a 'hard' or 'soft' manifestation of ecotourism. 'Hard' variants of ecotourism involve small groups visiting remote environments over long periods and usually undertaking physically and mentally demanding activities. Hard ecotourists expect little in the way of tourism infrastructure and are generally self-reliant. Conversely, 'soft' ecotourism is more akin to mass tourism, with short trips and unchallenging activities taking place in relative comfort with a high level of supporting facilities. The continuum, therefore, moves from a deep and engaged experience towards a more passive and shallow encounter as we move from hard to soft variants of ecotourism.

The ecotourism industry is made up of three broad sectors: tour operators, ecolodges and ecotourism attractions (Weaver, 2006). Within the tour operator sector, there has been a significant increase in specialist ecotourism provision, where operators are expected to commit to the five principles of ecotourism and to abide by one of a number of codes of conduct developed specifically for the ecotourism sector. Similarly, ecolodges have grown in popularity in recent years, offering varying levels of comfort but generally situated close to protected environments, built in vernacular style using local materials and using green building and energy technologies. Ecolodges are typically owned by local communities or entrepreneurs. Finally, ecotourism attractions have been developed to facilitate access to protected environments and so have proved popular with the softer end of the ecotourism continuum. Examples of these attractions include tree-top walkways which allow visitors to experience rainforests without the need to erode the forest floor.

One of the key issues in the provision of ecotourism products such as the ones outlined above is, of course, the question of quality control – how can potential ecotourists be sure that the operator or ecolodge that they are using really does adhere to ecotourism principles? The ecotourism industry has been the most active of the tourism sectors in trying to introduce industry-wide quality-control mechanisms. Many such initiatives exist, both for the whole ecotourism industry and for specific sub-sectors, such as the small group of tour operators who operate in the Antarctic regions. Font and Buckley estimated in 2001 that there were over 260 such voluntary programmes in existence. This wide range of initiatives has led to confusion for consumers who in a recent survey suggested that the broad array of ecolabels meant that it was difficult to identify legitimate certification programmes (Honey, 2005). Probably the best-known and respected programme is Australia's Ecocertification Programme which is run by Ecotourism Australia and has been in operation since 1996. It has now been exported from its Australian base to become the International Ecotourism Standard. Tour operators, accommodation providers and visitor attractions can apply for accreditation that adheres to eight central principles, each with its own core and advanced indicators. In order to receive accreditation, an ecotourism product must meet 100 per cent of the core criteria. Additionally, operators who wish to achieve advanced accreditation need to further satisfy at least 75 per cent of the advanced criteria. Operators are subjected to an audit during the three years in which their accreditation is valid. Accredited operators are able to use the Eco Certification logo which is, according to Ecotourism Australia:

> a globally recognised brand which assists travellers to choose and experience a genuine and authentic tour, attraction, cruise or accommodation that is environmentally, socially and economically sustainable. The Eco Certification Programme assures travellers that certified products are backed by a strong, well-managed commitment to sustainable practices and provides high quality nature tourism experiences. (Ecotourism Australia, 2008)

Despite its ethical credentials and these laudable attempts to move towards a universally accepted standard, ecotourism is still considered by some critics to be a problematic concept. Firstly, the typical characteristics of the ecotourist suggest that this is a type of tourism favoured by relatively affluent, well-educated, middle-class consumers who may simply be attempting to distinguish themselves from mass tourists, rather than demonstrating any deeply-held beliefs about environmental conservation. Thus, instead of being concerned with the environment, they are more interested in the status that such exotic holiday experiences will bring, something that the tourism industry well understands in its marketing of such holiday products. Brian Wheeller is critical of these 'egotourists' (Wheeller, 1994) and questions why ecotourism always seems to take place in far-flung destinations, necessitating international flights, as the following quotation illustrates:

> the ecotourist (and the supposedly eco-friendly firm) so concerned to ostentatiously behave sensitively in the vulnerable destination environment, is not generally so concerned about the danger to the overall environment ... Here convenience takes precedence over conscience – a car to the airport and a jumbo jet are hardly paradigms of virtue in the environmental stakes. (Wheeller, 1993: 125)

The paradox of ecotourism lies in the fact that as it becomes more and more popular, as it undoubtedly is, it will become increasingly difficult to provide. At the heart of ecotourism is an understanding that developments are small in scale and tour groups limited in number. As ecotourism continues to grow, this may become hard, if not impossible, to achieve.

See also: *ethical tourism, indigenous tourism, rural tourism, sustainable tourism.*

FURTHER READING

A good, current introduction to the ecotourism industry can be found in Higham's *Critical Issues in Ecotourism: Understanding a Complex Tourism Phenomenon*, and in the latest edition of Fennell's *Ecotourism: An Introduction*. The International Ecotourism Society's website (www.ecotourism.org) contains many useful resources for students.

RECOMMENDED BOOKS

Fennell, D. (2003) *Ecotourism: An Introduction,* 2nd edition. London: Routledge.
Higham, J. (2007) *Critical Issues in Ecotourism: Understanding a Complex Tourism Phenomenon.* Oxford: Butterworth-Heinemann.
Zeppel, H. (2006) *Indigenous Ecotourism: Sustainable Development and Management.* Wallingford: CABI.

Ethical Tourism

Ethical tourism is a form of tourism that has been specifically designed to encourage both the tourism industry and tourists to consider the ethical implications of their actions and avoid participation in activities which contribute to ethical abuses in tourism destinations.

In the widest sense, ethics is a strand of the study of philosophy that is concerned with what is right and what is wrong. The application of ethics to the business and practice of tourism has a fairly recent history and ethical tourism is often closely associated with the concepts of **sustainable tourism** and **ecotourism**, both of which are focused on the impacts that tourism may have on the wider context within which it operates. Ethical tourism, therefore, is a form of tourism that strives to treat the environment, host communities and employees in an ethical manner.

The study of ethics has traditionally been seen as a theoretical discipline but, within the last 40 years, there has been a move towards a more applied use, firstly with business ethics developing as a response to the abuse of power and business scandals. 'Consequently, applied ethics has evolved both in business and in society as a whole to include a number of key areas related to human well-being and development, including business, the legal and medical professions, the biosphere and environment, and, accordingly, tourism' (Fennell, 2003: 177).

Although tourism ethics are considered a branch of applied ethics, it is also useful to understand the theoretical approaches to the study of the discipline. Broadly speaking, the theory of ethics has two approaches – deontology and teleology.

> *Deontology* is about the *right behaviour* for humans, based on rules which may be derived from theological doctrine or social contract. Ethical conduct is, therefore, associated with doing one's duty and following correct procedures.
> *Teleology*, on the other hand, is about *good behaviour* which is not based on rules but on securing the best possible outcome, whatever the means may have been. Within teleology, we find two associated theories – hedonism and utilitarianism. Hedonism is concerned with the greatest pleasure for the individual and utilitarianism strives for the best outcome for the greatest number. Both of these theoretical approaches can illuminate the study of tourism business, hosts and visitors, as will be demonstrated later.

Researchers believe that the tourism industry and academics have been slow to grasp the importance of ethics (Fennell, 2003, 2006), preferring instead to concentrate on the 'impacts' of tourism, especially those affecting the environment. The UK-based charity, Tourism Concern, has redressed this with its campaigns for a more ethical tourism industry in the areas of cultural conflicts, displacement, water abuse, working conditions, exploitation of women and child sex tourism, as well as environmental damage. Tourism Concern report that, for example, more than one million children are sexually abused yearly by tourists and that millions of young people are exploited in tourism-related labour. Much-needed water is directed away from local communities to keep golf courses green in South-East Asia and many peoples have been forced off their lands to create national parks and tourist resorts (Tourism Concern, 2008).

However, despite the very obvious abuses described above, the application of ethics to tourism has always been highly problematic as the tourism industry is extremely fragmented, with a diverse range of stakeholders. Attitudes to what constitutes ethical behaviour will differ between tourists, tour operators and host community, and as international tourism necessitates exposure to different cultural and religious belief systems, it is not always clear which value systems tourists will apply in a destination. In an attempt to address these issues, a wide variety of codes of ethical conduct have been developed by the tourism industry, governments and associations, for the benefit of tourists, hosts, governments and tour operators. According to Malloy and Fennell (1998: 454), such codes of conduct 'are designed to inform individuals of acceptable and/or unacceptable behaviour in a particular context' and have been developed in recent years as a reaction to a variety of ethical transgressions, both within and outside the tourism industry.

Goodwin and Francis (2003) suggests that codes of conduct fall into two categories – codes of ethics (based on values) and codes of conduct (related to actual practice in specific settings). Some recent examples of tourism codes of conduct are provided below to demonstrate the wide range of agents and authorities and intended audiences:

- Code of Conduct for the Protection of Children from Sexual Exploitation in Travel and Tourism (produced by End Child Prostitution and Trafficking/UNICEF/UNWTO) – this code was developed by international organisations, and is aimed at a wide range of interest groups.
- Tourist Guide Code of Conduct and Ethics (produced by the Provincial Government of the Western Cape, South Africa) – this code was developed by regional government and specifically aimed at tour guides.
- Code of Conduct for Arctic Tourists (produced by the World Wildlife Fund) – this code was developed by a global wildlife charity for the education of tourists to the Arctic. It includes advice on conservation, sustaining biodiversity and local economies and safety.

In addition to the issue, industry or place-specific codes described above, the international tourism industry now has a Global Code of Ethics published by the World Tourism Organisation (WTO) in 2001. This is described as 'a comprehensive set of principles whose purpose is to guide stakeholders in tourism development: central and local governments, local communities, the tourism industry and its professionals, as well as visitors, both international and domestic' (WTO, 2001). The code consists of nine articles setting out a range of ethical issues, and a final article explaining procedures for implementation and referring disputes to the WTO's World Committee on Tourism Ethics. This includes the relationship between tourists and local residents; the satisfaction and fulfilment of tourists; sustainable development; the enhancement of cultural heritage; maximising the benefits of tourism for the destination and its stakeholders, including communities; the freedom of movement for tourists; and the rights of workers in the tourism industry.

There are now many ethical tourism codes of conduct in existence and they have come under criticism for being too platitudinous, overly generic, too inclusive and difficult to enforce (Malloy and Fennell, 1998: 454). Certainly, for ethical codes to be successful, there is a need for highly motivated consumers who are prepared to follow rules governing their conduct. But what are consumers' attitudes to ethical tourism? Undoubtedly, ethical consumerism has grown in recent years with the rising popularity of fairly traded goods in supermarkets and an increase in interest in farmers' markets and locally sourced food. A number of studies have been carried out among consumers to ascertain their attitudes towards ethical tourism consumption. These studies show that while the majority of holidaymakers choose their destination on the basis of price, weather, amenities and accommodation, a small but growing number report that they are concerned with ethical issues within their holiday destination and the ethical credentials of tour operators (Mintel, 2005 and 2007). Mintel's 2005 report suggests that 17 per cent of the travelling population can be classified as 'ethical tourists' and the most recent report predicts that the responsible travel market will grow by 25 per cent year on year (Mintel, 2007).

The 2007 Mintel report also found that 9 per cent of their respondents expressed a desire to volunteer on an aid or conservation project as part of a future holiday. Although ostensibly a laudable concept, volunteer tourism has been criticised for the egoism of its participants, who are simply looking for gap-year adventures to put on their CVs, and for the sponsoring organisations who are becoming more corporate in the marketing and management of these experiences (Weaver, 2006).

There are certainly far more tour operators, large and small, selling holidays which are aimed at the ethical consumer. The website Responsible Travel, for example, which was launched in 2001, represents 270 tour operators who meet their specified criteria for ethical procedure and who have environmental, social and economic policies (Responsible Travel, 2008).

FURTHER READING

David Fennell's 2006 text *Tourism Ethics* gives a very good introduction to this area of study. Interested readers should also consult the *Journal of Sustainable Tourism* for current research in the field. The Responsible Tourism website is interesting for the industry perspective on ethical issues, and Tourism Concern is a useful source of information on international campaigns. Patullo and Minnelli's *The Ethical Travel Guide* (2006) gives many examples of ethical tourism destinations and activities.

RECOMMENDED BOOKS AND ARTICLES

Fennell, D. (2003) *Ecotourism: An Introduction*, 2nd edn. London: Routledge.
Fennell, D. (2006) *Tourism Ethics*. Clevedon: Channel View.
Weaver, D. (2006) *Sustainable Tourism: Theory and Practice*. Oxford: Butterworth-Heinemann.

e-Tourism

> *e-Tourism refers to the application of new technologies to activities within the tourism sector, such as the bookings of package holidays, flights, hotels and the provision of visitor information.*

New information technologies, in particular computer networks and the internet as mechanisms for processing, analysing, storing, retrieving and disseminating information, have transformed tourism since the 1990s. According to Buhalis (2003: 3), these technologies 'increasingly empower and enable both tourism consumers and suppliers to communicate, enhance awareness of needs and offers, inform, negotiate and develop bridges to reduce distance and cultural and communication gaps'.

The current technologies used in the tourism industry have their roots in the 1950s when airlines developed computer reservations systems (CRSs) to handle schedules and bookings for individual airlines. These were used until the 1970s when global distribution systems (GDSs) began to be developed to handle information on numerous carriers as well as passenger details. Licences to operate these GDSs were sold to travel agents, and the systems Galileo and Amadeus were launched in Europe in 1987. GDSs played a vital role in the globalisation of the tourism industry and most travel agents in the main tourism generating regions of the world are linked to the four leading GDSs – Amadeus, Galileo, Sabre and Worldspan (Page and Connell, 2006). Of course, at the same time as these GDSs were being developed, the internet and the World Wide Web (WWW) were also under development. These two terms are often used interchangeably, but technically the internet refers to the global network of computers (hardware), while the World Wide Web describes the software which enables us to utilise the Internet.

All traditional sectors of the tourism industry (for example, airlines, car hire companies, hotels, tour operators, travel agencies and destination management organisations among others) have now shifted their operations online, recognising that information communication technologies and the internet give them a variety of benefits. These benefits include the opportunity to increase internal efficiency, interact directly with consumers, offer a more personalised product and widen their geographical reach by increasing points of sale. The internet also provides the ideal environment for selling products at the last minute. Along with these traditional tourism players, newcomers to the industry, such as the budget airlines, were able to exploit the potential of the internet from the mid-1990s onwards and companies such as EasyJet now sell their flights solely online.

Because of the intangible nature of tourism services, consumers cannot inspect the product at the point of sale and so the tourism industry and consumers are highly dependent on good-quality information. Buhalis suggests that 'timely and accurate information, relevant to consumers' needs is often the key to satisfaction of tourist demand. Therefore information technologies provide the backbone that facilitates tourism' (Buhalis, 1998: 411). It is this ability to provide instant access to information and an interactive environment which has made the World Wide Web so well suited to the tourism environment. What also makes this technology so significant is that unlike other information technologies such as CRSs and GDRs, which were controlled by tourism suppliers, the internet is open to all. This means that, potentially, consumers can go directly to tourism suppliers (for example, airlines and hotels) and purchase products without the need for the travel intermediaries – tour operators and travel agents. They can put together individually tailored packages from the comfort of their own homes, unrestricted by travel agency opening times, and can plan travel at the last minute. Increasing numbers will be able to arrange their own travel independently as recent government statistics show that 65 per cent of households had access to the internet in 2008, a rise of 7 per cent from the previous year (National Statistics, 2009a). It was thought that this would lead to the disintermediation of the tourism industry and there were concerns that travel agents would become redundant. However, what has in fact happened is that a new breed of tourism e-mediaries has emerged to service customers (see below) and traditional travel agencies have adapted to meet the needs of the burgeoning e-tourism business environment. Buhalis and Licata (2002) and Buhalis (2005) provide an overview of some of these new tourism e-mediaries, which include:

Single suppliers
Single suppliers such as airlines and hotel chains now use the online environment, not only to distribute their own products, but also to offer additional services such as travel insurance, car hire and destination information.

Travel agencies
New web-based travel agencies such as Expedia.com and ebookers.com have emerged, offering a range of travel products for sale online. Offline agencies such as Thomas Cook have also developed their online provision to reach as wide a range of potential customers as possible.

Last-minute agencies
The perishable nature of the tourism product has led to the emergence of last-minute agencies such as last-minute.com who sell discounted holiday, gift and experience products online with very short lead-times. The closer the departure date, the better the deal available to consumers.

Destination management organisations
These organisations (either public sector or partnerships) plan, manage and coordinate the various functions of a visitor destination (see **destination management**) and increasingly have a web-based presence to market destinations, provide visitor information and facilitate the booking of local accommodation and events.

e-tourism

The era of e-tourism has therefore presented new challenges for traditional travel agencies and prompted a shift in focus within these tourism intermediaries. A recent report by Mintel suggests that 25 per cent of a sample population of 2000 adults had used a traditional travel agent to make a booking in the years 2006–2008. Eighteen per cent used travel agents to book an overseas package holiday and 7 per cent used an agent to book a flight or accommodation only. Of those using a travel agent, the greatest proportion were from the ABC1 socio-economic group and were consumers without children. They also tended to be within the age ranges of 25–34 or 55–64 (Mintel, 2008). The report also indicated that consumers were using travel agents as a source of information – 19 per cent visited to look at brochures and speak to staff about their holiday options. Consumers, therefore, seem to be reluctant to consult a travel agent for the booking of individual flights and accommodation but are more likely to use an agent to book an overseas package. This reflects the fact that although more and more UK households have access to the internet, there are still some perceived barriers to buying holidays online. According to Page and Connell, these barriers may include the credibility of the online retailer, the accuracy of information provided and security issues around online payment (Page and Connell, 2006).

The internet is also used extensively by some consumers to research destinations, compare prices and consult online customer feedback sites such as TripAdvisor.com, although they do not actually make their bookings online. This suggests that there is still a role for travel agents and, in particular, for those that can provide high-quality information and independent advice. Mintel sees this role as being akin to 'the middle-man as lifestyle guru. Upmarket travel agents can increasingly position themselves as a luxury service for those who have high demands but lack the time or will to do it themselves and are able and willing to pay for high-quality, personalized attention' (Mintel, 2008: 4).

It is clear to see that e-tourism is here to stay, as information technology has revolutionised the distribution of tourism products and allowed consumers to experience a greater degree of flexibility and independence in their travel arrangements. In 2005, travel was one of the largest UK e-business markets, with £59 in every £100 being spent on wholesale, retail, catering and travel goods (National Statistics, 2009b). Ever-widening access to the internet will increase this further, but information technologies cannot provide for every need and it would seem that there will still be a role for the well-qualified and knowledgeable travel professional in the future.

See also: destination management

FURTHER READING

Dimitrios Buhalis is the leading academic writing in the field of e-tourism and his 2003 text *eTourism* is to be recommended as a good introduction. Readers might also want to consult O'Conner's (1999) *Electronic Information Distribution in Tourism and Hospitality*.

RECOMMENDED BOOKS AND ARTICLES

Buhalis, D. (2003) *eTourism*. Harlow: Prentice-Hall.

Buhalis, D. (2005) 'Information technology in tourism', in C. Cooper, J. Fletcher, A. Fyall, D. Gilbert and S. Wanhill (eds), *Tourism Principles and Practice*, 3rd edn (1st edn, 1993). Harlow: Prentice-Hall. pp. 702–36.

Buhalis, D. and Licata, M.C. (2002) 'The future eTourism intermediaries', *Tourism Management*, 23: 207–20.

O'Conner, P. (1999) *Electronic Information Distribution in Tourism and Hospitality*. Wallingford: CABI.

Experience Economy

> The term 'experience economy' refers to a proposed new economic era based, not on the delivery of services, but on the staging by businesses of memorable experiences. Contemporary consumers in this new economy are highly motivated to consume meaningful experiences and are prepared to pay for them.

The tourism industry has always been in the business of providing experiences for visitors but in recent years, the staging of experiences has taken on a much more central role within the industry and the wider service and retail sector, so much so that it has been claimed that we have now entered a new economic era where experience is everything. The *experience economy* was hailed as the new economic era by Pine and Gilmore's studies in 1998 and 1999. In their analysis, the experience economy is the fourth economic stage in human progress: first, in the agrarian era, we extracted commodities from the earth, then during the industrial era, we manufactured goods. The industrial economy then gave way to the third economic era, the service economy, where services were delivered. Then, argue Pine and Gilmore, the experience economy evolved, where the main economic offering is the staging of experience. They differentiate experiences from services as follows:

> experiences are a distinct economic offering, as different from services as services are from goods. Today we can identify and describe this fourth economic offering because consumers unquestionably desire experiences and more and more businesses are responding by explicitly designing and promoting them. (Pine and Gilmore, 1998: 97)

The authors illustrate the concept of the emerging experience economy by likening it to the evolution of the birthday cake. In agrarian societies, parents would have made cakes from basic ingredients grown locally. In the industrial era, busy mothers might have bought a pre-packaged cake mix, and in the service era the cake may have been ordered from a bakery. Now, in the experience economy, the child's whole birthday party, including cake, is often outsourced to a fast-food restaurant or entertainment complex that will stage a memorable event for the children on behalf of their parents (Pine and Gilmore, 1998).

Pine and Gilmore take a fairly narrow view of experiences in that they believe an experience is only truly valued if it is paid for. Thus, they make the case that a wide range of businesses, from airlines to banks and shopping malls, could stage experiences that customers are willing to pay for and which will bring the consumer and the provider closer together. To help those businesses who wish to provide for the increasingly experience-hungry consumer, the authors have suggested some basic experience design principles based on what they believe to be the key characteristics of experiences. Firstly, experiences have two dimensions – one being the level of customer *participation* (from active to passive) and the other being the level of *connection* between the customer and the experience (ranging from absorption to immersion). Thus, a symphony audience might be passive in their enjoyment, while a skier would be active in the experience of their sport. Similarly, a viewer may be absorbed in watching a film on television at home but the same film experienced in a 3D cinema with surround sound may make the experience more immersing. The most engaging and memorable experiences are those that involve the customer in active participation in an event in which they are fully immersed. The authors then go on to suggest a number of principles to help providers design such experiences – these principles include the provision of a compelling theme to unify the offering, the use of positive cues to affirm the nature of the experience for the customer, the provision of memorabilia as a tangible reminder of the occasion and, finally, the engagement of all five senses to stimulate customers (Pine and Gilmore, 1998).

The tourism industry, traditionally concerned with the provision of standardised travel, accommodation and catering services, is of course embracing the contemporary experience economy and providing more and more tailored and unique experiences for visitors (see, for example, **special interest tourism**). Lofgren believes that this new economy is highly integrated and combines 'tourism, retail trade, architecture, event management, the entertainment and heritage industries as well as the media world under a common umbrella' (Lofgren, 2003). Walt Disney, considered by Pine and Gilmore to be an 'experience-economy pioneer', (1998: 99) has, of course, been in the experience business since the 1950s but it has only been in recent decades that the true significance of this new economy is being embraced by the tourism and heritage sectors, as outlined below.

Visitor attractions

Visitor attractions are increasingly promoting the experiences that they provide, rather than concentrating on the educational or aesthetic qualities of the offer. Thus, visitors expect to be actively rather than passively engaged with the attraction and to have an emotional, sensory response to their visit. London's newest visitor attraction, which opened in February 2008, has been named 'The London Bridge Experience' and exhorts its visitors to 'experience stunning special effects, animation and real actors who will show you what London Bridge was really like in times gone by. Interact with the characters, join in with your fellow travellers and experience the journey of a life-time' (London Bridge Experience, 2008). However, it is not just in newly developed attractions where experience is central – museums, those most traditional of attractions, have also entered into the experience economy and become, as Richards suggests, 'Experience Factories' (2001b: 62). The new approach to museum display and interpretation, the New Museology, that evolved in the 1990s, set in motion a different approach to museums and their visitors based on a new emphasis on social history and collective experience (Hart Robertson, 2006). Thus, museums have introduced sensory, participative displays, encouraged engagement and reminiscence and entered the popular cultural tourism industry which, according to Prentice (2001), is essentially experiential, often driven by the desire for insight rather than formal learning as a basis for understanding.

Destinations

An interesting aspect of the evolving experience economy is the rapid expansion of the events industry, with its accompanying proliferation of undergraduate and postgraduate courses being offered in this sector. Many tourism destinations are setting themselves up as stages for experiences and events using both traditional venues and more impromptu spaces such as city streets, squares and plazas (Richards, 2001b). London's newly semi-pedestrianised Trafalgar Square has been used for a large number of events, concerts and festivals in recent years and Edinburgh is a prime example of a city which uses a year-long programme of festivals and events to augment its traditional historic appeal.

Specialist tour operators

While there is still a market for mass-produced package holidays to Mediterranean beach destinations, a growing number of special interest tour operators are now offering individually tailored products for visitors who wish to use their holidays as a means of gathering unique experiences, whether in visiting far-flung destinations, encountering rare animal species or meeting remote tribal peoples in exotic settings. These holidays are discreetly packaged to allow the visitor to feel that they are central in engineering their encounters, but nonetheless the specialist tour operator is in the business of staging experiences and it is a business that is growing annually (see **special interest tourism**).

Tourism marketing

National and regional tourism marketing is increasingly appealing to the experience-seeking visitor with campaigns that emphasise individual engagement with the sights, sounds, smells, taste and feel of a place rather than the more traditional aesthetic appeals of heritage or landscape. England's national tourist board, Visit England, is currently using the concept of 'experience' as one of the main strands in its brand positioning of England as a holiday destination. It has identified three types of experience that convey the essence of England: 'real experiences' (conveying continuity and belonging), 'fun experiences' (including social activities and adventure) and 'indulgent experiences' (concentrating on accessible luxury, relaxation and pleasure) (Hayes and MacLeod, 2007; VisitEngland, 2004). Interestingly, Visit England has recently been renamed Enjoy England, thus turning the rather passive action of visiting into the more engaged activity of enjoyment.

Experiences have indubitably come onto tourism's centre stage within the last two decades and there are more experience-stagers working in the industry than ever before. However, Richards (2001b) warns us that to take the narrow view that experiences are only valued if they have been bought is to miss out on the importance of many of the spontaneous happenings that characterise any tourist trip. These chance encounters often cost nothing and yet can be the most memorable aspects of a visit. We must also bear in mind that individuals consume an experience through the lens of their own perception and so no event will be the same for all visitors. People bring different expectations, cultural awareness and even attention spans to an experience, which will alter how it is perceived. In effect, the visitor becomes co-producer of the experience itself.

See also: festivals and events tourism, special interest tourism

FURTHER READING

Apart from familiarising themselves with the very accessible seminal texts by Pine and Gilmore listed below, students may also wish to look at Boswijk et al.'s *The Experience Economy: A New Perspective*, which includes a number of useful business cases, some with direct relevance to students of tourism management.

RECOMMENDED BOOKS AND ARTICLES

Boswijk, A., Thijssen, T. and Peelen, E. (2007) *The Experience Economy: A New Perspective.* Harlow: Pearson Education.

Pine, B.J. and Gilmore, J.H. (1999) *The Experience Economy.* Cambridge, MA: Harvard University Press.

Prentice, R. (2001) 'Experiential cultural tourism: museums and the marketing of the new romanticism of evoked authenticity', *Museum Management and Curatorship*, 19 (1): 5–26.

Richards, G. (2001) 'The experience industry and the creation of attractions', in G. Richards (ed.), *Cultural Attractions and European Tourism*. Wallingford: CABI. pp. 55–69.

experience economy

Festivals and Events Tourism

> *Festivals and events tourism covers attendance at traditional or contemporary celebrations of culture, which can include music, dancing, gastronomy, arts and sports. Such events can be one-off or may take place at the same time every year, and can last from one day to several days.*

Festivals have been a cultural phenomenon for thousands of years, and were traditionally connected to celebrations at certain points in the religious, cultural or agricultural calendar. Festivals tended to be, first and foremost, religious celebrations involving ritualistic activities. In Ancient Greece, festivals were occasions on which deities could be worshipped, and prayers offered for success in battle or a good harvest. In late-mediaeval times in Europe, festivals took on a more secular character, and tended to celebrate human achievements instead. Picard and Robinson (2006) suggest that during the Grand Tour of the eighteenth and nineteenth centuries, festivals gave animation to 'foreign' townscapes and landscapes. Often, festivals would serve as a means of affirming local culture or traditions, and offered communities the chance to promote their cultural identity. Festivals also help to support and promote local artists and to offer a concentrated period of high-quality artistic activity.

Adams (1986) notes that festivals and tourism have had a long history of mutual benefit. Festivals have proliferated since the growth of mass tourism in the post-war period with the explicit intention of encouraging tourism. Picard and Robinson (2006: 2) suggest that festivals 'whether as "traditional" moments of social celebration or as constructed and highly orchestrated events, have been absorbed into the expansive stock of "products" that tourists desire'. Rolfe (1992) demonstrated that over 50 per cent of arts festivals in the UK originated during the 1980s, and that this growth was at least partly aimed at increasing tourism in many tourist cities. Today, although many festivals aim to cater primarily for the local community, they succeed nevertheless in attracting tourists, and many new festivals are created with a tourist audience in mind.

Since the late 1960s, the number of newly created festivals has increased significantly (Picard and Robinson, 2006). The aim of many festivals is to enhance the image of an area and to 'put it on the map'. Hughes (2000) noted, however, that many festivals which did not set out to attract tourists, have done so anyway. Festivals clearly have a higher concentration of visitors in areas of a country that are already established tourist destinations, and the majority of festival organisers therefore design the programme content with the attraction of tourists in mind. Kirschenblatt-Gimblett (1998) suggests that festivals are the ideal way for tourists to engage with a destination and to experience a sense of place. Zeppel and Hall (1992: 49) state that:

> Festivals, carnivals and community fairs add vitality and enhance the tourist appeal of a destination. Festivals are held to celebrate dance, drama, comedy, film and music, the arts, crafts, ethnic and indigenous cultural heritage, religious traditions, historically significant occasions, sporting events, food and wine, seasonal rites and agricultural products. Visitors primarily participate in festivals because of a special interest in the product, event, heritage or tradition being celebrated.

Tourism can even help to revive festivals and events which have fallen into disuse. The Venice Carnival, for example, was discontinued in 1769, but was revived in 1980 as a community and tourist festival, partly in order to address problems of seasonality, as it traditionally took place in February.

Festivals can take numerous different forms, and the most common are listed below. Included also are events, which have become more and more popular in recent years.

- carnivals
- arts festivals (e.g. dance, theatre)
- music festivals
- food and wine festivals
- religious festivals
- circuses
- sporting events
- mega-events (e.g. Olympic Games)
- cultural events (e.g. European Cultural Capital).

Traditionally, carnivals were born out of the oppressive context of European imperialism, colonisation and slavery (Alleyne-Dettmers, 1996), but they have, however, become increasingly celebratory. Bakhtin (1965) described carnivals as releasing spectators and participants from the constraints of everyday life to engage in sensuous, hedonistic and licentious pleasure. Large numbers of tourists are keen to experience carnivals, to enjoy the spectacle and to free themselves from their everyday personae. Examples include the Rio Carnival in Brazil, the Trinidad Carnival in the Caribbean and Notting Hill Carnival in London.

Miles (1997) describes the 'polyphonic' nature of carnivals and festivals, suggesting that it is the ideal forum for representing a multiplicity of perspectives and the expression of ethnicity. This is especially true of Asian Mela Festivals. The term 'Mela' is derived from a Sanskrit word meaning 'gathering', and is used to describe a range of community events in the Asian sub-continent. The cultural activities included in Mela are many and varied, incorporating (among others) music, dance, fashion, food and sometimes film. Melas have gradually developed from small-scale community-based events in India to national celebrations of diasporic cultures in Western countries. Like Caribbean carnivals, Melas have come to symbolise all that is 'colourful' about diaspora, transforming ethnicity into a cultural showcase for growing numbers of white and tourist audiences (Carnegie and Smith, 2006). A number of gay events (e.g. Gay Mardi Gras in cities such as San Francisco, Sydney and London) are also becoming increasingly popular, both with the gay and mainstream market (see **gay tourism**).

Music festivals, especially pop and rock festivals, such as Glastonbury in the UK, are popular with young audiences. WOMAD (World of Music, Arts and Dance) is a global festival which aims to bring together and to celebrate the music, arts and dance of a diverse range of countries and cultures throughout the world. It has taken place in many different countries since its inception in 1982. Food and drink festivals, such as the Munich Bier Fest, have always attracted large numbers of people, but now wine festivals are becoming equally, if not better, attended. Whereas music festivals tend to be somewhat globalised (i.e. inviting mainly internationally known artists), food and drink festivals can help to showcase and sell local products to tourists. Religious festivals are often colourful enough to attract tourists, but care must be taken that the religious and spiritual significance is not compromised by the presence of tourists who may not understand the significance of certain rituals, or may behave inappropriately. Circuses are travelling shows or may be a permanent feature of a destination. One of the most popular and spectacular in recent years has been Cirque du Soleil, which originated in Canada, but which offers a multi-cultural spectacle of exceptionally high quality. The artistes are from different countries and represent the best of their profession. Sporting events are also growing in popularity, and may include cultural activities. For example, all Olympic Games are now required to run a parallel Cultural Olympiad. World Cup Football is another mega-event which is desirable for host destinations because of the high-profile nature of the event.

Festivals and events are full of animation, vibrancy and spontaneity. They are often multi-locational so can be taken *to* people wherever they may reside, or to areas of high tourist concentration. Programming is fluid and flexible and can be adapted to the local environment, its communities and their cultures. In terms of socio-cultural impacts, festivals can play a key role in local community development, as they tend to be more socially inclusive than other forms of culture, and are often viewed by festival directors and residents alike as expressions of cultural diversity and identity. Festivals can become the quintessence of a region and its people. Quinn (2005) outlines the benefits of festivals in the context of regeneration. These include contributing to the democratisation of culture, celebrating diversity, animating and empowering communities, and improving quality of life.

However, festivals are usually temporary, fleeting or elusive experiences, which can fail to sustain or support cultural continuity if they are not repeated. This is why festivals are ideally repeated annually. Another problem is that as festivals become increasingly 'international', they often lose their roots and connections to specific localities. Small community festivals are often described as being more engaging for local people than large mega-events, but they generally fail to attract tourists and are, therefore, unlikely to be commercially viable in the long term unless extensive local funding is available. There are also problems of loss of authenticity, compromising of artistic integrity or trivialisation of culture. Some of the problems for festivals and events management are summarised below.

- Who has ownership of festivals and events can be significant (i.e. local people, public sector or commercial businesses).
- Mega-events often create a legacy of huge debts but very few local benefits.
- Financial and commercial imperatives can sometimes take over from social, cultural and educational objectives of festivals.
- Consistent funding or sponsorship on an ongoing basis (i.e. annually) is difficult to secure.

- A festival may be predominantly community-orientated or tourist-orientated, but these orientations are not always compatible.
- Festival activities can lose their local roots and local interest if they become too international, tourism-orientated or commercial.
- Ethnic and minority events (e.g. carnivals, gay pride, Melas) can be appropriated by agencies or visitors who are not part of, or are not sensitive to, those groups' needs and culture.
- Festival and event destinations can become too overcrowded at certain times of the year, and locals and even visitors may stay away as a result.

Quinn (2005) notes the need for better research and more holistic management if festivals are to succeed in providing positive benefits for locations and their inhabitants. Issues of appropriation and local ownership are complicated by the desire or need for increased publicity, political and financial support, and tourism development. Paradoxically, however, these are usually essential to the future continuation of many festivals and events.

See also: arts tourism, heritage tourism, gastronomic tourism, indigenous tourism

FURTHER READING

There are several recent books about the management of festivals and events, for example, Allen et al.'s *Festival and Special Event Management*, which is already into its fourth edition. Ali-Knight et al.'s *International Perspectives of Festivals and Events: Paradigms of Analysis* offers a diverse range of case studies. For a more sociological and anthropological approach, see Picard and Robinson's *Festivals, Tourism and Social Change: Remaking Worlds*. It is also useful to refer to the work of the International Festivals and Events Association (www.ifea.com).

RECOMMENDED BOOKS

Ali-Knight, J., Robertson, M., Fyall, A. and Ladkin, A. (2008) *International Perspectives of Festivals and Events: Paradigms of Analysis*. Oxford: Butterworth-Heinemann.
Allen, J., McDonnell, I., O'Toole, W. and Harris, R. (2008) *Festival and Special Event Management*. Chichester: John Wiley & Sons.
Picard, D. and Robinson, M. (eds) (2006) *Festivals, Tourism and Social Change: Remaking Worlds*. Clevedon: Channel View.

Film and TV Tourism

The term 'film and TV tourism' describes tourism visits prompted by seeing a location on television or at the cinema. This form of tourism also includes visits to places associated with film and television characters or celebrities.

The popular media of film and television have enormous influence on consumers' lives and this influence also extends to tourists' destination choices. Just as literary figures and authors can lure visitors to particular sites (see **literary tourism**), so popular television programmes and successful films can create tourism destinations out of a wide range of locations. This type of tourism has only been researched in recent years with authors referring to this activity as 'movie-induced' or 'film-induced' tourism (Beeton, 2005; Busby and Klug, 2001; Riley, Baker and Van Doren, 1998). Although films and television programmes are equally influential in attracting visitors, they appeal to different types of visitor and the duration of their influence varies. An avid fan of a long-term television soap opera may have a different relationship with its location than a visitor prompted to visit a region because of a recent viewing of a spectacular movie. Similarly, a longstanding television programme such as the UK's *Coronation Street*, which has been broadcast since 1960, has had a much longer span of TV-induced tourism to its location than a film might have.

As suggested in the definition above, film and TV tourism is not simply about visiting locations depicted in the media. There are various themes and forms of film and TV tourism. Beeton (2005) and Busby and Klug (2001) suggest that these can include the following:

On location
- Visiting locations of films or TV programmes (*Monarch of the Glen* country in the Scottish Highlands; *Harry Potter* film locations in the UK).
- Visits to the homes of film or TV celebrities (visits to 'Hollywood Homes of the Stars').

Commercial attractions
- Attractions constructed from film themes (the *Heartbeat Experience*, Whitby, UK).
- Guided tours to various film locations (*Sex and the City* tours in New York; *Sound of Music* tours, Salzburg, Austria).
- Movie tourism packages (*Lord of the Rings* themed package tours).

Stand-in locations
- Tourism visits to places where a film or TV programme is set but not actually filmed (*Braveheart*, set in Scotland but mainly filmed in Ireland).

Off location
- Film studio tours to view the filming process (Paramount Studios, Los Angeles).
- Film-based theme parks (Universal Studios, Los Angeles).

Events
- Film premieres and festivals (Cannes, Edinburgh, London, Venice).

Armchair travel
- TV travel programmes (*Pole to Pole*, BBC; *The Long Way Down*, BBC).

The diversity of the media-based experiences described above suggests that film and TV tourists are not necessarily a homogeneous group driven by similar motivations. For some visitors, travelling to a specific site may be akin to a pilgrimage – Monty Python fans, for example, have a semi-spiritual experience when visiting Doune Castle in Scotland, the location of *Monty Python and The Holy Grail* (Beeton, 2005). Other visitors may be attracted to a place because of the glamour associated with a specific celebrity or lifestyle portrayed, as in the popular *Sex and The City* tours, which encapsulate the shopping and brunching life of a group of New York women. Others may identify on a more emotional level with a site (for example, the nostalgia associated with visiting locations of the popular 1970 children's film, *The Railway Children*), while others will visit sites out of a general interest, for example visitors to Yorkshire may find themselves wandering in and out of *Heartbeat*, *Last of the Summer Wine* or James Herriot country as part of a wider visit to the county.

Many regions who wish to capitalise on the benefits of media-based tourism have created partnerships between tourism organisations and local film commissions to encourage the use of locations for filming and to publicise the resulting productions. The London film commission, Film London, the London tourism organisation, VisitLondon and various London boroughs have produced and promoted a series of Movie Maps depicting the locations featured in a number of recent films based in the capital. On a similar note, one of the British Tourist Authority's most successful publications was their Movie Map of Britain, which was first produced as a brochure in 1996, later becoming an interactive website.

These examples of destination marketing techniques result in additional tourism activity which, in turn, brings about a series of positive and negative impacts. All tourism activity brings benefits and problems but film and TV tourism is believed to exert a series of effects on destinations that are unique to this form of visitation. Media-based tourism can bring additional income and jobs to an area and in particular can provide opportunities for selling souvenirs/merchandising and spin-off services such as themed tours and services. The profile of an area can be raised, as in the case of the city of Sheffield, which became an unlikely tourism destination in the wake of the popularity of *The Full Monty*. Kim et al. (2007) discuss the role that a Korean TV series entitled *Winter Sonata* played in improving the perception among Japanese visitors of Korea as a holiday destination. A successful film or TV programme can also assist a country or region in its destination marketing. The New Zealand government was very proactive in using the *Lord of the Rings* trilogy in its national tourism campaigns, and even appointed a 'Minister of the Rings' to maximise the considerable benefits from film-induced tourism (Beeton, 2005). Such success cannot be guaranteed, however, as Frost (2004) illustrates with his case study of the unsuccessful attempts in Victoria, Australia, to capitalise on the 2003 film, *Ned Kelly*.

While some destinations actively intervene to maximise media-related tourism, other regions may be surprised to find themselves at the centre of a film-based tourism boom. As this form of tourism is often difficult to plan, some destinations find that they are subjected to an unsustainable number of visitors. This might result in environmental damage, loss of privacy for the host community or an unwelcome change to the traditional visitor base. The small fishing port of Tobermory on the Isle of Mull, in the Western Isles of Scotland, found itself at the centre of a highly specialised tourism boom when it was used as the setting for the popular children's television programme, *Balamory*. The facilities on this small island were unsuited to large numbers of families, and tourism operators felt disinclined to alter their product to satisfy what might be a fickle market (Connell, 2004, 2005). The lure of film- or TV-based tourism might not last long, so it would be unwise to base long-term planning on what could be a passing trend. The actual filming process itself might also exert impacts on the environment, as in the case of the remote Thai beach used in the filming of *The Beach*, which was bulldozed and widened to accommodate the needs of the production team (Beeton, 2005). The film also opened the once pristine region to endless streams of backpackers keen to thrill to the adventure and romance of their own beach experience.

We have already seen that a film or television programme can bring different types of visitors to a destination, but it could also encourage altered behaviour in tourists. The World Heritage Site of Angkor in Cambodia was used as the location for the computer-game-based adventure film, *Tomb Raider*, and film-induced tourists to the site were found to be climbing on the ancient temple walls in an attempt to emulate the heroine, Lara Croft. This type of media exposure is not seen to be consistent with conservation plans set out for the site (Winter, 2002). Inappropriate visitor behaviour can also extend to the actual removal of part of a site for souvenirs, and street signs and other iconic items have been repeatedly removed from some film and television locations.

Finally, as with **literary tourists,** some visitors to locations may feel some disappointment with the perceived **authenticity** of sites visited. The romantic locations depicted in the very popular film *Notting Hill* would be very difficult to find on the real London street of the same name.

The importance of the simulated image, the fleeting nature of media-based tourism, the blurring of the distinctions between reality and illusion and the role of celebrity have led some commentators to suggest that film and TV tourism is a clear example of **post-tourism**. In contemporary post-modern culture, where post-tourists operate, real places become commodified and turned into spectacles to be consumed by the ever-present **tourist gaze**, as the visitor views locations as if they were giant cinema screens.

See also: *arts tourism, authenticity, cultural tourism, literary tourism, post-tourism*

key concepts in
tourist studies

FURTHER READING

Sue Beeton's recent text *Film-induced Tourism* is the first sustained exploration of film and TV tourism and is a very useful introduction to the field. A number of case studies are to be found in the journal articles listed below, which cover a range of theoretical and practical issues associated with media-based tourism. Both Tony Reeve's (2003) *The Worldwide Guide to Movie Locations* and the website www.movie-locations.com provide useful details on film-related destinations for the film and TV tourist.

RECOMMENDED BOOKS AND ARTICLES

Beeton, S. (2005) *Film-induced Tourism*. Clevedon: Channel View.
Busby, G. and Klug, J. (2001) 'Movie-induced tourism: the challenge of measurement and other issues', *Journal of Vacation Marketing*, 7 (4): 316–32.
Riley, R., Baker, D. and Van Doren, C. (1998) 'Movie induced tourism', A*nnals of Tourism Research*, 25 (4): 919–35.

Gastronomic Tourism

> *Gastronomic tourism includes visits to destinations which are motivated primarily by an interest in indigenous national or regional gastronomy, and can include sampling food and drink, learning about production processes, buying food- or drink-related products, or attending cookery courses.*

Gastronomic tourism is not new in the sense that tourists and travellers have always eaten food in locations which are not their home. However, travelling with the *specific* motivation to learn more about national and regional cuisine, to sample certain foods or drinks, to purchase them or to enjoy cookery courses, is a relatively recent phenomenon. Hall and Mitchell (2005a) suggest that the combination of food, wine and tourism have been popular since the early nineteenth century with the opening of the first restaurants, but it it was traditionally expensive and only for an élite. The first wine trails and roads were developed in Germany in the late 1920s, and encouraged people to enjoy a number of products within one region while travelling around. Although the Second World War in Europe brought a temporary halt to leisure travel, there was a renewed enthusiasm for food when rationing ended. Since the 1960s, interest in wine and food has grown with the increasing publication of cookery books and the showing of cookery programmes on TV. Although there was not much real tourism until the 1970s, people were becoming receptive to the idea of tasting and learning about different cuisines. The changing role of women in Western societies has meant that cooking has become more of a leisure activity for both genders, rather than a compulsory domestic chore for women. Celebrity chefs tend to have a large following, and many tourists will travel simply to eat in the restaurant(s) of their favourite chef, or to visit a region that they have endorsed. Gastronomic tourism is still very much the premise of a minority, however, and a certain degree of social status tends to be attached to gastronomic knowledge and preferences.

Popular destinations in gastronomic tourism tend to be those with a distinctive and good quality cuisine. This would include not only traditional destinations like France and Italy, but increasingly countries such as Thailand and India, which offer a more exotic gastronomy. In the case of wine tourism, European destinations – France, Italy, Spain, Germany and Portugal – are facing major competition from so-called 'New World' wine-producing countries – South Africa, Australia, Chile and New Zealand. Wine tourism is a sub-set of gastronomic tourism and might include visits to vineyards, wineries, wine festivals, wine shows, wine museums, even wine spas (e.g. Caudalie in France, or 'City of Wine' in El Ciego, Spain).

The globalisation and fusion of cuisine (e.g. the Australian tendency to combine European and Asian flavours) has meant that many changes have been made to traditional and indigenous gastronomy. Migration patterns have led to a range of cuisines in most major world cities, but also a growth in the fast-food movement (e.g. MacDonalds) which can overshadow national and regional culinary distinctiveness. Hall and Mitchell (2005b), however, suggest that economic and cultural globalisation is the third stage in an ongoing process of transformation and hybridisation of cuisine. European mercantilism in the late 1400s to 1800s resulted in new foodstuffs being brought by ship back to Europe from other continents, and large-scale migrations from the seventeenth to the twentieth century, including European settlement in colonies, post-war migrations, decolonisation from the 1960s, and recent immigration (e.g. from Central and Eastern Europe), have all contributed to gastronomic change and development. There is still a strong link between national and regional identity and cuisine, but there is also a growing acceptance of the interesting fusions that can be created through the merging of the global and the local.

Food is an important place-marker in tourism promotion. The climatic conditions, culture and history of a region shape the character of the food that is produced. Gastronomy is often said to be a sub-sector of **cultural or heritage tourism** for this reason. This link between location and gastronomy has been used in a number of ways in tourism, including promotional efforts based on distinctive or 'typical' regional or national foods. Food can also be used as a means for guiding tourists around regions and countries, for example in the form of trails (Hjalager and Richards, 2002).

The impacts and benefits of gastronomic tourism for regions can include an increased demand for food-related products, the building of brand loyalty, marketing intelligence for producers and suppliers, educational opportunities for visitors and residents, regional and local employment creation, extension of the tourists' stay in an area, wider distribution of spending, and the protection of intellectual property. The latter issue has become increasingly important in the global marketplace, as many producers struggle to retain the unique identity of their products. New laws and regulations are therefore needed to preserve the use of certain brand names and labels (e.g. Champagne in France or Tokaji wine in Hungary).

Gastronomic tourists are usually keen to sample products which are indigenous to a country or region (unlike mass or package tourists who may seek out their own national cuisine even while abroad). All tourists tend to eat at least three times per day, but it is only a minority who consider this to be a primary focus of their holiday. Hall and Mitchell (2005a) suggest categorising gastronomic tourists as follows:

- **Gourmet tourists** – visit expensive or highly rated restaurants or wineries
- **Gastronomic/culinary tourists** – interested in wider issues such as the culture and landscape which produce food and wine
- **Cuisine tourists** – interested in specific cuisines from a country or region.

Gastronomic tourists (like most **special interest** tourists) tend to be wealthier and better educated than average, travel without children, and are usually in the AB (upper/middle) or C1 (lower-middle-class) groups.

The research by the authors in Hall et al. (2000) suggest that wine tourism is mainly short-stay (3–4 days), non-seasonal and enjoyed by couples aged 30–50 without children, who tend to travel in groups. Motivations include tasting and buying wine, enjoying a day out, socialising, learning about wines, relaxation and landscape.

Hall and Mitchell (2005a) state that only 3 per cent of international tourists could be described as gastronomic tourists, but Enteleca Research & Consultancy (2000) provided an analysis of tourists which implies that far more tourists enjoy gastronomy as a secondary motivation and could therefore be targeted by food producers or suppliers:

- food tourists (6–8%)
- interested purchasers (30–33%)
- the un-reached (15–17%)
- the un-engaged (22–24%)
- laggards (17–28%).

The study concluded that food has an important role for about half of the tourists surveyed. 'Food tourists' are the most dedicated group, and local food has an important role in their destination choice. For 'interested purchasers', food contributes to holiday satisfaction and they sample local food when the opportunity arises. 'Un-reached tourists' believe that food can contribute to the enjoyment of their holiday, but they seldom buy local foods. The 'un-engaged' and 'laggards' are those who have limited or no intention to try local food.

Erik Wolf (2008), president of the International Culinary Tourism Association, a non-profit group representing more than 500 tourism businesses in 19 countries, described how World Travel Market Research had revealed that more than half (53 per cent) of tourists ranked eating traditional dishes as a 'very important' or 'important' part of their holiday. Of British people, 86 per cent said they enjoyed local foods when abroad and would skip meals in the hotel or resort to try out local restaurants. This implies that the latent demand for gastronomic tourism could be much higher than previously thought.

In recent years, a number of factors, such as changes of lifestyle, are affecting the development of gastronomic tourism. Many people are trying to eat healthier foods and many have switched to vegetarian or special diets, which hotels and restaurants need to accommodate. Capitalist working patterns usually mean that traditional long lunches are not an option for most workers, so a shift to fast food or snack bars has increased. In addition, chain hotels, restaurants and cafés tend to offer standardised or globalised food, rather than local specialities. Menus in tourist destinations are frequently adapted and simplified to accommodate tourists' tastes (e.g. making Thai food less spicy). The Slow Food Movement was established in 1989 to counteract fast food and fast life, the disappearance of local food traditions and people's dwindling interest in the food they eat, where it comes from, how it tastes and how food choices affect the rest of the world (Slow Food Movement, 2008). Although many tourists prefer the predictability and 'safeness' of international cuisine or fast food, gastronomic tourists most certainly do not. The richness, diversity and quality of national, regional and local cuisine is their primary motivation for travelling to a particular location.

See also: *cultural tourism, heritage tourism, special interest tourism*

FURTHER READING

In recent years, there have been more journal articles and book chapters written on this subject than whole books, but it is still worth looking at Hjalager and Richards' *Tourism and Gastronomy*; Hall et al.'s *Food Tourism around the World: Development, Management and Markets* and Boniface's *Tasting Tourism: Travelling for Food and Drink*. The Association for Tourism and Leisure Education has a Special Interest Group on Gastronomic Tourism (see www. atlas-euro.org for details of their research, publications and meetings).

RECOMMENDED BOOKS

Boniface, P. (2003) *Tasting Tourism: Travelling for Food and Drink*. Aldershot: Ashgate.
Hall, C.M., Sharples, L., Mitchell, R., Macionis, N. and Cambourne, B. (eds) (2003) *Food Tourism around the World: Development, Management and Markets*. Oxford: Butterworth-Heinemann.
Hjalager, A. and Richards, G. (2002) *Tourism and Gastronomy*. London: Routledge.

gastronomic tourism

Gay Tourism

> *Gay tourism (sometimes termed GLBT or Gay, Lesbian, Bi-Sexual and Transgender Tourism) is about developing products and activities which appeal to these segments, or creating safe, sympathetic destinations where it feels comfortable to be openly gay.*

Many destinations are increasingly recognising the benefits of attracting the so-called 'Pink Pound or Dollar'. According to Florida (2002), who developed a 'Gay Index' for cities, there are close connections between economic development and business growth, and high numbers of gay residents. The same is true of the tourism sector, where the slang term 'gaycation' has become common parlance for a vacation which includes a pronounced aspect of GLBT culture. The International Gay and Lesbian Travel Association (IGLTA) holds an annual world convention and four symposia in different tourism destinations around the world. Each symposium attracts over 100 representatives of tour agencies and travel publications that specialise in the gay and lesbian market (www.iglta.org). However, this subject still tends to be treated with a great deal of cautious 'tact' on the part of tourism theorists, very few of whom propose direct methods of targeting gay clients. This is perhaps true of the whole of the leisure industry which, while admitting that this is one of the most lucrative sectors to capture, does not blatantly (or only on very few occasions) acknowledge that their promotions are designed exclusively for the homosexual audience, for fear, perhaps, of potential heterosexual backlash.

However, it is clear that gay men in particular (much more than lesbians, bisexuals and transsexuals, who are still peripheral segments of this central market) travel more, spend more and have the largest amount of disposable income. According to a 2000 Tourism Intelligence International report, 10 per cent of international tourists were gay and lesbian, accounting for more than 70 million arrivals worldwide. This market segment is expected to continue to grow as a result of ongoing acceptance of GLBT people (Guaracino, 2007). They are highly discerning consumers, investing their travel dollars in suppliers and destinations that recognise their unique buying preferences and who offer them differentiated value.

However, it is worth considering which destinations and attractions are popular with gay tourists at present, as it should also be noted which ones are not at all gay friendly, as GLBT tourism is far from widespread. In most Muslim countries, it can be illegal to be openly gay, many parts of Africa have introduced new anti-homosexuality laws in recent years (e.g. Zanzibar in 2004) and much of the Caribbean is not gay friendly. Amnesty International once described Jamaica as 'suffering from an appalling level of homophobia'. The resort chain Sandals for years had a policy of not accepting same-sex couples, and only lifted this ban in 2004. There were also well-documented stories of gay cruises being banned from docking in some of the Caribbean Islands such as the Cayman Islands. Even in the UK, the government was still debating whether hotels should have the right to ban same-sex couples in 2005, but by 2006 anti-discrimination legislation was in place. Ironically, around the same time, Visit Britain (www.visit britain.co.uk) was actively promoting gay tourism with the caption: 'With our proud gay history, cutting edge culture and fashion, flamboyant cities and pulsating nightlife, isn't it time you came out … to Britain!'

Many large cities have a reputation for being gay friendly, especially San Francisco, Sydney, London, Madrid, New York, Amsterdam and, increasingly, the cities of South America such as Rio and Buenos Aires. Rio Carnival provides an ideal opportunity for dressing up and expressing one's true self. Buenos Aires was chosen to host the 2007 International Gay and Lesbian Football Association (IGLFA) World Championship because of its tolerance of homosexuality. Manchester in the north of England has a popular Gay Village, which has become the main focus of the city's vibrant nightlife. Indeed, a number of cities, both in Europe and internationally, can claim to have a gay quarter which has a thriving evening economy, not to mention daytime leisure and retail provision. Many English and European seaside towns are also actively promoting gay tourism as a means of establishing a new image or identity. Examples include Brighton, Blackpool and Bournemouth, which have all been promoted as gay destinations by the national and local tourism agencies. Sitges in Spain has also been a popular gay destination for many years, as well as some parts of the Canary Islands. Many new products have emerged in recent years, such as gay cruises, gay ski weeks or gay spas.

Gay parades and gay entertainment are among the many attractions of a 'cosmopolitan' city. Chicago, for example, has capitalised on the marketable qualities of its 'gay village', Halsted Street, as has Las Palmas de Gran Canaria, with its famous Drag Queen competition in the local carnival. The most significant examples of gay cultural events that draw a mainstream tourist audience, as well as a gay one, are the Gay Pride or Mardi Gras events. Originally, such events were highly politicised, and the marches which accompany such events still tend to be so. These were largely a forum for the gay community to present a united front, and to express and assert their identity and rights publicly. However, in most cases, the lively celebrations that follow are becoming more of a public party than anything else, unfortunately often resulting in the 'de-gaying' of public spaces and/or feelings of progressive alienation on the part of gay groups (Smith, 2003).

Decisions to 'go gay' are not to be taken lightly by any tourist resort, especially as a too blatant approach can quickly alienate other market segments. For example, Sitges in Spain and Brighton in the UK have become well-known gay tourism destinations, but this might mean that they fail to attract 'traditional' beach tourists (e.g. families with children). However, it can also have the opposite effect and attract even more tourists. For example, many women seem to feel 'safer' attending gay events than straight ones, as they are not threatened by the advances of straight men.

As in traditional promotion and publicity in the tourist market where the 'tourist gaze' is directed from the dominant perspective of the white heterosexual European male, the marketing in GLBT tourism tends to be dominated by the perspective of the white European homosexual male. This has been acknowledged by more than a few of the authors who have ventured to map the terrain of GLBT tourism, for example Waitt and Markwell (2006). This trend, towards a white male dominant vision, is reflected in web pages and publicity (books, brochures, travel guides, etc.) relating to gay tourism, and the celebration of 'gay parades' and pride festivals. This means that certain homosexual groups may still be excluded or marginalised because of their age, gender, nationality or skin colour.

'Gaycations' (or gay vacations/destinations) are decided on the basis of the reputation for gay friendliness, location close to known attractions plus recommendations by friends. Survey respondents answering questions with respect to travel preferences also state that online information is vital for planning their trip, since internet and networking have basically allowed for many to 'come out of the closet', thus producing the sexual revolution we are witnessing in the twenty-first century.

It might be asked why gay people need to go to specific destinations or to use gay-oriented facilities and services. Many GLBT tourists need the 'escape' of vacations to be the 'self' or the 'other' they cannot usually manifest due to family, work and religious restrictions. The 'liminal' realm of tourist destinations provides a release from everyday life and opens up areas for GLBT tourists to explore multiple possibilities (Turner, 1987) and alternative 'acceptable' notions of self. However, much remains to be studied about the implications and perceptions of gay tourism, not least the blurring of boundaries between gay tourism and **sex tourism**. It is often assumed that gay tourism and sex tourism are synonymous, which is an unhelpful assumption and serves to fuel even more unnecessary prejudice.

See also: identity, sex tourism

FURTHER READING

On this, as in many other semi-taboo topics in tourism, it is often better to consult the specialised websites for gay and lesbian travel. However, many mainstream books are starting to emerge, such as Waitt and Markwell's *Gay Tourism: Culture and Context*, as well as Clift et al.'s *Gay Tourism*. The work of Howard Hughes also focuses increasingly on gay tourism, especially *Pink Tourism: Holidays of Gay Men and Lesbians*.

RECOMMENDED BOOKS

Clift, S., Luongo, M. and Callister, C. (eds) (2002) *Gay Tourism: Culture, Identity and Sex*. London: Continuum Books.
Hughes, H.L. (2006) *Pink Tourism: Holidays of Gay Men and Lesbians*. Wallingford: CABI.
Waitt, G. and Markwell, K. (2006) *Gay Tourism: Culture and Context*. New York: Haworth Press.

gay tourism

Geography of Tourism

> *The geography of tourism usually refers to the physical and cultural geography of consumption, supply, demand and transport in tourism.*

The geography of tourism is dominated by a number of key themes, which relate to location, place and space, human and cultural characteristics, and the movement of people or **mobility.** This includes the modes of transport which are used to carry them from one location to another. The geography of tourism is also concerned with the flows of tourism from generating countries to destinations. These can be heavily influenced by economic and political factors, with the flows of tourism traditionally being from Western developed countries to less developed countries. As a result, debates relating to the globalisation of tourism and the standardisation of culture are closely connected to geography, as tourism is often said to homogenise an environment or destroy a sense of place.

Aitchison, MacLeod and Shaw (2000) discuss the geographies of leisure and tourism, which they suggest include different geographical discourses. These include colonial geographies, which map regional territories and assign multiple meanings to the same locations; systematic geographies, which can create physical boundaries around nation states, or can create spaces which are not freely accessible to all peoples (e.g. women, ethnic minorities, homosexuals); landscape evaluations, which decide how land should be used or how it should be valued; tourism geographies, which consist of tourism destinations such as seaside resorts, their life cycles and patterns of visitation; structuralist interpretations, which recognise the frameworks and institutions controlling tourism landscapes; and post-colonial geographies, which reflect on the constructions of tourism destinations as exotic and the people within these landscapes as the Other (see **self and other**).

Hall and Tucker (2004) show how colonial thinking and discourse are far from over in contemporary tourism, especially as many Europeans may be nostalgic about imperialism, and may idealise it. The flows of Western tourists therefore often go in the direction of former colonies, perhaps because of a nostalgia for an earlier, more 'glorious' era in a country's history, as well as the familiarity of architecture, food, language and general culture. The British and American markets still tend to move in their leisure time to places where English is widely spoken, the capacity to communicate in their mother tongue being an essential part of the relaxation. The same could be said of Spain (and the Spanish) with Latin America or the Caribbean, or, for that matter, the French and their former colonies (Morocco being a prime example).

However, the geography of tourism, especially economic and political geography, is constantly being rewritten. Although dominated for the last 60 years by European preferences and trends, as transport systems have evolved, tourism has moved further afield, and tourists now come from countries like China and India, with very different consumer trends and patterns. The cultural geography of consumption and 'consuming places' is partly dictated by gender, age, social status, physical fitness, communicative ability and religion, as well as nationality. The geography of tourism is also defined by types of tourism or vice versa. Therefore, we tend to divide tourism into geographical packages: urban, rural, coastal, island, domestic, international or 'pleasure periphery', according to Hall and Page (2005), two of the greatest exponents of the New Geography of Tourism. Climate also influences tourist movements considerably. People who live in the colder regions of the north of Europe tend to gravitate towards the warmer climes of the south in their holiday periods.

Climate change is a major factor influencing the geography of consumption of tourism. The areas most affected by the 2004 Asian Tsunami have taken some time to recover from the blow to their tourism trade. Typhoons, monsoons, hurricanes, forest fires and excess exposure to extreme temperatures are also significant de-motivators to tourism. Political and religious incidents also change the physical pattern of consumption of tourism (see **crisis management**). After the September 11 attacks, the USA took some time to climb back up into the top tourism ranks. The Balkans, Iraq, Iran and Afghanistan have been practically wiped off the list of potential geographical venues for tourism, with only the first of these timidly making its way back into the sector. Palestine, the Lebanon and Israel generally suffer the same fate.

Economic developments can also produce significant changes in geographical movement, with people gravitating towards the United Kingdom or the USA hit by recession when these destinations may have been perceived as too expensive in the past. Dubai and the Emirate States are also an example of 'glittery' places previously perceived as being outside the possible economic sphere of most, much like Las Vegas in the past, but now topping the list of chosen resorts. The Eurozone is prohibitively expensive at present, and survives thanks to the rise in Chinese and Japanese tourism.

The geography of tourism is also very much concerned with space and place, which includes concerns about standardisation and globalisation. As a consequence, a relatively new form of tourism, known as Geotourism, has emerged. Geotourism is tourism that sustains, or even enhances, the geographical character of a place, such as its culture, environment, heritage and the well-being of its residents. Geotourism is a form of special interest tourism which is linked to **sustainable** and **ecotourism**, but also to **heritage** and **cultural tourism**. It encompasses both cultural *and* environmental concerns, as well as the local impact tourism has upon communities and their individual economies and lifestyles. Geotourism can become a way of promoting and funding geoconservation – that is, the protection of landscapes and their unique features. The visitors' interests should go beyond an aesthetic appreciation of landscape and focus on the understanding, preservation and conservation of the site.

Early definitions of geotourism in the 1990s were closely linked to the visitation and interpretation of geological and geomorphical sites or so-called 'geosites', which provided a form of 'recreational geology' (Hose, 2005). However, the concept of geotourism seems to have become broader in recent years, and was reintroduced publicly in a 2002 report by the Travel Industry Association of America and *National Geographic Traveler* magazine. This report stated that National Geographic senior editor, Jonathan B. Tourtellot, and his wife, Sally Bensusen, had coined the term in 1997 in response to requests for a term and concept more encompassing than **ecotourism** and **sustainable tourism.** Geotourism incorporates the concept of sustainable tourism and the idea that destinations should be preserved for future generations, but at the same time allows for enhancement that protects the character of the locale. Geotourism also adopts a principle from ecotourism, which is that tourism revenue can be used to promote conservation. This includes not just the natural environment, but history and culture as well (National Geographic, 2008).

Geotourism is focused on the distinctive character of a location, and aims to retain its geographical character or sense of place; this means the whole place, including its historic structures, traditional and contemporary cultures, landscapes, gastronomy, arts and crafts, as well as local flora and fauna. Development should enhance this sense of place, and so globalised and standardised facilities (e.g. chain hotels, fast-food restaurants) and generic architecture are discouraged. This should benefit visitors and local residents alike. Geotourism aims to promote a virtuous circle whereby tourism revenues provide a local incentive to protect what tourists are coming to see, thereby not following the typical pattern of 'each man kills the thing he loves'. Geotourism embraces principles of sustainability with an integrated and long-term approach to destination development and management. The National Geographic (2008) summarises the main characteristics of geotourism and has also created a Geotourism Charter based on 13 principles (see www.nationalgeographic.com/travel/sustainable/about_geotourism.html). Many countries have started to develop and promote geotourism, including the USA, Canada, Australia, Norway, Iran, Nepal, Ecuador, Costa Rica and Greece.

The Travel Industry Association of America (2002) undertook some research called 'the Geotourism Study' on the kind of travellers who are likely to display the right attitude to be attracted to geotourism. The study identified eight traveller segments or profiles from the 154 million Americans who had taken at least one trip in the previous three years. The results showed that there are at least 55 million Americans who could be classified as 'sustainable tourists' or 'Geotourists'. The top three segments were:

- geo-savvys (16.3 million adult travellers)
- urban sophisticates (21.2 million)
- good citizens (17.6 million).

All three groups are guided by a high awareness of the world around them, and they are likely to seek trips which help to protect and preserve the ecological and cultural environment, and which afford them authentic travel experiences. In addition, the other segments identified represent close to 100 million travelling Americans who could be moving in that direction.

It could be argued that geotourism is just a fusion or repackaging of existing concepts (**sustainable tourism, ecotourism** and **cultural tourism**), but the label could be appealing to the growing number of travellers who are interested in the conservation of beautiful and unique landscapes, and the continuity and authenticity of local cultures.

See also: crisis management, mature tourism, mobility, neo-colonialism

FURTHER READING

Worldwide Destinations: The Geography of Travel and Tourism by Boniface and Cooper is worth reading, together with the work of Michael Hall (e.g. Hall and Page, *The Geography of Tourism and Recreation: Environment, Place and Space*). *Geography of Travel and Tourism* by Jackson and Hudman, in its most recent edition, is also useful.

RECOMMENDED BOOKS

Boniface, B. and Cooper, C. (2004) *Worldwide Destinations: The Geography of Travel and Tourism*. Oxford: Butterworth-Heinemann.
Hall, C.M. and Page, S.J. (2005) *The Geography of Tourism and Recreation: Environment, Place and Space*, 3rd edn. London: Routledge.
Jackson, R.H. and Hudman, L.E. (2002) *Geography of Travel and Tourism*. New York: Delmar Learning.

Health and Wellness Tourism

This consists of forms of tourism which focus on activities and practices which contribute to personal health and wellness, including physical, mental, psychological and emotional domains.

Health and wellness tourism are among the oldest forms of tourism. Ancient civilisations as far back as 5000–1000 BC practised many of the therapies which are found in spas today (e.g. Ayurveda, Chinese medicine, Thai massage). Greeks introduced water treatments to the Roman Empire and the Romans built some of the first spas in Europe. Hebrews engaged in ritual purification through immersion in the Dead Sea; the Ottoman Empire built Turkish baths; and the first forms of thalassotherapy (visits to sea water resorts) took place in the eighteenth century. The first spa resorts appeared in the USA in the early nineteenth century and there was an intense development of international destination, resort and hotel spas in the latter part of the twentieth century to complement the already existing medical heritage spas.

Nature plays a significant role in health and wellness in many countries, such as those which have a sea coast and can offer products like thalassotherapy or seawater-related treatments (common in Europe), or the Dead Sea, which is the main natural healing asset in the Middle East. Mountains are another feature which has always attracted health visitors, especially the Alps in Europe. Jungles and national parks (e.g. in Central and South America, Africa) make ideal locations for adventure and eco spas, which are a growing trend. Even deserts (e.g. in the Middle East or North Africa) are being used as locations for yoga and meditation holidays. Many countries have natural healing assets such as medical, thermal and mineral waters (Central and Eastern Europe), special muds, caves, mountains, climate, etc. These countries tend to have a long history of medical tourism and are often only just starting to move into more leisure-based wellness tourism.

There has clearly been a growth in the pursuit of health and wellness tourism in recent years, which is reflected in the proliferation of spas, wellness hotels and retreat centres (for meditation, yoga, stress management, life coaching, etc.). This is supported by changing definitions of health, and a shift from passive approaches to more active ones (people want to improve their lifestyles so that they can remain healthier into old age). The widely accepted definition of health is that of the World Health Organization (WHO, 1948), which states that 'health is a state of complete physical, mental and social well-being and not merely the absence of disease or infirmity'. Health is much more than not being ill. Besides the body, it relates to one's emotions, thoughts and feelings. The concept of wellness takes this idea even further, and those tourists who are already well rather than ill, and do not require medical treatment, are more likely to opt for wellness trips. Wellness as defined by the National Wellness Institute (2007) is 'an active process of becoming aware of and making choices toward a more successful existence'. Wellness is supposed to create harmony in mental, physical, spiritual or biological health in general, and has stronger ties with changing lifestyle than with curing a specific disease. In contrast, medical tourism tends to deal with physical conditions and diseases, and may consist of rehabilitation or recuperation in a medical spa, or even having surgery.

We can therefore make a distinction between health, wellness and medical tourism and some of the products and activities which are included in these categories. Health tourism is the overarching category within which wellness and medical tourism can offer different experiences. For example:

> **Wellness tourism:** includes leisure and recreation (beauty treatments, sports, pampering in spas); holistic activities (yoga, meditation and spiritual activities in retreats or ashrams); and perhaps medical wellness where the tourist/patient is focused on improving health rather than curing a specific medical condition (diet and lifestyle advice, occupational wellness in hotels or clinics).
>
> **Medical tourism:** includes surgery (cosmetic, dentistry, operations in clinics or hospitals); therapeutic treatments (rehabilitation, healing in medical spas); and medical wellness where the tourist/patient may be treated for a specific medical condition (diabetes, obesity, depression) in specialised clinics or hotels.

It can be seen that, at one end of the spectrum, wellness tourism can deal with people's spiritual lives in holistic tourism, while, at the other end, the focus is mainly on the physical body in therapeutic and surgical medical tourism. However, increasingly more visitors are interested in balancing body, mind *and* spirit, and many spa and hotel resort facilities are starting to offer a whole range of health tourism activities and treatments.

The market for health tourism varies according to different activities undertaken, but some general patterns are also in evidence. If health tourism is defined broadly to include spirituality, then the market ranges from hippy backpackers who visit yoga ashrams in India or Buddhist meditation retreats in Thailand, to elderly tourists with specific medical and health problems in the heritage spas of Central Europe, to stressed-out executives visiting luxury spa resorts and hotels all over the world. However, the main trend for health tourism tends to be among professional women aged 45 on average. Sociological research carried out by Cleaver and Muller (2002) into the tourism behaviour of 'BabyBoomers' (those born immediately after the Second World War in Europe and the USA) suggests that this group is a key target for the health tourism sector. These consumers are often at their peak earning potential, have high education levels, enjoy increasing freedom from debt, have more time for travel and a greater desire for 'self-fulfilling' activities. However, there is also a concerted effort being made in the health tourism sector to attract more men, more families and younger people (although not always simultaneously, as mixing markets is not usually an effective strategy). Arguably, all health tourists are becoming self-aware, active seekers of enhanced well-being, health and happiness. Of course, health is not a static concept and is subjective and relative, thus always in flux. The needs of health tourists will clearly vary enormously at different times and stages of their lives.

Typical types of health products, locations and visitors include the following:

- Traditional spas (e.g. in Central and Eastern Europe) offer water-based healing and treatments to older people (55+) with specific health problems.
- Hotels and day spas (e.g. in the UK, USA, Australia) offer beauty and pampering treatments to high-income visitors, usually professional women aged 30+.
- Purpose-built recreational spas (e.g. in Austria, Germany) offer water-based leisure and entertainment, as well as massage and other treatments to individuals, couples and families with children.
- Seaside resorts and thalassotherapy centres (e.g in France, Israel) offer seawater-based treatments to mid- or upper-income groups.
- Holistic retreat centres (e.g. in Greece, Spain) offer a range of activities which help to balance body, mind and spirit. The average market is professional people aged 30–55.
- Yoga centres (e.g. in India, USA, Canada, Europe) offer yoga holidays to mainly professional women aged 40+.
- Meditation retreats (e.g. in Thailand, India) attract independent travellers, backpackers and 'soul-seekers' who undertake meditation courses for several days or weeks.
- Pilgrimage centres (e.g. in Spain, France) attract religious and non-religious seekers, mainly from older age groups, but increasingly the under-30s. Many pilgrims travel alone.

- Medical centres (e.g. in Hungary, South Africa, India) provide essential or cosmetic surgery for visitors who are mainly over 40, female and from developed countries where healthcare is more expensive.

In terms of product development, some destinations develop organically because of their spiritual traditions (e.g. Goa in India, Chiang Mai in Thailand and Byron Bay in Australia) and attract visitors in an untargeted, 'ad hoc' way. Others develop purpose-built centres for spa treatments, medical procedures or holistic practices, and target specific markets. Although many forms of health tourism are becoming more globalised and can be found anywhere (e.g. massage, saunas, steam rooms, fitness activities), there are still regional and cultural variations in health tourism. Even medical tourism, which could in theory be practised anywhere, tends to take place in countries which are cheaper than the tourists' own country, but may also specialise in specific procedures (e.g. dentistry in Hungary, sex-change operations in Thailand, cosmetic surgery in South Africa or South America). More traditional forms of health tourism in Central and Eastern Europe still focus on physical and medical treatments, mainly in spas. In Asia, the relationship between body, mind and spirit is more important than in Europe, and therefore activities such as yoga, meditation and massage tend to be integrated into everyday life and culture. Scandinavians often bathe in ice-cold water for health reasons, and saunas are a part of everyday life for the Finnish and many Russians. Indigenous peoples and tribal groups in Africa, Australasia and the Americas (Native American Indians, Aborigines, Maori) traditionally bathe in hot springs for spiritual reasons and use herbal medicines. The recent trend seems to be for Western tourists to seek solace in Eastern philosophies and therapies (Chinese medicine, Buddhist meditation, Indian Ayurveda, Thai massage). Such alternatives already pervade many Western societies, but tourists are often just as keen to visit the origin of the practice. There is also a move towards visiting more natural environments, to enjoy organic food and to use herbal and plant remedies. Many locations in Australia, Asia and Central or South America are developing eco spas, which can cater for these changing needs. Therefore, despite the globalisation of health tourism, there are still many reasons to travel to different parts of the world to experience specific health practices.

See also: religious and spiritual tourism

FURTHER READING

There are very few books specifically on the subject of health and wellness tourism, but two have recently been published. These are Smith and Puczkó's *Health and Wellness Tourism*; and Jafari et al.'s *Wellness and Tourism: Mind, Body, Spirit, Place*. There was also a special edition of the *Journal of Tourism Recreation Research* in 2006 on *Wellness Tourism*. There are several books on spa management, but most of these do not refer to tourism.

RECOMMENDED BOOKS

Jafari, J., Bushell, R. & Sheldon, P. (eds) (2008) *Wellness and Tourism: Mind, Body, Spirit, Place*. New York: Cognizant.

Smith, M.K., and Puczkó, L. (2008) *Health and Wellness Tourism*. Oxford: Butterworth-Heinemann.

Heritage Tourism

> *Heritage tourism focuses on historic attractions, buildings and objects, as well as intangible forms of culture such as the traditions and lifestyles of communities.*

Graham et al. (2000) differentiate between the terms 'past', 'history' and 'heritage'. The past is concerned with all that has ever happened, whereas history is the attempts of present-day historians to explain selected aspects of the past. Essentially, heritage is the contemporary use of the past, including both its interpretation and representation. Increasingly, however, the concept of heritage has become associated with the commercialisation or commodification of the past with the growth of the heritage industry. As a result, there has been some contention over the extent to which the past or history should be exploited or distorted as a resource for entertainment in the form of heritage. Hewison (1987)

heritage tourism

expressed concern about the apparent elaboration of historical facts for the purposes of heritage 'entertainment', whereas others (e.g. Urry, 1990/2002) fully embrace the idea of 'edutainment', the combination of education (formal or informal) and 'entertainment'. Heritage tourism is generally based on the latter concept, and even museums and sites which would prefer not to go down this route are sometimes forced to because of insufficient public funding.

The traditional view of heritage tourism was that it was inherently exploitative. Larkham (1995: 86) differentiated between the concepts of preservation, conservation and exploitation as follows:

- *Preservation* involves the retention, in largely unchanged form, of sites and objects of major cultural significance.
- *Conservation* encompasses the idea that some form of restoration should be undertaken to bring old buildings and sites into suitable modern use.
- *Exploitation* recognises the value of heritage sites, particularly for tourism and recreation, and encompasses the development of existing and new sites.

However, it is increasingly being accepted that tourism and visitation are inevitable, and that they can even be welcome developments. Extra resources can be generated for conservation purposes, heritage attractions receive more attention and publicity, the profile of **indigenous** peoples can be raised and their traditions can even be revived as a result of tourist interest (e.g. dance, craft production). There is a growing awareness of the need to protect heritage landscapes in a sustainable way, and tools and techniques are improving all the time.

Heritage is so multi-faceted that it can range from historic artefacts to buildings through landscapes to people's stories of their past. Heritage attractions can include the following:

- built heritage attractions, such as monuments, historic buildings, architecture, archaeological sites
- natural heritage attractions, such as national parks, landscapes, coastlines or caves
- religious heritage attractions, such as churches, cathedrals, temples, mosques, synagogues, as well as pilgrimage routes and cities
- industrial heritage attractions, such as mines, factories, industrial landscapes

- literary heritage attractions, such as the houses or home towns of famous writers
- artistic heritage attractions, such as the landscapes and environments which inspired artists
- cultural heritage attractions, such as traditional festivals, events, dance or folk museums.

With such a diverse range of attractions, the management of heritage tourism can be a complex process. The main challenge is maintaining the balance between conservation and visitor management. Conservationists allow some adaptation to heritage, but they are not always open to extensive visitation or tourism development. The management of tourism in composite urban environments (e.g. historic cities) clearly requires a more integrated approach than individual heritage sites. Policies and planning decisions need to be integrated into a broader urban development context, and conflicts of interest between urban planners, tourism developers, conservationists and the local resident population need to be addressed. Historic towns are inhabited by living, working communities, and should not be viewed simply as historic attractions to be fossilised or turned into living museums by the tourism or heritage industries for the benefit of visitors.

Tourist numbers at some of the world's heritage attractions, especially World Heritage Sites (WHSs) and historic cities, are becoming a cause for concern. WHSs are designated by UNESCO and represent some of the world's most unique cultural and natural heritage. Leask and Fyall (2006) suggest that there is often over-exposure of the World Heritage Site 'brand', which is gradually leading to saturation for many sites. There is now arguably a form of mass heritage tourism which is difficult to control. UNESCO stipulates that WHSs should be made available to the widest possible number of people, but many major attractions are finding it increasingly difficult to balance the conservation of the site and the accommodation of visitors. This process is clearly complicated when local communities are part of the landscape (e.g. in historic cities or cultural landscapes). Consequently, each WHS is required to have a management plan, which outlines its policy towards conservation, visitors and local issues. The diversity of WHSs means that the management of them cannot be standardised too much, and management plans must aim to address the unique features and specific nature of individual sites. The fate of heritage sites which are not on the WHS list rather depends on the site owners' management philosophy and financial position, but in general they struggle even more to protect and develop the heritage.

As well as the World Heritage Site list, there was also a project to create a list of the new Seven Wonders of the World, as some of the old ones no longer exist. Therefore, the public were able to vote online for the sites they thought should be included. The cultural sites voted for in 2007 were:

- Chichen Itza (Mexico)
- the Colosseum (Italy)
- Machu Picchu (Peru)
- the Statue of Christ (Brazil)
- the Great Wall of China
- Petra (Jordan)
- the Taj Mahal (India).

By 2011, the seven natural wonders of the world will also have been voted for, with Federico Mayor Zaragoza, the former Director of UNESCO, as the main judge (see www.new7wonders.com).

UNESCO has also developed a Convention which helps to protect intangible cultural heritage (ICH). This decision was partly based on concerns about the cultural effects of globalisation, the disappearance of unique traditions and languages, and the increasing recognition of the importance of intangible heritage for many non-Western cultures. The Convention states that the ICH is manifested, in the following domains among others:

- oral traditions and expressions including language as a vehicle of the intangible cultural heritage
- performing arts (such as traditional music, dance and theatre)
- social practices, rituals and festive events
- knowledge and practices concerning nature and the universe
- traditional craftsmanship.

Brown (2003) describes how the protection of intangible heritage can be complicated by the fact that **indigenous** people are often secretive about their traditions. Many indigenous groups fear that their cultural heritage will be appropriated by powerful outsiders, and are therefore reluctant to release information. Indigenous peoples and tribal groups have their own special problems relating to the protection of their traditions, culture and heritage. Traditionally, they inhabited certain landscapes which may since have been appropriated by developers. In addition, industrial, transport and tourism development threaten to encroach further on their heritage. Excess visitation can lead to acculturation or permanent changes in indigenous cultures, as residents start to adapt their practices to suit tourists' interests or become influenced by tourist patterns of behaviour.

However, it is not only indigenous and tribal groups whose heritage is disregarded or inadequately protected. Samuel (1994) suggests that heritage tends to reflect the ruling aesthetics of the day, mirroring public taste and what society values at the time. This means that it is inherently biased and elitist, and has traditionally reflected the tastes of white, middle-class, male Europeans. It is only because of the influence of post-modern thinking and cultural politics that efforts have been made to value the heritage of minority and ethnic groups in society. Even the social history of everyday people was traditionally overshadowed by royal or military history, and men's history has always been researched more intensively than women's. However, heritage sites and museums are increasingly focusing on the heritage of a wider range of people. The post-modern pluralisation of history and its interpretation and representation have led to a growing appreciation of industrial, agricultural and popular folk heritage. Although funding is limited and decisions still need to be made about what to support and represent, the process is becoming more democratic.

There are also interesting discussions about the nature of heritage interpretation. Some theorists have suggested that heritage tends to sanitise, glorify or soften the past. For example, Swarbrooke (2000) suggests that many museums are tending to focus on 'soft' heritage in a deliberate attempt to avoid conflict and controversy. It is common in tourism to follow this pattern, as many visitors want to be entertained rather than shocked or horrified in their leisure time. Schouten (1995) suggests that the visitor is looking for an experience, rather than the hard facts of historical reality. However, Tilden (1977) argues that the interpretation of heritage should aim to provoke, shock and move people. Tunbridge and Ashworth (1996) and Lennon and Foley (2000) provide an in-depth analysis of the concept of '**dark**' or 'dissonant' heritage and the heritage of atrocity, which is, by its very nature, sensitive and controversial, emotive and sometimes shocking.

Heritage can be used in various ways for the purposes of tourism. One example is of 'living heritage', where actors are employed to re-create or re-enact the past, usually in costumes. Although there are concerns from historians and conservationists about the 'historical accuracy' of this form of heritage, it is increasingly popular, and members of the public can even join in. For example, battle re-enactment is a hobby for many people in Europe.

Overall, it can be seen that heritage tourism is becoming one of the world's major growth sectors and, as a result, more people are concerned about the conservation and interpretation of the past. However, traditional processes and practices are gradually being replaced by more democratic ones, which recognise the diversity of heritage and include a wider range of peoples and their cultures.

See also: cultural tourism, dark tourism, indigenous tourism, urban tourism

FURTHER READING

In addition to the numerous books on **cultural tourism** (see separate entry), there have been many publications on heritage studies, heritage management and, more recently, heritage tourism. Examples include Graham et al.'s *A Geography of Heritage: Power, Culture and Economy*, and Boyd and Timothy's *Heritage Tourism*. Several books have focused on sub-sectors of heritage, such as World Heritage Sites (see Leask and Fyall's *Managing World Heritage Sites*. It is also worth referring to articles in the International *Journal of Heritage Studies* and the *Journal of Heritage Tourism*.

RECOMMENDED BOOKS

Boyd, S. and Timothy, D. (2002) *Heritage Tourism*. London: Prentice-Hall.

Graham, B., Ashworth, G.J. and Tunbridge, J.E. (2000) *A Geography of Heritage: Power, Culture and Economy*. London: Arnold.

Leask, A. and Fyall, A. (eds) (2006) *Managing World Heritage Sites*. Oxford: Butterworth-Heinemann.

key concepts in tourist studies

Identity

Identity is concerned with how we see ourselves, whether individually, collectively or as a nation. This shapes all of our value systems and ideology, influencing where and how we travel or why.

Identity is a rather fluid concept, especially in the post-modern, global era. Globalisation and the invasion of virtual time and space have had serious repercussions on identity at both an individual and a collective level. The mobilities, fluxes and flows caused by the blurring of physical boundaries on territories, geographical and political reorganisation, voluntary and obligatory movements of individuals and flows of information and capital, of the network society, have triggered redefinitions of identity at multiple levels of society and social organisation.

Sarup (1996) describes how identity construction is based on theories such as socialisation or role theory, ideology (e.g. state apparatus), discourse theory, and disciplines and technologies of the self. There is no such thing as a homogeneous identity; all are multiple or hybridised. Sarup describes how more traditional theories of identity construction were linked closely to the dynamics of class, gender and race. However, the complexities of psychological and sociological factors must also be taken into consideration.

The relationship between tourism and identity has been the focus of several studies, either directly or indirectly, for example Lanfant et al. (1995), who state that:

> Tourism, particularly 'cultural tourism', is often considered by international organisations as a pedagogic instrument allowing new identities to emerge – identities corresponding to the new plural-ethnic or plural-state configurations which are forming. (1995: 4)

Lanfant questions the extent to which the forming of identities is motivated by ideology. Tourism has frequently been described as an imperialist or hegemonic power, and identity has become a product to be manufactured, packaged and marketed like any other. As Lanfant argues, most identities are constructed in relation to others (see **self and other**).

Without a strong sense of their own identity, host societies are likely to succumb to the temptations of commercialisation, and lose sight of their traditions (Hart Robertson, 2005).

Burns (2005) discusses the creation of social identities in the context of tourism. He quotes Said (1978), who suggests that perceptions of race, nation and ethnicity can engender simplistic or stereotyped views of the 'Other'. Commercially constructed identities used in the travel industry are frequently based on these stereotypes, which may be covertly or even overtly racist and exploitative. They may also provide simplistic and idealised images which correspond to the tourists' fantasies (see **sex tourism**). In a later work, Burns and Novelli (2006) discuss the critical discourse of tourism and tourists as they relate to social and cultural identities. This includes the complex social milieu in which tourism takes place, where culture, people and their histories and lifestyles become part of the tourism product. They argue that the implications of this process are not fully understood within tourism literature and research, with culture being described on the one hand as vulnerable and fixed, waiting to be 'impacted' on by tourism and, on the other hand, being seen as vibrant and easily capable of dealing with globalisation and modernity trends. Clearly, it depends very much on the context, and the nature and stage of tourism as to how well destinations can withstand threats to their identity.

In her book, *Identity Tourism: Imaging and Imagining the Nation*, Pitchford (2007) examines the role of tourism in the construction of national identity. This includes the historical and cultural narratives which are used to create national stories and to counter negative, external perceptions. For this, certain media are required, and tourism is one such medium. Identity tourism is described as incorporating both ethnic and heritage tourism, museums, heritage centres, performances and other attractions in which collective identities are represented, interpreted and constructed.

Issues of identity construction have been a major consideration for post-socialist countries and new nation states such as former Central and Eastern European destinations (including the former USSR and Yugoslavia). This is particularly significant when considering the projection of image through marketing and promotional literature. It is difficult to decide which aspects of the culture to focus on, especially as socialist heritage may be dissonant for local residents but fascinating for visitors. However, identity creation is much more than just a commercial marketing exercise. The assertion of new and distinctive identities is highly politicised and linked to complex social and cultural forces.

Identity formation and projection is also particularly complex in neo-colonial countries (see **neo-colonialism**). Internationally, there has been a growing interest in the development of **indigenous tourism,** which, if managed effectively, is often viewed as a means of revitalising or reinforcing the cultural traditions and identity of indigenous communities (this is true of many native communities in Australia, New Zealand, North America and some parts of Asia and Central and South America). Many indigenous people (especially young people) are rediscovering their cultural traditions and identity as a result of tourist interest.

Castells (1997) defines three types of constructs of identity, at both individual and collective levels. First, there is what he calls 'legitimising' identity, produced top–down, and introduced by the dominant institutions or state structures, to extend and rationalise their authority and domination. Places (and people) have strong or weak, central or peripheral identities (and, thus, a projected market image), depending upon their tangible domination of political circumstances and power, their legitimisation and authority at a world level. In the modern world, the more urban a place is, the more central its identity and power. Such central identities are usually given concrete and tangible expression through monuments or icons, symbolic of the power and sense of place of the destination, and by extension, central experiences to be lived in the tourist's life cycles: the Statue of Liberty and the White House, the Eiffel Tower, and Versailles, the Colosseum and the Vatican, or the Tower of London, and Buckingham Palace, to name only a few. Books such as *1,000 Places to See Before You Die* (Schultz, 2003) give added legitimisation to these destinations. Central destinations with powerful tangible icons or draws, promoting the dominant world view of sights to see have an authoritative brand image and, thus, are associated or identified by the tourist as 'musts' on the tourism circuit.

The second 'identity' defined by Castells (1997) is the logical spin-off of the central/peripheral dichotomy. 'Resistance' identity is given where any individual or community steps out of the mainstream, central vision to assert an alternative, central way of being, forming initially minority lobbies of identity politics. The definition of the resistance identity necessarily refers to the mainstream, underlining the difference between 'them' and 'us'. Examples include Catalonia or the Basque country in Spain, for example. Sometimes, the assertion of resistance identity is so strong that it might pose a threat to tourists or tourism (e.g. the bombings by ETA in the Basque country). In the UK, Scotland, with its tangible heritage of castles, including Balmoral, and its projected intangible heritage, such as the Loch Ness Monster or Braveheart, has a relatively positive resistance identity vis-à-vis England. There are many other examples of resistance identities, ranging from the ethnic resistance in Montenegro, for example, to the biological, gender resistance of 'gay pride' (see **gay tourism**). Traditional masculine and feminine roles have been largely emptied of meaning (at least, in the West), with greater fluidity of gender identity than ever encountered before in previous generations. In tourism, the increased fluidity in gender identity has produced female consumption of male prostitution (see **sex tourism**), Gay or Pink Dollar Tourism (see **gay tourism**), and a re-mapping of the geography of tourism (see **geography of tourism**) according to 'safeness' of manifestation of difference.

The third process of identity construct defined by Castells is 'project' identity, which normally arises out of resistance identity, where the individual, for example a feminist challenging the very structure of the patriarchal system and capitalist production, moves from definition by resistance to definition by challenge of the established order. On another scale, the Dalai Lama is, perhaps, a fine example of project identity, challenging the legitimisation of world order and identity through war, with identity defined through peace and compassion. Although it is almost half a century since the Dalai Lama fled Tibet after a failed uprising against Chinese rule, his palace in Lhasa has recently been restored as a tourist attraction.

Post-modern societies have blurred social and geographical boundaries leading us to a society where the individual's identity and interests are determined by what he or she consumes, and goods are valued for their symbolic as well as their use value (e.g. by identifying them with celebrities and role models). Consumer identities or lifestyles change with age and maturity (see **mature tourism**), just as the images and identities of a destination change. The same person may begin their tourist experience as a backpacker (or allocentric, according to Plog's terminology) and end up as a time-share or second-home owner (possibly medio/psychocentric in Plog's terminology), thus moving from mobility motivated by new experience, to mobility based essentially on stability and security.

Consumer identities cross national and international borders, as well as cyberspace. Thus, tourists may be heavily influenced by other tourists, even though these are often in a virtual space (e.g. Blog communities). The internet has allowed for these communities of people with shared interests to interconnect and to redefine their identities through technology and tourism, as well as shaping the identities of destinations through shared perceptions.

FURTHER READING

The work of Pitchford, in *Identity Tourism: Imaging and Imagining the Nation*, and that of Burns and Novelli in *Tourism and Social Identities* are especially useful in the tourism context. Many other sources about identity can be found in sociology, anthropology and other disciplines. See Sarup's *Identity, Culture and the Postmodern World* and Castells, *The Power of Identity*.

RECOMMENDED BOOKS

Burns, P.M. and Novelli, M. (2006) *Tourism and Social Identities*. Oxford: Elsevier.
Lanfant, M., Allcock, J.B. and Bruner, E.M. (1995) *International Tourism: Identity and Change*. London: Sage.
Pitchford, S. (2007) *Identity Tourism: Imaging and Imagining the Nation*. Oxford: Elsevier.

Indigenous Tourism

> *Indigenous tourism involves visiting native or indigenous people, such as tribal groups or ethnic minorities in their natural habitat.*

The terminology used to describe the kind of tourism where tourists visit local people in their natural habitat has been variously referred to as 'ethnic', 'tribal', 'native' or 'Aboriginal', though Butler and Hinch (2007) prefer to use the umbrella term 'indigenous'. Indigenous groups are described as being distinct in terms of their culture and identity, relative to dominant groups in mainstream society. This may include their traditions, their language, their political systems and institutions, and their ties to natural environments and territories.

Indigenous tourism usually involves visiting native or indigenous people, such as tribal groups or ethnic minorities. This may be in an area that is a national park, a jungle, a desert or a mountainous region. More often than not, it will be a remote and relatively fragile location that is not easily accessible to the average tourist. However, the notion of a natural habitat is a somewhat controversial one, as many indigenous peoples have been forcibly removed from their original homelands as the land was 'required' for other purposes (e.g. mining, deforestation). Thus, many tourists may instead visit indigenous peoples such as Native American Indians in specially created reservations.

In recent years, tourists have become more and more interested in the culture, traditions and lifestyles of indigenous peoples. Even without face-to-face contact with indigenous groups, tourists are increasingly keen to purchase indigenous arts and crafts as souvenirs, as well as enjoying the cultural displays and performances that seem to constitute an integral part of the tourist experience. Many tour operators are now capitalising on the exoticism of indigenous, ethnic and tribal groups. Activities such as hilltribe, mountain or desert trekking are becoming increasingly popular, especially in some of the emerging destinations of the world such as South-East Asia and Central America. Those tourists who venture in search of traditional and ethnic cultures in remote locations are often motivated partly by an anthropological desire to learn more about communities under threat from global forces, but also to satisfy their need for cultural experiences of an authentic nature. The growth of **ecotourism** has also led to increasing interest in the preservation and protection of indigenous peoples, their habitat and their culture (Zeppel, 2006). Although ecotourism is a form of tourism that was originally more concerned with environmental than cultural issues, its development encourages the use of indigenous guides, local products and local resources.

Indigenous tourism can take a number of different forms and can focus on many different activities. These can include the following:

- indigenous ecotourism (e.g. in jungles, rainforests and mountain areas such as those of Central America or Asia)
- wildlife and safari tourism (e.g. in the national parks of Kenya or Tanzania where the Maasai people live)
- hilltribe tourism and trekking (e.g. in the villages of Thailand or Vietnam)
- Bedouin or desert tourism (e.g. in the deserts of North Africa or the Middle East)
- Inuit tourism (e.g. in countries close to the Arctic Circle such as Greenland, Canada or Alaska)
- village tourism (e.g. on the islands of the South Pacific).

- reservation tourism (e.g. American Indian reservations in the USA or Canada)
- Aboriginal or Maori tourism (e.g. in Australia and New Zealand).

The impacts of these forms of tourism can be significant, as most of the environments in which they take place are fragile. Tourism may encroach not only on the natural habitat of indigenous peoples, but on the entire ecosystem (e.g. flora, fauna). Irreversible changes may take place in the environment, and cultures may also be affected by the process of acculturation, whereby the dominant culture (that of the tourists in this case) starts to influence and cause changes in the local culture (that of indigenous people). Although the interest of tourists in the local culture can also help to support that culture and has sometimes led to the revival of dying traditions, care must be taken that the local people still feel in control of their destiny.

Tourism is only one factor in the changing lifestyles of indigenous peoples. Mining, deforestation, road building and civil war are all responsible for threatening their long-term survival, and many are still subjected to racism, persecution and violence. The legacy that remains for many indigenous people is often one of poverty, deprivation and social exclusion. Indigenous issues are highly politicised because the majority of ethnic and tribal groups are fighting for their cultural survival in an increasingly globalised world, usually without access to adequate political or legal protection and support. Consequently, a number of international and national organisations are working for and with indigenous peoples to protect their interests, and many of these encourage tourism development as a way of gaining international recognition and support.

Butler and Hinch (2007) have developed further their previous book on *Tourism and Indigenous Peoples* (1996), which focused mainly on the impacts of tourism on indigenous lifestyles and cultures, and now demonstrate the shift towards more active participation of indigenous peoples in tourism development. Certain forms of community-based tourism can offer indigenous peoples the chance to move towards greater political self-determination if local control is maximised. Zeppel (2006) describes how indigenous peoples often run cultural ecotours, ecolodges, hunting and fishing tours, cultural villages and other nature-orientated facilities and services. This can help the people to supplement their subsistence lifestyle and aid the transition to a cash economy. Many such ventures are developed and controlled by indigenous peoples, and they are not merely on the margins.

The extent of indigenous involvement in, and control of, indigenous tourism development is very variable, and will depend very much on the context in which development is taking place and the degree of local and governmental support. Although indigenous people were traditionally rarely given complete control or ownership of tourist sites or attractions, there have been definite moves towards consultative, cooperative and even sole management. Cooperative arrangements can be highly beneficial as long as indigenous peoples are treated as equal partners. Ultimately, the majority of indigenous peoples are likely to be seeking the kind of empowerment that enables them to move towards sole ownership and management of tourism venues and initiatives. However, better support is often needed in terms of funding, education and business skills training.

The profile of indigenous tourists is changing rapidly. In the past, the market was largely composed of allocentric (**identity**) tourists, that is, adventurous or intrepid individuals seeking the unexplored and the untouched. Although many activities such as hilltribe, mountain or desert trekking are still mainly dominated by the independent backpacker market, other forms of indigenous tourism (cultural heritage, arts and crafts, and village tourism) are now starting to form part of mainstream tourism packages. In fact, wildlife tourism on indigenous tribal lands in countries like Kenya and Tanzania has become a mass tourism phenomenon.

The ubiquitous cultural performances, displays and arts and crafts markets also indicate the growing significance of indigenous culture for the tourism product. There has also been an increasing globalisation of indigenous cultures, with Aboriginal art, for example, being sold on the internet. The growing interest in indigenous culture and arts and crafts tourism raises important questions about concepts such as **authenticity** and commodification. Tourists' interest in indigenous arts and culture can help to support cultural continuity or the revival of traditions, but it can also compromise the authenticity of the art form. Indigenous culture sometimes needs to be presented to tourists in a simplified format which then compromises the art form. Many tourists just want a taste of local culture, not a lengthy performance of dancing, singing or music which requires considerable concentration or phenomenal endurance (e.g. all-night performances of Kathakali dance in Hindu temples in India). Tourists rarely understand local dialects, so translations of songs or plays may be provided, or some kind of interpretation offered.

However, the authenticity of arts and crafts is considered to be very important for the majority of indigenous tourists, and they may want to be assured that the product they are buying is made by a local craftsperson and reflects traditional methods and a design which is characteristic of the local area. Of course, the commodification and mass production of tourist souvenirs is widespread, but many craftspeople are now using government-approved stamps of authenticity to protect local production and to reassure tourists seeking authentic products. Fair trade initiatives are also being set up in order to protect local producers from exploitation, and more emphasis is being placed on local training needs.

Indigenous exhibitions are also being shown in world-famous museums. However, the interpretation of indigenous collections or exhibitions is often left in the hands of non-indigenous peoples who may or may not understand fully the culture and traditions with which they are dealing. Traditionally, the culture of indigenous peoples has been fossilised in museum exhibitions or viewed with nostalgia, implying that it has vanished or disappeared, rather than being dynamic and ongoing. However, museum exhibitions are now increasingly focusing on the 'truth' of indigenous and colonial history, as well as attempting to represent and interpret indigenous traditions and culture more accurately.

Over the past few decades, indigenous peoples have increasingly been afforded the kind of political, legal and economic support that is imperative for their future survival. Rather than being perceived as dying species, there is a growing appreciation of their resilient and dynamic cultures and traditions, and a recognition of the need to protect them. Although land use remains perhaps the most controversial and unresolved issue, a great deal of progress has been made in other areas of indigenous development. Tourism can be viewed as one of the most positive forces for change in terms of economic benefits, conservation measures and the protection or revitalisation of cultural traditions. The key concepts of local empowerment, self-determination and control need to be adhered to, but if tourism is managed responsibly and ethically, its contribution to the cultural survival of indigenous peoples can be invaluable.

See also: *cultural tourism, ecotourism*

FURTHER READING

Indigenous tourism has become the subject of several books and journal articles in recent years. For example, Ryan and Aicken's *Indigenous Tourism: The Commodification and Management of Culture*; and Butler and Hinch's *Tourism and Indigenous Peoples: Issues and Implications*. These contain a number of interesting case studies from around the world. Johnston (2005) also examines many of the practical issues relating to indigenous tourism development in *Is the Sacred for Sale? Tourism and Indigenous Peoples*. Reference should also be made to the website of the organisation 'Survival – The Movement for Tribal Peoples' (www.survival-international.org).

RECOMMENDED BOOKS

Butler, R. and Hinch, T. (eds) (2007) *Tourism and Indigenous Peoples: Issues and Implications*. Oxford: Butterworth-Heinemann.

Johnston, A. (2005) *Is the Sacred for Sale? Tourism and Indigenous Peoples*. London: Earthscan Ltd.

Ryan, C. and Aicken, M. (eds) (2005) *Indigenous Tourism: The Commodification and Management of Culture*. Oxford: Butterworth-Heinemann.

Zeppel, H. (2006) *Indigenous Ecotourism: Sustainable Development and Management*. Wallingford: CABI.

Literary Tourism

key concepts in tourist studies

> **Literary tourism describes tourism activity that is motivated by interest in an author, a literary creation or setting, or the literary heritage of a destination.**

Literary tourism has a number of dimensions as the definition above suggests. Tourists enjoy visiting birthplaces, burial sites, museums, literary trails and other sites associated with authors or literary creations. William Worsdworth's cottage, Thomas Hardy's birthplace and Shakespeare's tomb are all popular visitor destinations in the UK. Tourists also enjoy attractions with more generic literary associations such as Jamaica Inn on Bodmin Moor in Cornwall or the guided literary pub tours of Edinburgh.

The representations of countries and their culture within literature can also inspire visits – package tourists to Spain may not necessarily think that their visit has been inspired by the works of Hemingway, Laurie Lee or Robert Graves but their attitudes and perceptions of the country may have been subconsciously created by their reading of these texts.

Literary tourism is of course not a new activity and many of the important sites on the seventeenth and eighteenth century Grand Tour of Europe were literary shrines (Buzard, 1993). Early Grand Tourists followed the trail of the classics, visiting landscapes described by Virgil, Horace and Cicero. Later, the Romantic poets provided the inspiration as visitors travelled the continent, inspired by the poets Byron and Shelley (Towner, 2002). These tourists were highly educated, elite travellers with the cultural awareness and financial resources necessary to make such travels. Some of today's literary tourists may resemble these earlier travellers – and there is certainly an assumption that an interest in literary themes may still be the preserve of the educated middle classes – but literary tourism has also been more widely popularised in recent years. This is undoubtedly due to the prevalence of more accessible film versions of classic texts (see **film and TV tourism**), best-selling novels with a tourism tie-in, such as the Da Vinci Code Trail and the upsurge in popularity of children's fiction. J.K. Rowling's fictional wizard, Harry Potter, won the Tourism for England Award in 2002 for rescuing English tourism in the aftermath of the foot-and-mouth epidemic, which effectively closed off much of the English countryside. The fame of the Harry Potter books inspired a rush of tourism activity among young literary tourists and their families which was further extended when the film versions of the book appeared on screen.

It is difficult to make general assumptions about the characteristics of the literary tourist but they seem to be motivated to visit places either by a deep and well-informed interest in a writer or their works or by the more generic aesthetic or historic qualities of a site. Authors have described visitors as either literary 'pilgrims' or more general cultural tourists. The original literary Grand Tourists were certainly pilgrims, prepared to travel long distances to emulate their favourite poet or author, and researchers have found some evidence of a similar level of dedication in contemporary tourists (Herbert, 1996). However, the more generalist visitors inspired by interest, curiosity and pleasant environments now greatly outnumber the pilgrims. But even these more general visitors will have an emotional or imaginative link with these places, as – albeit if they have little in the way of biographical insight into the author's life – they will no doubt have absorbed associations through film, television and other media.

Authors tend to agree that literary tourism sites fall into three broad categories (Fawcett and Cormack, 2001; Herbert, 1996 and 2001; Robinson and Andersen, 2004; Tetley and Bramwell, 2002):

- the factual site
- the imaginative site
- the socially constructed site.

Factual sites have a real connection to a writer's life and are usually places where authors were born, lived, produced their works, died and were buried. Examples include Jane Austen's house at Chawton in Hampshire, or Robert Burns' birthplace in Alloway, Scotland. At these sites, the attraction for the visitor is straightforward – to see the actual desk where favourite novels were written, or to witness the humble beginnings of a writer's life, has an immediate appeal.

The second category of literary destination is the more imaginative site which provides the setting for the novels, plays or poems. The Dublin streets of James Joyce's *Ulysses*, 221b Baker Street in London, fictional home of Sir Arthur Conan Doyle's Sherlock Holmes, or the areas around South Shields in Tyneside from where Catherine Cookson's literary characters hailed are all popular tourist destinations. But of course many places are both the home of the writer and the inspiration for the work, and in these situations there may be a blurring of **authenticity** as real sites elide with more romantic imagined places. Two examples of such places are the Yorkshire Moors of the Brontës and Prince Edward Island in Canada, home and inspiration to Lucy Maud Montgomery for her famous series of *Anne of Green Gables* novels. In both cases, the lives and real homes of the female authors get confused with those of their famous literary heroes and heroines, which may in fact result in disappointment with visitors encountering mundane reality rather than the romantic settings of their imagination. (Fawcett and Cormack, 2001; Tetley and Bramwell, 2002).

The third type of literary site represents those that have been deliberately created in order to attract visitors. The newly opened *Dickens World* in Chatham in Kent is an example of this type of development, as is *The World of Beatrix Potter* in Windermere, Cumbria. Indeed, an association with a famous literary figure or character allows a destination to develop a wide range of themed visitor attractions as has happened over a long period of time in Stratford-upon-Avon with its range of Shakespeare-themed facilities, from the officially sanctioned (the Royal Shakespeare Company) to the more informal souvenir shops and tea-rooms. A number of literary trails have also been created, encouraging visitors to make journeys that include biographical as well as more imaginative sites (MacLeod et al., 2009). There are trails that present the lives of Thomas Hardy,

George Eliot, Agatha Christie and Robert Burns, which have a generally biographical focus, but also trails that interpret the literary creations themselves such as the Da Vinci Code Trail (based on Dan Brown's best-selling novel) and the Harry Potter Trail. The film versions of both of these literary works give added focus and appeal to such trails. Finally, we can also add to this category the book town or literary town. These destinations promote their association with authors and literary characters, for example Dublin and James Joyce, or Edinburgh and Walter Scott. Pride in the literary reputation of an area can take the form of literary festivals, as is the case in Hay-on-Wye, Cheltenham and Wigtown. Visitors come to these places because of literary activities and for the opportunity to visit specialist bookshops.

Literary tourism sites are usually domestic buildings and are therefore not always capable of handling large numbers of visitors. If an author receives a sudden surge of interest due, for example, to a popular TV adaptation, the literary site may simply not be able to cope with the large numbers generated. There may also be management challenges associated with accommodating a range of visitors with very different needs – literary pilgrims who wish to absorb every detail of the 'shrine', and coach-driven tourists on a convenient stopping-off point. In this respect, the literary tourism destination resembles the **spiritual tourism** site.

See also: authenticity, film and TV tourism, special interest tourism

FURTHER READING

The collection of essays in Robinson and Andersen's (2004) text provides a good range of examples of literary tourism and the introductory chapters set out clearly the various theoretical approaches and provide a useful introduction to literary theory. Buzards' works1993 work gives a comprehensive overview of the role of literature in the development of European tourism, and an analysis of the cited works listed below will give readers a grounding in current research in the area.

RECOMMENDED BOOKS AND ARTICLES

Buzard, J. (1993) *The Beaten Track: European Tourism, Literature and the Ways to Culture 1800–1918*. New York: Oxford University Press.

Fawcett, C. and Cormack, P. (2001) 'Guarding authenticity at literary tourism sites', *Annals of Tourism Research*, 28 (3): 686–704.

Robinson, M. and Andersen, H. (eds) (2004) *Literature and Tourism: Essays in the Reading and Writing of Tourism*. London: Thomson International.

literary tourism

Mature Tourism

Mature or Third Age Tourism usually refers to the BabyBoomer or BoBous generation of tourists from the Western developed countries aged 55+, who are travelling in ever-increasing numbers.

The United Nations (2002) has predicted that by 2050, one in every five persons will be aged 60 or older, and that by 2150 this ratio will be one in every three persons. Over the last half of the twentieth century, 20 years have been added to the average lifespan in the developed world, bringing global life expectancy to its current level of 66 years. Of course, there are national variations, but in most major tourism-generating countries, the life expectancy is higher than average.

Many over 55s may be retired already, and it is becoming increasingly common, especially in Western developed countries, for travel to be an integral part of the retirement experience. In contrast to previous generations, BabyBoomers (the generation born immediately after the Second World War in Europe and the USA) or BoBous (half Bohemian, half Bourgeois) are living longer, remaining active for longer and have more disposable income. For this reason, the accepted terminology used to describe tourists who are aged 55+ tends to be either 'mature tourists' or 'third age tourists', perhaps more flattering than 'grey tourist' or 'senior tourist', terms which are also commonly used for the over-60s. According to socio-economic studies, any person over the age of 50 is at his/her maximum earning rate, with the possibility of having paid off their mortgage and having covered all major financial output for family dependants (be they the previous or the younger generation), thus leaving them with more discretionary income and more independence and freedom to travel. Mature tourists are therefore one of the largest and most lucrative groups of travel-related consumers.

The World Tourism Organisation's (WTO) *Recife Charter on Senior Tourism* in 1996 was the first document of its kind to make the explicit connection between senior or mature tourism and quality of life. The declaration also called for a research agenda to examine such a linkage, as most studies had thus far tended to view those who had retired simply

key concepts in tourist studies

as a market niche with disposable income who could travel out of season, or else had considered this growing sector of the population solely in terms of another type of tourist (see Dann, 2001). In this work, the author suggests that senior tourism may provide a chance for friendships or romantic relationships with people of a similar age, and opportunities for new experiences and reflection, thereby fostering a sense of purpose. He also states that tourism may allow seniors to escape feelings of physical suffering, impending death or diminished social status that may surround them while at home.

Moscardo (2006) uses research from the USA and Australia to show the current strong demand and travel preferences of mature tourists in these countries. However, she notes that it is often difficult to differentiate the wants and needs of this particular segment from other age groups. Dann (2001) suggests that seniors tend to participate in different activities from younger tourists (e.g. socialising with other travellers, visiting cultural and historical destinations, travelling with a guided tour group). They may desire the nostalgic qualities of less-developed locales or require special care services or resources if they have physical disabilities. Nevertheless, mature tourists are by no means a homogeneous group. The results of factor analyses by Cleaver et al. (1999) led to the identification of seven travel-motive segments for senior tourists, labelled (in order of relative size):

- nostalgics
- friendlies
- learners
- escapists
- thinkers
- status-seekers
- physicals.

It is worth referring to this article in order to note that senior travellers are potentially as diverse as any other market segment. However, a few common characteristics can be identified. Horneman et al. (2002) carried out a study which profiled older travellers, and concluded that mature tourists:

- stay longer at the destination
- spend more time planning
- visit friends and relatives more often.

mature tourism

Other research showed that mature travellers may tend to prefer package tours, especially coach and cruise ship options. Long-distance driving to warmer locations may also be common. Mature tourists are also tending to become more and more active (Moscardo, 2006). Tourism Queensland, Australia, carried out some research on what they called 'grey' or 'seniors' tourism in 2002. They concluded that seniors:

- on the whole (76 per cent) feel travel is important to maintaining general health and well-being
- tend to spend a higher percentage of their discretionary income on travel than younger people
- tend to budget carefully and are conscious of value for money when travelling
- typically spend more time planning holidays than younger travellers
- are larger consumers of travel information than young people
- are more likely than younger people to travel in off-peak periods
- are more likely than younger travellers to demonstrate brand loyalty, including using favourite tour guides and choosing holidays based on past travel experiences
- are motivated by spending time with family and friends, getting a break from routine and visiting places that have always been of interest
- seek reassuring information on available medical facilities, opportunities for personal assistance and health insurance when travelling.

Age-sensitive aspects, such as health assistance, grading of physical challenges and climate susceptibility should be subtly factored into any product designed for this group. However, it has also been recognised that certain factors tend to limit or constrain travel by older people. These include:

- safety/security concerns
- health issues
- available time
- cost
- family responsibilities
- poor information about suitable options.

(Moscardo, 2006)

Other meanings of mature or third age tourism can also be found, for example, referring to the Three 'S' (Sun–Sea–Sand) resorts which have reached maturity on the Mediterranean, the resorts that Butler (1980) refers to in his famous Tourism Life Cycle Model article. These mature resorts, which, after over 40 years of activity, have reached a degree of standardisation of little appeal to a highly experienced tourist, now have to consider policies and programmes designed at regeneration. Interestingly, one of the main ways of doing this is by attracting mature tourists who can visit during the low season, or perhaps purchase second homes there.

Third age tourism can also be used to refer to familiarity with IT, where the tourist controls the market thanks to the third revolution of the modern world, IT and internet, changing it from a supply-led industry to a demand-led business. It has produced the overnight transformation of the mass tourism package into the individualised 'dynamic package', put together by the consumer himself or herself, often with the help of new online companies, who cultivate loyalty through their specialised knowledge of the consumer's needs. It has also produced the new phenomenon of 'word-of-mouth' publicity through internet blogs. In terms of internet use by mature tourists, Cho's (2002) research reveals that mature travellers who use the internet are more likely to be younger, have higher annual household incomes, and have higher levels of education than mature travellers who do not use the internet. Also, the results indicate that mature travellers who are still working are more likely to use the internet than those who are not working.

FURTHER READING

In 1999, there was a special edition of the journal *Tourism Recreation Research* edited by Pearce and Singh. However, there have since been many journal articles about 'Mature', 'Senior', 'Grey', or 'Third Age' tourism (see especially those by Graham Dann). The book chapter by Moscardo (2006) mentioned here is also a useful one.

RECOMMENDED ARTICLES

Cleaver, M., Muller, T.E., Ruys, H.F.M. and Wei, S. (1999) 'Tourism product development for the senior market, based on travel-motive research', *Tourism Recreation Research*, 24 (1): 5–11.

Dann, G.M.S. (2001) 'Senior tourism and quality of life', *Journal of Hospitality and Leisure Marketing*, 9 (1/2): 5–19.

mature tourism

115

Horneman, L., Carter, R.W., Wei, S. and Ruys, H. (2002) 'Profiling the senior traveller: an Australian perspective', *Journal of Travel Research*, 41: 23–37.

Moscardo, G. (2006) 'Third-age tourism', in D. Buhalis and C. Costa (eds), *New Tourism Consumers, Products and Industry: Present and Future Issues*. Oxford: Butterworth-Heinemann. pp. 30–9.

Mobility

> **The term mobility refers to our ability to move. It is often used in association with transport and so is an important tourism concept. Mobility also refers to flows of information, foreign investment and social strata which are also of relevance to travel and tourism.**

Mobility, the ability to be mobile, has always been central to the concept of tourism, and the history of mass tourism has consequently been bound up with developments in mobility and transportation. Although the elite had always managed to travel from the earliest days of the Grand Tour onwards, it was the introduction of the trains and then cheap charter flights that brought mobility and tourism to the masses. From the times of Thomas Cook and the coach tour, partly replaced by the train, the boat, then the plane (or the private car), the means of transport available have defined how and where we travel. Urry (1995) has suggested that to be mobile is to be part of the modern world and certainly the ability to travel has changed the way that people view their world. At a time when travellers were forced to walk or ride, their knowledge of the land that they were crossing would be deep and intimate. When the railways brought speed, this 'flattened' the landscape viewed from the train window, creating a standardised transit route with all attention focused on the destination of the journey. Mobility is therefore 'responsible for altering how people experience the modern world, changing both their forms of subjectivity and sociability and their aesthetic appreciation of nature, landscapes, townscapes and other societies' (Urry, 1995: 144).

The disciplines of transport studies, sociology, human geography, leisure studies and migration studies have always engaged with research within the field of mobility, although Hall (2005) suggests that tourism studies have only recently embraced these ideas. This may be due to the problems inherent in defining tourism – for example, much leisure research focuses on activities within or near the home, whereas we tend to research tourism from the perspective of international travel, ignoring more local activities. However, many other types of mobility are now coming under the scrutiny of tourism researchers, for example:

> travelling for education both in the short and long term, business travel, health tourism, leisure shopping, second home travel, daytrips, the combining of work and travel, and amenity orientated migration. (Hall, 2005: 23)

These newer forms of mobility challenge the established pattern of tourism of individuals leaving home for a specified period (usually one or two weeks), staying at a destination and then returning home. The notion of the 'global nomad' (Richards and Wilson, 2004) also introduces new forms of mobility in a globalised world (also see **backpacking**). These travellers represent the rootlessness of contemporary society in their somewhat aimless travels across the globe, made easier by the reduced cost and time involved in long-haul travel. Thus, 'the global nomad crosses physical and cultural barriers with apparent ease in the search for difference and differentiation and in this way the … nomad is placed in opposition to the "tourist" caught in the iron cage of the modern tourism industry' (Richards and Wilson, 2004: 5). Thus, globalisation eases the nomads' travel but what attracts is the opportunity to interact with local culture and difference. The resulting 'glocalisation' is, as Bauman (1998) suggests, best thought of as a restratification of society based on the free mobility of some and the place-bound existence of others. Tourist flows, for example, are mainly uni-directional (e.g. West to East, or developed to less-developed countries). Those from the developed nations of the world may feel that it is their right to travel unimpeded across the globe but this is by no means a universal right. The originating market regions for tourism are still concentrated in Europe, the Americas, and Asia and the Pacific.

In the age of virtual reality and communication technology, mobility, of course, means much more than merely vehicles of transport. Mobility (often referred to somewhat pejoratively as 'flux', or positively as 'flow') is associated with information transfer, with changes in circumstances

mobility

and identity, with promotion of the individual in society ('upward mobility'), with voluntary and unimpeded movement of workers from one country to another in search of work, with migration, and, of equal importance to tourism, mobility of foreign investment.

Traditionally, in tourism, it was the consortium of airlines, tour operators and travel agencies that governed where and what was developed in the travel industry, with access controlled exclusively by them. With greater mobility and flow of information made available by the internet and IT, access to travel information has been freed from the restrictive corset of the multinationals, giving rise to low-cost flights and access to resorts which were not on the 'official' map before (see **e-tourism**). This greater flow or mobility of information, including the possibility to travel virtually to the accommodation booked before the actual visit, has allowed for greater consumer control over the tourism market, plus greater spending and distribution of the economic benefits of tourism in the destination, thus reducing leakage. This greater consumer freedom has produced more mobility of the service industry, with greater flexibility of small and medium-sized enterprises as the result of a demand-led scenario in tourism, as opposed to a supply-led tourism industry.

It is not only technology which is due to produce changes in mobility in the future. Climate change and exacerbated drought situations, plus crop failures, have resulted in mobility, in the form of illegal migration to escape poverty, on a scale never witnessed before. Most of the migratory movement has tended to gravitate towards Europe, mainly from Africa and Latin America. Money remittances from family members working in Europe represent the major source of income for many families in Latin America and Africa. This mobility has also been favoured by the ageing population in Europe, in need of specialised medical services and attention that are not available at an affordable price in their home regions. Illegal migrant mobility has also benefited the tourist industry which is intensive in unskilled low-cost labour, above all in the areas where 'all-inclusive' packages are on offer, demanding scarce outlay on large amounts of human resources. Low labour costs have also produced a greater movement of foreign investment to areas such as India and China, thereby producing both greater affluence among certain sectors of society and a consequent rise in demand for foreign travel, which is perceived as part of a higher-status middle-class lifestyle.

From the earliest days of mechanised transport, technology has allowed for the annihilation of time and space (Aitchison et al., 2000), making destinations appear increasingly close and widening our expectations of where we can travel to. London to New York was once considered to be a long-haul flight but is now seen as a reasonable journey to make for a weekend. The speed of our communications technology has also contributed to our sense that we are living in a global village with instantaneous social and financial transactions. These changes in our perspectives of time and space have allowed for innovative mobility proposals to flourish, such as Virgin's proposed spacecraft, Virgin Galactic, for pleasure cruises to the outer stratosphere. Conversely, nostalgia has flourished in some tourism markets with cruise liners and classic train journeys providing travel at less accelerated speeds. Here, slow mobility allows the traveller time to watch the slowly passing scene in a world where quality time is a luxury. In these situations, the very act of travel becomes the holiday itself.

Of course, mobility can also be examined from the perspective of 'reduced' mobility and this is also a major concern in the contemporary tourism industry. The design of transportation infrastructure, accommodation, destination resorts, visitor attractions and interpretation must all encompass accessibility for those of impaired mobility and this can be a major challenge, particularly in historic or natural environments.

See also: *backpacking, e-tourism, geography of tourism*

FURTHER READING

Readers will find Hall's book *Tourism: Rethinking the Social Science of Mobility* to be thought-provoking. Sheller and Urry's text *Tourism Mobilities: Places to Play, Places in Play* will also be of interest. One of the most useful sources however, is the journal *Mobilities*, which is published by Taylor & Francis.

RECOMMENDED BOOKS

Hall, C.M. (2005) *Tourism: Rethinking the Social Science of Mobility*. Harlow: Pearson.
Sheller, M. and Urry, J. (2004) *Tourism Mobilities: Places to Play, Places in Play*. London: Routledge.
Urry, J. (1995) *Consuming Places*. London: Routledge.

mobility

Neo-colonialism

> *Neo-colonialism is a term used to describe the operations of capitalist forces in the era when colonial empires are no longer in existence. Instead of using force, neo-colonialist powers employ economic, financial and trade policies to dominate less powerful countries. Third World tourism is considered by many to be a form of neo-colonialism.*

Colonialism in the past was related to the spread of empires and the need to dominate ever greater areas of territory in order to prove power and dominion. The last great empire, as such, the British Empire under Queen Victoria, produced 'colonialism' in the shape of the Commonwealth. One of the last bastions of colonialism, Hong Kong, was ceded only recently back to 'local' rule, whereas Canada, Australia, New Zealand and parts of Africa are still cutting the bonds of colonialism in the form of the Commonwealth. Colonialism implied secession of a territory and control over the institutional structures being exerted from a foreign land, often through local delegates or representatives. The domination was usually exerted by the West and the North invading the East and the South. In its crudest form, colonialism in the past led to foreign masters enslaving the local population.

The legacy of colonialism, decolonisation and freedom from foreign rule for many countries – above all in Africa – has been widespread governmental corruption and foreign debt. The international institutions, such as the World Bank and the IMF, capitalist powers (including nations, former colonisers and corporations) and, in particular, the USA, use neo-colonialism to control other nations. They use economic, financial and trade policies to dominate less powerful nations where before they physically occupied them. The Structural Adjustment Plans (SAPs) are usually proposed to write off debt, but lead to greater rather than lessened poverty, drastic reductions in public spending, and focus on resource extraction and export production. The SAPs then promote another form of neo-colonialism, widespread foreign investment, taking advantage of the Third World countries as vast reservoirs of cheap labour and raw materials, causing economic leakage and 'demotion' of local staff due to imports of trained middle managers from abroad, thereby preventing the development of these countries into self-sufficient economies. This closes the circle of neo-colonialism, making the Third World nations dependent upon aid from the richer nations and, therefore, forced to allow their policies to be dictated from abroad in order to survive.

One of the main new survival strategies, adopted at both community and national levels, as much in the Caribbean as in Africa, has been the promotion of tourism. However, although proposed as a development strategy, most tourist resorts are controlled by foreign investors and outside corporations. Coupled with the promotion of all-inclusive packages purchased in the tourists' home countries, a phenomenon referred to as 'leakage', this can lead to the deterioration rather than the enhancement of the natural and social environment and balance.

The debate about whether tourism is like a new form of neo-colonialism or imperialism has been prominent since the 1970s (e.g. see Nash, 1977; Turner and Ash, 1975). There is justifiable concern that tourism is, and will remain for the foreseeable future, dominated by Western developed nations, rendering host nations dependent and subservient to their needs. Tourism still flows predominantly from the developed to the developing world. The local populations are unlikely to travel outside their immediate environment, therefore their role will never be more than that of serving tourists. They will never experience what it is like to be 'guests', and so they may feel subordinated and relegated to the status of little more than servants to wealthy Westerners.

Many of the theories relating to the discussion about tourism as a new form of imperialism have their origins in economic development theory. Economists have focused traditionally on core–periphery theory and the growth–dependency relationships between host nations and their Western 'benefactors'. Dependency is viewed as a process whereby the indigenous economy of a developing country becomes reorientated towards serving the needs of exogenous markets (Hall, 1994). The notion of core–periphery relationships is used within dependency theory to highlight this unequal, often exploitative, relationship. Nash (1989) described imperialism as the expansion of a society's interest abroad. Metropolitan centres or cores (usually former imperial nations) exercise their power over peripheral nations or regions of the world. Mathieson and Wall (1992) suggested that three economic conditions substantiate the claim that tourism is a new form of imperialism or colonialism. These are that:

1 Developing countries grow to depend on tourism as a means of securing revenue.
2 A large proportion of expenditures and profits flow back to foreign investors and high leakages occur.
3 Non-locals are employed in professional and managerial positions.

This debate is particularly pertinent to former colonies such as in the Caribbean where tourism appears to be reasserting itself as a new form of colonialism. Burns (1999: 157) describes how, for dependency theorists, development and under-development are two sides of the same coin: surpluses from the exploited countries generated, first through mercantilism and later through colonialism, had the combined effect of developing the metropolitan countries and leaving the peripheral countries under-developed.

Craik (1994) noted that ex-colonies have increased in popularity with tourists, and the 'detritus' of post-colonialism has been transformed into tourist sites. Hall and Tucker (2004) suggest, for example, that many post-colonial islands are described as 'paradise', which merely reinforces Western ideas of a romantic 'other', and erotically charged imagery may also be used of local 'exotic' people. The majority of authors in Hall and Tucker (2004) show how colonial thinking and discourse are far from over in contemporary tourism, especially as many Europeans may be nostalgic about imperialism, and may idealise it. As a result, they are attracted by their own myths and fantasies about colonial landscapes, buildings and people.

Third World countries in particular are far divorced from the reality of the industrialised landscape of the First World and are, thus, seen as more primitive and culturally exotic. The commodification of 'alternative tourism' in all-inclusive packages (ostensibly for reasons of security) in closed resorts, allows the tourist to appropriate a more acceptable foreign reality, albeit practically 'virtual', in the destination, and even to see themselves as benefactors of the national economy. One form of tourism that arguably perpetuates imperialistic relationships of exploitation and dependency is **sex tourism.** The international tourism market continues to be dominated by consumers from the North and the West. For the organised tourist, the Other in the tourist resort and in the service industry, is, to many effects, the native of colonial times. Literally, on the 'other' side of the world (West/East, North/South), everything becomes possible and every taboo can be broken. The main reasons for the unprecedented growth in mass sexual tourism include worsening poverty and the persistence of patriarchal, sexist societies. Sex tourism is arguably part and parcel of the same process of neo-colonial 'othering', whereby local people are depicted (and sold) as being exotic/erotic objects of the tourist gaze. Local and indigenous women and men are often rendered subservient to the needs of wealthy, powerful Western tourists. Poverty-stricken villagers are sometimes persuaded to sell their young children to the sex tourism industry as a means of ensuring their family's future survival.

Neo-colonial tourism is clearly based on economically and politically unequal and exploitative relationships, but there are also numerous social and cultural issues which need to be considered. Many of these relate to the (re)interpretation of colonial heritage, which may be dissonant or meaningless to local people. For example, Fisher (2004) in Hall and Tucker (2004) cites the case of Levuka in Fiji, where many local residents believed, that old colonial buildings should be knocked down and replaced by functional ones. Very few considered them to be representative of Fijian history. They also believed that the place where buildings were located would somehow retain its 'spirit', regardless of whether the buildings were still there. This is in stark contrast to European conservationists who would preserve the buildings at all costs. African native peoples are usually less concerned about tangible heritage (i.e. buildings), placing more emphasis on intangible legacies. This means that the values of indigenous societies and those of tourism developers and tourists are often radically different, making host–guest relationships in neo-colonial countries even more difficult to manage.

FURTHER READING

One of the best and most recent books on the subject of tourism and neo- or post-colonialism is by Hall and Tucker – *Tourism and Postcolonialism*. Earlier seminal work wwhich has focused on tourism as a form of imperialism includes that of Nash (1977, 1989), and the article by Craik on 'peripheral pleasures'.

RECOMMENDED BOOKS AND ARTICLES

Craik, J. (1994) 'Peripheral pleasures: the peculiarities of post-colonial tourism', *Culture and Policy*, 6 (1): 153–82.
Hall, C.M. and Tucker, H. (eds) (2004) *Tourism and Postcolonialism*. London: Routledge.
Nash, D. (1977) 'Tourism as a form of imperialism', in V. Smith (ed.), *Hosts and Guests: The Anthropology of Tourism*. Oxford: Blackwell. pp. 33–47.

neo-colonialism

> **Planning here is the controlled and integrated development of tourism in such a way that positive impacts are maximised and negative impacts are minimised.**

Tourism is an attractive development option for many countries because it brings important economic benefits (see **economics of tourism**). However, economic considerations often overshadow or outweigh social or environmental ones, as governments see tourism as a quick and easy route to growth. However, this can backfire if negative impacts adversely affect the destination, visitors stop coming, or the destination becomes dependent on tourism and some kind of crisis destroys it (see also **crisis management**).

Some typical negative impacts of tourism include the following:

Economic	Environmental	Socio-cultural
Economic over-dependence on tourism	Damage to vegetation	Conflicts and misunderstanding of respective cultures
Tourism controlled by too many foreign operators and investors	Ecological disruption	Feelings of exploitation on the part of locals
	Water pollution	
	Air pollution	
Tourism feels like a new form of imperialism or colonisation	Architectural pollution	Congestion of facilities and creation of 'tourist enclaves'
	Waste-disposal problems	
Too much emphasis on tourism at the expense of other industries	Damage to archaeological and historic sites	Social problems exacerbated by tourism
	Congestion	Demonstration effect (imitation of tourist behaviour by locals)
Creation of unstable and inadequate employment conditions for local people	Land-use problems	Eventual erosion of social fabric
		Over-commercialisation of culture and loss of authenticity

In the early days of mass tourism, developments tended to take place without much advance planning. This meant that destinations developed in a random and ad hoc way, merely responding to demand rather than considering long-term impacts. There was little consideration of the economic, environmental, social or cultural needs of an area and its population, so negative impacts were created, and ultimately many destinations stagnated, declined and became unattractive to visitors. Plog (1974) suggested that this pattern was an inevitable part of tourism. Butler's (1980) tourism life-cycle model is frequently used to illustrate the potential fate of destinations:

- exploration
- involvement
- development
- consolidation
- stagnation
- decline *or* rejuvenation.

While this model has since been reviewed, many destinations still fail to learn from the mistakes of the past and go through the same cycle. However, in recent years, most destinations accept that a tourism plan is a necessary requirement in order to develop tourism in a sustainable way (see **sustainable tourism**). This often takes the form of a so-called Master Plan, which is usually a 5–7-year plan which provides a series of steps and guidelines for planning tourism in stages or phases. It is usually written by private consultants in collaboration with international and government agencies. A typical planning team might look like this:

Core members	Additional members
Tourism development planner	Environmental specialist
Tourism economist	Anthropologist/sociologist
Tourism transportation/infrastructure planner	Human resources expert
Marketing specialist	Hotel specialist
	Engineer
	Architect/designer

Planning can technically take place at all levels. Inskeep (1991, 1994) outlined the different priorities of planning at different levels of tourism. He emphasised the fact that international or regional planning usually focuses on cross-country marketing or the coordination of tours and transport. National planning tends to focus on the coordination of tourism with other sectors of the economy, or the spatial distribution of tourism. Sub-national planning is more detailed, and focuses on impact management (e.g. environmental, economic and socio-cultural) and local accessibility.

However, Master Plans normally apply to a country or a region of a country. There may be some international-level planning where countries share natural resources (e.g. a sea, a mountain range or waterfall, for example), or regional planning (e.g. in the Caribbean or South Pacific), but generally it is more practical to plan for each country separately. This is because of different size, geography, resources, political structure, social structure and cultural traditions. Different approaches will also be needed, depending on whether the country is a developed or less developed country, a landlocked country or island, a politically stable or unstable country, etc. When planning for a region or local area of a country, the typology of the destination will make a difference too (e.g. whether it is coastal, urban, rural, mountainous, spa-based).

If tourism is properly planned, then the following positive impacts can be created:

Economic	Environmental	Socio-cultural
Creation of employment	Conservation of natural areas	Stimulus for conservation of cultural heritage
Foreign exchange benefits	Conservation of historic and cultural sites	Revitalisation of traditions and customs
Improved standard of living	Incentive for 'cleaning up' local area	Development of cultural facilities
Expansion of other economic sectors	Enhancement of the local environment	Renewal of cultural pride
	Improvement of local infrastructure	Cross-cultural exchange
	Increasing local awareness of environmental concerns	Opportunities for the emancipation of women

The chosen approach and process will be important. Different approaches to development traditionally focused on physical or economic planning, but increasingly the social and cultural elements have become equally, if not more, important. The main objectives for developing tourism need to be established for each destination, for example maximising economic benefits, enhancing the environment, improving quality of life for local residents, ensuring visitor satisfaction, improving destination image. The main stakeholders need to be identified and consulted, for example public, private and voluntary sectors, as well as local residents and visitors. Public sector agencies may need to regulate private sector ones to ensure development is controlled and ethical. Financial resources need to be guaranteed before development takes place. Timescales should be realistic, and ongoing monitoring of development should take place in the form of impact analysis and research (e.g. environmental impact analysis; feedback from local residents and visitors).

Inskeep (1994) provides a checklist for planning tourism at national and regional level. This includes being specific about the development objectives and what should be achieved by or through tourism. There is clearly a need to undertake a feasibility analysis and to make recommendations for environmental and infrastructural developments. Appropriate forms and scales of tourism should also be identified. Emphasis should be placed on the existing and potential tourist attractions, services and facilities and how they could be improved or developed. The economic, environmental and social impacts of tourism also need to be considered so that the benefits are maximised and damage is limited. Market research and forecasting are also essential to ensure that demand exists and is compatible with the type of planned development. Finally, all plans should be monitored and evaluated throughout the implementation stage and ideally on an ongoing basis.

Unfortunately, many factors can affect tourism planning, and even if an ethical and sustainable plan is written, this does not necessarily mean that it can or will be implemented. Governments may not have the means to implement plans or may be corrupt; development may not be adequately regulated by law; consultants or private sector agencies may act unethically or withdraw from projects; communities may resist development and fail to cooperate; visitors may mistreat the destination; crises such as a natural disaster or terrorism may strike at any time.

There are also concerns that Master Planning is not the ideal form of planning for many destinations, as a 5–7-year plan lacks flexibility and the consultants who write the plan are not usually those who implement it. Therefore, attention has been paid to other forms of planning, for example 'third way' planning or incremental planning. Burns (2004) suggests that there can be a 'third way' in tourism planning which is politically and socially specific, is inter and intra-sectoral, is realistic about what can actually be achieved, tackles problems and impacts as they arise, considers who exactly the beneficiaries, are and considers economic, social and cultural diversity. Incremental planning aims to be responsive to the development of tourism in a destination, its impacts, and the experiences of local people and visitors. The following table outlines some of the differences between Master Planning and Incremental Planning:

Master Planning	Incremental Planning
Rigid and inflexible	Integrated approach
Planner as expert	Planner as facilitator
Top-down	Bottom-up
'Global' planning	'Local' planning
Homogenising	Considers diversity
National boundaries	Multi-level
Gap between planning and implementation	Implementation integrated into plan

Incremental planning constantly reviews and monitors development, but this makes it a far more expensive and time-consuming process, which many destinations cannot afford. However, many planners are starting to be more realistic and sensitive about what can or should be achieved in tourism, and new planning paradigms are being considered. There is not one single planning paradigm which can work for all destinations, so plans must be adapted to suit different countries and contexts. Planning should be integrated into wider political and socio-economic change. Awareness is needed of stakeholder power structures and agendas, and an understanding is required of new social and cultural literacies (i.e. those of local communities and visitors). There is no such thing as a perfect destination, but with careful planning, developers can certainly move closer to creating **ethical** and **sustainable tourism**.

See also: crisis management, economics of tourism, ethical tourism, sustainable tourism

FURTHER READING

There are many good books on the subject of tourism planning, including Edgell's *Tourism Policy and Planning: Yesterday, Today and Tomorrow* and Mason's *Tourism Impacts, Planning and Management*. The book by Var and Gunn, *Tourism Planning: Basics, Concepts and Cases*, and any books by Inskeep are still seminal works. It is also worth consulting the following websites, as these organisations are actively involved in national and regional tourism planning: World Tourism Organisation (www.world-tourism.org), World Travel and Tourism Council (www.wttc.org) and Pacific Asia Travel Association (www.pata.org).

RECOMMENDED BOOKS

Edgell, D. (2007) *Tourism Policy and Planning: Yesterday, Today and Tomorrow*. Oxford: Butterworth-Heinemann.

Mason, P. (2003) *Tourism Impacts, Planning and Management*. Oxford: Butterworth-Heinemann.

Var, T. and Gunn, C. (eds) (2002) *Tourism Planning: Basics, Concepts and Cases*. London: Routledge.

Post-tourism

The post-tourist or post-modern tourist is a consumer who embraces openly, but with some irony, the increasingly inauthentic, commercialised and simulated experiences offered by the tourism industry.

The concept of the post-tourist has developed in response to consumer attitudes and preferences in the post-modern era. The term seems to have been coined by Feifer (1985), and has been used subsequently by Urry (1990/2002), Rojek (1997) and others. The post-modern world is characterised by globalisation, hyper-consumerism, the **experience economy** and new developments in technology. Consumers have numerous choices and possibilities, and often undertake seemingly incompatible activities simultaneously in order to capitalise on this array of opportunities. Post-modern tourism has therefore been described as a form of 'pastiche tourism' (Hollinshead, 1997: 192) or 'collage tourism' (Rojek, 1997: 62).

According to a report by Tyrell and Mai (2001), experiences and memories now mean more to contemporary consumers than products, and they emphasise the need for innovative approaches to development, which satisfy the needs of individualistic 'money rich/time poor' consumers. Their report builds on the work of Pine and Gilmore (1999), who discuss the experience economy, in which businesses compete to create unique and memorable experiences for customers. Post-tourists are likely to be responsive to experience-creation, and often the more fantastical the better. They are familiar with new technology and are especially responsive to media. The profile of the post-modern tourist is discussed by both Urry (1990/2002) and Walsh (1992). They describe how many post-modern consumers receive much of their travel knowledge through media representations. They cite Feifer (1985) who described the post-tourist as one who does not even have to leave the house in order to view the typical objects of the **tourist gaze**. The simulated tourist experience is brought into their living rooms through television travel shows, internet sites and software programmes.

Post-tourists have very different views and expectations from more conventional or traditional tourists, e.g. cultural tourists. For the post-tourist, tourism has become playful: 'the post-tourist knows that they are a tourist and that tourism is a game or a series of games with multiple texts and no single, authentic tourist experience' (Urry, 1990/2002: 100). Post-tourists accept multiple interpretations of history and culture, and do not see the need to differentiate between 'high' and 'low' culture, embracing contemporary, popular culture (e.g. pop music, theme parks) as much as traditional or folk cultures. They also do not always make a distinction between reality and fiction, mainly due to the growth in simulated experiences, virtual reality and the creation of fantasy experiences. Post-tourists recognise the fact that culture is often contrived and inauthentic, and may wholeheartedly embrace inauthentic experiences, being drawn to 'hyperreal' attractions (e.g. theme parks, leisure centres or shopping malls), simulacra (e.g. Santa Claus' Lapland), or, as described by AlSayyad (2001), sites of 'authentic fakery' such as Las Vegas or manufactured heritage theme parks of 'fake authenticity'. Kirschenblatt-Gimblett (1998: 9) suggests that the post-modern world has become a kind of museum of itself: 'Tourists travel to actual destinations to experience virtual places.'

Rojek (1993) described the post-tourist as having three main characteristics. These are:

- an awareness of the commodification of the tourist experience, which the post-tourist treats playfully
- the attraction to experience as an end in itself, rather than the pursuit of self-improvement through travel
- the acceptance that the representations of the tourist site are as important as the site itself.

This means that the post-tourist can freely enjoy the escapism afforded by tourism and the diversity of entertaining experiences. He or she may also take as much pleasure in a replica monument or a visual representation of a site as in the site itself.

Rojek (1993) also suggests four kinds of tourist site which tend to feature in the landscape of post-modernism and are visited by post-tourists:

- blackspots (the commercial development of sites of atrocity, such as graves, war zones, massacre, assassination or accident sites)
- heritage sites (these are not always authentic in their interpretation of the past, instead offering a sanitised, glorified or entertaining version of history)
- literary landscapes (e.g. places which have become famous because they feature in an author's works, but which are often fictional)
- theme parks (these combine all aspects of global culture, new technology and media).

Smith (2005) refers to one form of post-tourist, and that is the 'new leisure tourist'. It is suggested that this is a relatively young breed of tourist, who is seeking escapism, entertainment and fun. Disposable income levels are relatively high but time is generally short. Although comfort and security are sought, the tourism experience should afford an element of excitement or thrill. This might be in the safe confines of a hotel, resort or themed attraction. Typical attractions might include visiting adventure lands, cyberworlds or simulated environments. New leisure tourists enjoy landscapes that correspond to Barber's (1995) concept of 'McWorld', where a number of familiar global brands are clustered under one roof. It is of no consequence that such attractions could be located anywhere, it is the experiences gained which count. The new leisure tourist differs significantly from traditional visitors like cultural tourists. There is no pretension of being interested in local societies and cultures; instead, simulated environments may be preferred. For example, many theme parks simulate environments like Egypt's Valley of the Kings, an Arabic souk or the jungles of Africa, without the inconvenience of further travel, and offer 'safer' experiences there.

There is clearly a considerable difference between the profiles and motivations of different types of tourists. For example, whereas cultural tourists are actively seeking authentic cultural experiences and interaction with local people, post-tourists tend to enjoy more simulated experiences, believing that truly authentic places and cultures are impossible to find. When it comes to new leisure tourists, they are actively looking for fake authenticity and simulated worlds. They simply want to have fun and be entertained, whereas cultural tourists may be on an educational or self-development quest. Post-tourists and new leisure tourists are positively playful in their approach and may not easily distinguish between fantasy and reality. They may be unaware of, and would certainly not be offended by, commercialisation.

It is debatable as to how far the concept of the post-tourist is typical of the modern era, and to what extent it is merely lifestyle or life-stage-driven. Tourist profiles are never fixed or static, and people may choose to be a cultural tourist at one time and a post-tourist or new leisure tourist at another. For example, single people and childless couples may be more likely to pursue cultural activities than families with young children or teenagers, who often seek out post-tourism attractions. At certain points in time, people might prefer to seek escapism, entertainment and fun than education (e.g. when life and work have become particularly stressful). Thus, post-tourism is also driven by life-stage and mood, and typologies can only indicate collective trends rather than individual preferences and proclivities. A profile of the post-tourist is therefore tentatively offered in the box below.

Typical Profile of a Post-Tourist

- Relatively young (18–45 years)
- High disposable income
- Compulsive consumer
- Time pressured
- Individualistic/independent
- Escapist on holiday but work-obsessed at home
- More interested in entertainment than education or self-development
- Experience-collector
- Enjoys luxury, comfort, security
- A thrill-seeker but in a controlled environment
- Short attention span
- Interested in new technology and media
- Fascinated by the cult of celebrity

(Adapted from Smith, 2005)

It is clear that post-tourism is dominated by consumers who are short of time but keen to engage in as many activities as possible in order to maximise their precious leisure experiences. Their high disposable incomes allow them to take more and more holidays, and to be more discerning and demanding in their tastes. Consequently, the desire for comfort, luxury and quality of service is paramount, but so too is the need for escapism, entertainment and fun. Post-consumers are clearly keen to leave home and the demands of work behind, but destinations are required to become more and more sophisticated and exciting in order to attract them. Therefore, fantastical tourism projects are being developed as a means of differentiating and branding destinations in a competitive marketplace. Attractions which are typically visited by the post-tourist are listed in the box below.

Typical Post-Tourist Destinations

- Post-modern, cosmopolitan cities like Los Angeles
- Fantastical destinations like Las Vegas or Dubai
- Theme Parks
- Fantasy attractions (e.g. Santa Claus Land)
- Film and TV studios or settings
- 'McWorlds' or global entertainment zones (e.g. mega shopping malls)

Future post-tourists are likely to be older, with even more time and money on their hands. As everyone becomes more technologically literate and media-orientated, it will be interesting to see how the attractions sector responds. Although there have been many debates about the sustainability of destinations like Dubai, which have been criticised for being environmentally unfriendly or for employing slave labour, these man-made, simulated and virtual environments are the least vulnerable to the impacts of mass tourism. Therefore, perhaps ironically, unreal and inauthentic post-tourism destinations may offer the most sustainable form of tourism development in the future!

See also: *experience economy, tourist gaze*

post-tourism

133

FURTHER READING

There are no books specifically on the concept of the post-tourist, but reference is made to this phenomenon in the works of several authors: Feifer's *Going Places: The Ways of the Tourist from Imperial Rome to the Present Day*; Urry's *The Tourist Gaze: Leisure and Travel in Contemporary Societies*; and Rojek's *Ways of Escape: Modern Transformations in Leisure and Travel.*

Feifer, M. (1985) *Going Places: The Ways of the Tourist from Imperial Rome to the Present Day*. London: Macmillan.

Rojek, C. (1993) *Ways of Escape: Modern Transformations in Leisure and Travel*. London: Macmillan.

Urry, J. (1990) *The Tourist Gaze: Leisure and Travel in Contemporary Societies*. London: Sage.

Regeneration

> **Regeneration is the renewal of an environment which has declined economically, environmentally and socially. Typical strategies include developing 'flagship' projects, such as cultural attractions or events, which draw in tourists and act as catalysts for further investment and development.**

The phenomenon of regeneration has become increasingly prominent on government agendas in recent years, particularly in those countries that have suffered a significant level of economic or industrial decline. The term regeneration is often considered synonymous with 'revitalisation' (bringing new life to), or 'renaissance' (being reborn). It necessarily implies an initial *de*-generation. The Department for Culture, Media and Sport (DCMS, 2004) described regeneration as 'the positive transformation of a place – whether residential, commercial or open space – that has previously displayed symptoms of physical, social and/or economic decline'. This definition makes the point that the concept of regeneration is mainly applied to areas that are being *re*-developed after industrial decline, and does not really apply to those that are in the process of industrial development. Thus, the term has generally been used in the context of developed Western countries (e.g. Europe, USA, Canada, Australasia). However, increasingly, the term is being applied to economic, environmental and social development programmes in all cities, including those in Asia such as Hong Kong, Tokyo, Hanoi,

Kuala Lumpur and Bangkok. It also seems to refer to new cultural and creative areas of cities, waterfronts and entertainment zones.

Regeneration is often described as a process that aims to revitalise areas of cities or resorts that have declined, using a range of tools (property, business, retail or arts development) to enhance an area. Urban regeneration strategies were largely developed initially in response to the post-war decline of cities, and the rising inequality, poverty, crime and unemployment that blighted inner cities in particular. The de-industrialisation process and subsequent global economic restructuring in the late 1970s and 1980s also acted as a catalyst for the development of urban regeneration strategies for many cities in the USA and Western Europe. Increasingly, it has been used as a way of attracting tourists to cities or areas of cities which were previously not considered to be tourism destinations. As stated by Maitland (2007: 25):

> Tourism, leisure and cultural activities are now seen as a natural and integral part of the way in which cities in developed economies make their living, and an obvious element in strategies for regeneration and economic development.

The concept of regeneration in tourism has often been applied to seaside resorts which have moved through Butler's Life Cycle Model (1980). There are few traditional resorts in Europe that did not experience the decline and stagnation engendered by de-industrialisation and changing consumer tastes from the 1950s onwards. This eventually resulted in tourist dissatisfaction and tarnished images, not to mention environmental damage and languishing economies. Agarwal's (2002) critical analysis of Butler's model suggests that a restructuring thesis can rather help to understand the post-stagnation phase of resort development. She suggests that when the restructuring thesis is applied to tourism, it can help to make sense of the economic options available to resorts in terms of their future regeneration. Hence, strategies such as environmental or service quality enhancement, product diversification, specialisation or repositioning can be employed to help counteract decline. A combination of strategies may be employed, or resorts will select the approach that is most appropriate for the nature and character of the destination. Bull (2001) suggests that some resorts may do well to consider alternative development and diversification options once tourism has declined, and Walton's (2000) analysis of British seaside resorts emphasises their resilience and capacity for reinvention, but tourism is not heralded as necessarily being the panacea for regeneration. Indeed, tourism is not always considered to be at the centre of regeneration – perhaps just a welcome by-product of a longer process of economic redevelopment and image enhancement.

In addition to many interesting and exciting projects taking place in the USA, some of the most innovative approaches to urban regeneration can be seen in European cities such as Barcelona, Bilbao, Glasgow, Liverpool, Rotterdam and Lisbon. What many of these cities have done is to build incrementally on a series of initiatives, usually starting with one major catalyst or 'flagship' project (the Olympic Games, European Capital of Culture status, a major museum, gallery or conference centre), which puts it on the map and attracts visitors. The cultural attractions, venues and events that tend to be used to regenerate cities and attract tourists are listed below.

- 'flagship' projects (e.g. Expos, Olympics, Dome)
- development of 'cultural and creative quarters'
- new museums, galleries, theatres, conference centres
- construction of waterfront or dockland developments
- festivals and special events
- shopping centres or retail parks
- restaurants, bars, nightclubs, cafés
- theme parks.

Regeneration clearly does not happen overnight. It is an incremental process, and many former industrial, perhaps less aesthetically pleasing cities have had to accept that tourism may be a relatively late addition to their strategy. Businesses are unlikely to invest in cities that do not already show signs of economic growth or potential, just as tourists will only visit those cities that have significant attractions and ideally an infrastructure to match. Firstly, the local economy must be diversified and strengthened, especially where there has been industrial decline. Jobs may be created in the service sector or creative industries, as advocated by Florida (2002). But this may require government incentives for start-up companies or training to encourage entrepreneurship in the first place.

If tourism is to be encouraged, there may be a requirement for new infrastructural developments, such as transport and accommodation, especially if landmark buildings or 'mega-events' are not located centrally. Opportunities to increase length of stay and expenditure may be needed. Cities like Bilbao struggled in the initial stages of regeneration and tourism development, despite the apparent 'success' of the Guggenheim Museum, as there was little else for tourists to see or do once they had visited this one attraction. Smaller, supporting attractions may be needed, even if these are related only to shopping (a major motivating factor for most tourists), as well as a flourishing evening economy. However, animation is difficult to create in remote locations, especially if they are not frequented by local people either. Incentives may be needed, like more frequent public transport connections, guaranteed taxi services or closer links between hotels and attractions.

Although ephemeral events like festivals and events are tourist magnets, they are of temporary duration and may not have such a long-lasting impact as permanent attractions or iconic buildings. Having said that, Olympic and European City of Culture bids are required to include a detailed strategy for legacy and re-use. Barcelona is an example of a city that has managed this legacy admirably, constantly building new attractions on the former Olympic site. These days, with growing competition and changing consumer tastes, tourist destinations cannot afford to rest on their laurels. They must be constantly creative and innovative in their approach to the development and (re)branding of attractions. Some authors have suggested that there need to be more creative approaches to regeneration and tourism development. For example, Richards and Wilson (2007) advocate increasing the development of experiential creative spaces, creative spectacles and creative tourism. The tastes of the post-modern tourist or '**post-tourist**' are clearly changing, and increasing numbers of tourists are drawn to the excitement of 'hyper-real' experiences, often within enclavic bubbles, such as shopping malls, theme parks or leisure complexes. This is part of the 'playfulness' of tourism (Rojek, 1993). The production of such spaces therefore appears to be a prominent characteristic of post-modern urban planning, and thus an inherent part of regeneration.

If regeneration is successful, then the following positive impacts can benefit the location:

Potential Socio-Economic Benefits	Potential Environmental Benefits
• Employment creation • Education and training programmes • Infrastructural improvements • Housing developments • Improved safety and security	• Better use of land and public spaces • Clean-up operations • Reduced air and water pollution
	(Continued)

- Development of recreational and leisure facilities
- Cultural projects and initiatives
- Revenue from tourism development
- Improved internal and external image of city

- More green spaces and parks
- Street furniture and public art
- Conversion of industrial or derelict areas
- Heritage conservation

Nevertheless, regeneration can create problems if it is not managed carefully. When gentrification occurs, the cost of living rises in an area, and local people are priced out of their housing. Mega-events are frequently used to boost the tourism profile and image of a city, but the legacy is often one of high levels of debt, redundant buildings and a community that has been displaced or bypassed. Many projects have been copied in numerous locations (e.g. many cities wanted their own Guggenheim after witnessing the success of Bilbao), but the context and culture will determine the response of local people and visitors. Copycat schemes can rarely match the success of an original idea. There are also problems of standardisation or homogenisation in tourism developments, where certain developments are so globalised that they could be anywhere (e.g. a waterfront development, shopping mall or entertainment complex). If all tourism destinations start to look the same, then why travel?

The authors in Smith (2007) use case studies of regeneration initiatives to show how expensive mistakes can be avoided. For example, increasingly creative approaches to development and design are being taken; charismatic and dynamic leadership of regeneration projects is emerging; public spirited initiatives are complementing commercial ones; long-term outcomes are being planned for, especially in the context of sporting mega-events; local issues are being prioritised alongside international development and tourism projects; and integrated approaches to cultural and community planning are being implemented. Although culture and tourism were once seen to be the icing on the cake in regeneration schemes after economic and social issues had been addressed, evidence suggests that this situation is changing, and that more integrated approaches are being adopted. Indeed, cultural and tourism developments can become the catalysts

key concepts in tourist studies

for regeneration, sometimes providing a new level of hope for cities which have declined seemingly beyond all other hope. Flagship projects, events and festivals, innovative and iconic architecture, and the development of cultural and creative attractions can all help to raise the profile of cities and create unique branding opportunities. More importantly, they can help to strengthen economies and enhance social cohesion.

See also: *urban tourism*

FURTHER READING

There are many books about regeneration, especially urban regeneration, but very few of these focus on tourism. One exception is Smith's *Tourism, Culture and Regeneration*. It is also worth consulting **urban tourism** books (see separate entry), which tend to include regeneration as a major or minor theme.

RECOMMENDED BOOKS AND ARTICLES

Hallyar, B., Griffin, T. and Edwards, D. (eds) (2008) *City Spaces – Tourist Places: Urban Tourism Precincts*. Oxford: Butterworth-Heinemann.
Maitland, R. and Newman, P. (eds) (2008) *World Tourism Cities*. London: Routledge.
Smith, M.K. (ed.) (2007) *Tourism, Culture and Regeneration*. Wallingford: CABI.

Religious and Spiritual Tourism

Religious tourism focuses on the visiting of religious sites, monuments or destinations, with the primary aim of engaging with or intensifying a specific faith.

Spiritual tourism aims to explore the elements of life which lie beyond the self and contribute to body–mind–spirit balance. These may or may not have an affiliation to religion.

Religious tourism is not easy to define, and so the terms 'religious', 'faith', 'spiritual' or 'pilgrimage' tourism may be used interchangeably. Most religious sites, monuments and destinations also attract cultural heritage tourists who may or may not have a religious affiliation. Some tourists have multiple motivations – a visit to a religious site could be motivated by a religious belief, attraction to its architecture and an interest in its historical value all at the same time. Many research statistics aggregate religious and religious heritage tourism, resulting in problems with quantification. Religious tourism, in theory, only focuses on those visitors who belong to a certain religious group and travel primarily with the aim of furthering their knowledge of or engagement with a specific faith.

It is also difficult to provide typical profiles for religious tourists, as they can be practically any age, gender or nationality. The nature of the faith may determine what percentage of the population will engage in religious tourism (all Muslims, for example, are expected to complete the Hajj to Mecca at least once in a lifetime). Many countries can be described as more religious than others (e.g. Catholic countries such as Ireland, Italy, Poland, Portugal), whereas others have a high percentage of non-believers, such as Scandinavian and other northern European countries. These countries might still generate secular spiritual tourists, however.

In terms of religious tourism attractions, one of the best known classifications was published by Nolan and Nolan (1989). They identified three groups:

- pilgrimage shrines – places that serve as the goals of religiously motivated journeys from beyond the immediate locality
- religious tourist attractions – structures or sites of religious significance with historic and/or artistic importance
- festivals with religious association.

The study included sacred buildings of special value, not only in the architectural sense, but also because they are sites of special historic interest or because they are located in an idyllic landscape, and attract equal numbers of pilgrims and tourists (e.g. the Cathedral at Chartres and the island abbey of Mont Saint Michel in France). It also included buildings and monuments built as a result of religious urges, but not used for religious purposes. These are buildings and monuments erected in fulfilment of vows or out of gratitude for miracles that have occurred (e.g. the statue of Christ in Rio de Janeiro). Festivals with religious association attract large numbers of believers and non-believers because of their local colour and rituals (e.g. Holy Week). The destinations which attract the largest numbers of pilgrims or tourists of religious heritage tend to be those which appear in the Bible, Koran or other sacred texts.

Religious tourism has certain elements that distinguish it from other types of tourism. Tourists often travel in groups from the same faith or denomination with a knowledgeable guide, and the trips are sold through specialist suppliers, predominantly direct mail or Church/Temple/Synagogue channels. Seasonality is frequently less pronounced than for other forms of travel, although key dates in the religious calendar may lead to intensification in certain destinations. The seminar and conference market is growing in this sector (e.g. Assisi has a niche in the Catholic conference market). Moore (2007) suggests that there has been a shift from a 'poverty mentality' among religious travellers to an expectation of first-class accommodation. Although this might not be true of all religious tourists (e.g. pilgrims), the quality of facilities certainly seems to be improving.

Some forms of religious tourism, such as pilgrimage tourism, have even more specific characteristics. This form of religious tourism became popular during the Middle Ages, which were marked by journeys to holy or sacred places. The most common destinations of the period were Santiago de Compostela, Czestochowa and Rome. Pilgrimage is a physical journey, which often symbolises and reflects the life journey of the individual (Devereux and Carnegie, 2006). The pilgrimage market can attract specific religious tourists (e.g. Muslims to Mecca), but increasingly it attracts a more 'spiritual' market (e.g. Santiago de Compostela).

Pilgrimage became a subject of anthropological study for Victor Turner (1978), who argued that pilgrimage was a religious practice through which people entered a liminal state, having left the confines of their profane lives. Here they would also experience a feeling of 'communitas' with other pilgrims while normal social restrictions were temporarily suspended. Two edited collections on pilgrimage by Eade and Sallnow (1991) and Morinis (1992) take Turner's work as a starting point for homage and critique. They argue that, unlike the tourist who seeks the edge or the periphery, the pilgrim seeks the centre of his/her culture and society. Hannaford (2001) also develops a frame of criteria for pilgrimage which is structured around three major areas: (a) material, physical aspects, (b) personal experiential dimensions and (c) an ideational aspect, which highlights the difference between the *recreation* of the tourist and the *re-creation* of the pilgrim.

The main motives for a pilgrimage may include the following:

- to fulfil a commandment of a religion
- as an act of devotion at the site of a miraculous or significant event
- as a process in gaining remission of sins
- to pray and seek a cure for illness
- to attend a prayer meeting with a religious leader
- to witness a religious ceremony or performance
- for a family religious ceremony
- to go to a site where miraculous events are expected in the future.

Devereux and Carnegie (2006) add the following characteristics of pilgrimage tourists: 'aspiration to non-materialistic living', 'sense of altruism' (e.g. helping others) and, 'often willingness to endure hardship to reach spiritual goals'.

The act of pilgrimage demonstrates the blurring of boundaries between the religious and the spiritual. Heelas and Woodhead (2005) suggest that a slow but steady spiritual revolution is taking place in which secular spirituality is taking over from traditional religion. Some Western psychologists such as Freud believed that religion was detrimental to the emotional health of the individual. Others like Jung believed that spirituality was the essence of what it meant to be human. Indeed, the word 'spirituality' comes from the Latin 'spiritualitas', an abstract word, related to the Greek word 'pneuma' meaning breath, the essence of life. In **holistic and wellness** research, some researchers have developed 'wheels of wellness' (denoting an ideal balance of activities in life), some of which place spirituality at the centre (e.g. Myers, Sweeney and Witmer, 2000). Spirituality is a holistic discipline which is not limited to the 'explorations of the explicitly religious' but considers all aspects of the spiritual experience, namely, 'the psychological, bodily, historical, political, aesthetic, intellectual and other dimensions of the human subject of spiritual experience' (Schneiders, 1989: 693). Davie (1994) described spirituality as 'believing without belonging', which arguably suits more individualistic societies. Sociological research has suggested that the development of more individualistic cultures and societies has increased social alienation, resulting in a greater need for seeking spiritual solace.

Magyar (2008) has compiled a list of the most popular spiritual destinations around the world by collecting information from major spiritual, travel-oriented websites.

- Jerusalem (Israel)
- Mecca (Saudi-Arabia)
- The Vatican and Rome (Italy)
- Tibet, Nepal and Mount Everest
- Goa and Benares (India)
- Macchu Picchu (Peru)
- Egypt
- Mount Fuji (Japan)
- Navaho Region (USA)
- Rio de Janeiro (Brasil)
- Alaska (USA).

We can see that there are some destinations which are perhaps surprising – Alaska, for example, which is visited mainly because of its untouched nature and spiritual atmosphere. However, this proves that for many non-religious tourists, spirituality can be found in alternative places (e.g. nature and landscape).

Cohen (1996) describes how the quest for a 'spiritual centre' is an integral part of tourism, especially when people feel socially alienated. Traditional aspects of spiritual retreats have often been in the form of pilgrimages for religious tourists (Carrasco, 1996; Devereux and Carnegie, 2006), but the secular tourist may seek other forms of spiritual enlightenment. Spiritual tourism can include visiting religious sites or buildings, spiritual landscapes, pilgrimage centres, ashrams, retreats or gurus. The spiritual quest is seen as more abstract than a specifically religious one, focusing on the balance of body, mind and spirit. Tourists seek meaning, engagement and peace through a variety of different activities, such as meditation, chanting and breathing. Although some of these traditions may be derived from religious practices, they are likely to be multi-faith and hybridised (e.g. combining Buddhist meditation with Hindu mantras or Chinese martial arts).

Cohen (1996) distinguishes between different tourists' motivations and experiences, categorising them as recreational, diversionary, experiential, experimental and existential. While the first three categories of tourist are largely escaping routine, boredom or alienation, they are not necessarily expecting to *find* meaning elsewhere. In contrast, experimental tourists seek spiritual centres in different, alternative directions, often sampling and contrasting 'authentic' life or rituals in an attempt to find themselves. In many cases, they tend to be younger, 'post-modern travellers', hanging out in ashrams or Kibbutzes for some length of time, but can also include ageing hippies from the 1960s and '70s who never left the destination or, increasingly, 30-to-50-something, burnt-out, recuperating professionals. Existential travellers, on the other hand, tend to commit to one spiritual centre, residing there semi-permanently or visiting periodically on a kind of personal pilgrimage.

The characteristics of typical religious and spiritual tourists are summarised and contrasted below.

Religious Tourists

- Have affiliation to specific religion or religious group
- Have interest in quest for religious enlightenment
- Enjoy visiting specific religious sites and landscapes
- Empathise with other religious tourists, pilgrims and local communities
- Engage in ritualistic behaviour
- Ultimately seek religious union or salvation

Spiritual Tourists

- Likely to have 'multi-faith' empathy
- Have interest in personal spiritual development
- Enjoy visiting spiritual or mystical landscapes
- Seek interaction with local and indigenous communities
- May engage in rituals and ceremonies
- Hope for reconciliation of body, mind and spirit

It is clear that religious and spiritual tourism are closely linked in terms of activities, but the motivations of tourists may be very different. There is a long history in tourism of journeys contributing to spiritual enlightenment, but in post-modern societies these motivations may be increasingly of a secular nature.

See also: *health and wellness tourism*

FURTHER READING

There are many books about religion and spirituality, but only a few focus on tourism as well. Examples include Fernandes et al.'s *Religious Tourism and Pilgrimage*; Olsen and Timothy's *Tourism, Religion and Spiritual Journeys*; and Raj and Morpeth's *Religious Tourism and Pilgrimage Management: An International Perspective*. It is worth noting that many of the more recent publications tend to emphasise multi-faith and non-religious spirituality, in contrast to the traditional focus on Christian heritage sites.

RECOMMENDED BOOKS

Fernandes, C., McGettigan, F. and Edwards, J. (2003) *Religious Tourism and Pilgrimage*. Tilburg: ATLAS.

Olsen, D.H. and Timothy, D.J. (eds) (2006) *Tourism, Religion and Spiritual Journeys*. London: Routledge.

Raj, R. and Morpeth, N.D. (eds) (2007) *Religious Tourism and Pilgrimage Management: An International Perspective*. Wallingford: CABI.

Rural Tourism

> *Rural tourism describes forms of tourism activity that take place in countryside regions and which encompass local culture, traditions and industries as well as outdoor activities and experiences that are staged in an unspoiled rural setting. The local community plays an important role in providing the rural tourism product.*

Rural tourism has been popular across Europe since the end of the eighteenth century when tourists inspired by the Romantics would seek out rural retreats, in particular the Alps and the Lake District. However, this form of tourism really came into its own in the late twentieth century as a result of (a) the need to escape the city and the 'urban' environment, in areas where beaches do not abound and (b) the perceived need to reaffirm identity and national difference, in the face of growing unity and redefinition of geographical borders and frontiers. Rural tourism, as such, is not necessarily an international movement, but rather a domestic pursuit, with national tourism searching out its roots. It can also be seen as a type of nostalgia tourism in its search for the higher-quality aspects of life, contact with nature, good food and health.

Echoing the domestic nature of the rural tourism experience, the UK's Countryside Agency reported in 2001 that tourists spend £12 billion annually in the English countryside and that a quarter of all holiday stays by British people in England are in the countryside. However, they do go on to point out that rural images are also a very important tool in attracting overseas visitors (Countryside Agency/ETC, 2001).

Rural tourism is not necessarily the same as ecotourism or, for that matter, agricultural or agro-tourism although the terms are often inter-changed. The associations of rural tourism are clearly different from eco-tourism or agricultural tourism. Critics of ecotourism feel that this form of tourism is closely associated with public relations and marketing and perceived ecological values (see **ecotourism**). People who take 'green' tourism holidays are making a statement about their principles and lifestyles. People who go on rural tourism trips are not necessarily doing much more than looking for good food, good walks and peace and quiet. 'Eco-labels', eco-taxes and eco-tourism, in general, represent political stances and the promotion of 'green' and ecological values for sustain-able economic benefits. Working farm holidays, on the other hand, rep-resent the 'deep' ecologist's stance – immersion in the rhythm of work in the country as opposed to in the city, the aspect of leisure only being reflected in the change of 'environment'. Rural tourism, however, is a completely different leisure product. It is associated with lack of acoustic pollution, with contact with nature, gastronomic values, and traditional pursuits and crafts, 'slow' food, and a relaxed pace of life – in other words, the complete antithesis of life in the city. As such, it is inti-mately linked to the idea of community tourism, as the antithesis of the individual and isolated life led in the city. A lack of visual and acoustic contamination is absolutely vital to the success of rural tourism ven-tures, together with an unspoilt environment (in the widest possible sense of the word 'environment') and traditional architecture. Interaction with others is also central to the experience of rural and community-based tourism.

Page et al. (2001) suggest that rural tourism has a number of distin-guishing characteristics, which include the peace, quiet and solitude of remote locations. Tourists are often drawn to the landscapes, wildlife, culture and lifestyles of local communities, as well as being keen to escape urban life and to enjoy the fresh air. Another motivation might be to improve health and fitness through adventure and challenge.

Rural tourism can be related to the idea of empowerment of women, since the major crafts and activities carried out in rural tourism are dom-inated by women. As opposed to the major restaurants and catering busi-nesses in the cities, gastronomy is a female-dominated activity in rural areas, in general, and rural tourism, in particular. Rural tourism, then, is perhaps the most effective example of stakeholders being directly engaged in the shape, execution and profits made from the tourism product. As such, it tends to be the basis of community, pro-poor or **ethical tourism**.

The need for lack of visual contamination, together with a certain quality of infrastructure considered to be basic for comfort, means that there is greater recourse made to alternative energy and clean energy systems in new rural and community projects, in order to provide the water, drainage systems and basic comforts required to make the leisure stay as pleasant as possible. This, again, is an example of how tourism can be used to provide positive benefits and impacts, by bringing energy and water systems to areas where these are lacking.

Rural tourism, like other activities, differs according to where it is offered. In Europe, where life in the city is the norm for most, and the population is ageing, rural tourism represents a high-quality style of tourism, an escape from everyday life. As such, it can go hand in hand with wine tourism, **gastronomic tourism**, **health and wellness tourism**, and adventure tourism. In other parts of the world, however, where the economy is still largely rural, rural tourism offers a unique opportunity to come into contact with the local population, to 'belong' to a community for a short period of time. Rural tourism, if designed on a community basis with community consensus, allows for physical and cultural habitats to be protected.

To a very large extent, this was the concept of tourism promoted in the Brundtland Report, designed to mitigate poverty and to stimulate economic growth in the Third World. Agenda 21, produced at the Earth Summit in Río (1992), was an action plan, designed to move towards sustainable development through tourism evolving at a community level, based on environmental products, and working on the 'bottom-up' approach, as opposed to the hierarchical 'top-down' approach of most institutional development plans.

Shackley (1996) comments on these new approaches to tourism:

> Terms such as environmentally friendly tourism, sustainable tourism, ecotourism, responsible tourism, low impact tourism are just a few among many in common use ... These designate low impact tourism programmes which might result in some form of sustainable benefits to the destination area. (Shackley, 1996: 12)

Again, 'sustainability' relating to rural tourism and economic viability depends upon where it is offered, by whom, and what value-added complementary products are to be derived from the holiday experience. The developed world's offer of rural tourism still pales in comparison with the beach resort product, being largely restricted to short breaks, rented accommodation or themed events, such as 'Murder' weekends, spiritual retreats or health farms. The less developed countries' offer of rural tourism tends to be based on volunteer and pro-poor tourism, thus appealing to the tourist's conscience, and consisting in a longer-lasting relationship with the destination and, thus, a longer stay. Community, rural tourism may even be offered as part of a tourist's otherwise 'sophisticated' tourism package, allowing for a short immersion in the life of the exotic (or semi-dangerous) 'other' in the destination, such as a stay in a Maasai camp in the 'Real Africa' followed by a hot-air balloon trip over the Serengeti park, with champagne included. Clearly, the motivations of tourists attracted to such packages are very different from those of tourists who are looking for a true community-based rural experience.

While the benefits of rural tourism to both consumers and providers can be considerable, there are numerous challenges inherent in developing and managing the rural tourism product. Page et al. (2001) suggest that these might relate to the difficulties of undertaking research to establish the economic and market value of rural tourism. Rural communities are likely to have very different socio-demographic profiles and will therefore respond differently to tourism. Tourism development may not be appropriate for all regions, and it is difficult to manage the quality of the natural and cultural environment in order to maintain its attractiveness to visitors.

There is a need for rural regions and communities to be understood before rural tourism is developed. It is clear that rural areas are attractive to visitors and that tourism may be a useful tool for rural development. However, rural tourism will be most successful where it is embedded in a strong rural economy.

See also: *ecotourism, ethical tourism, sustainable tourism*

FURTHER READING

Readers will find Hall et al.'s *New Directions in Rural Tourism* to be useful. Interesting case studies can be found in Roberts' *Rural Tourism and Recreation: Principles to Practice*.

RECOMMENDED BOOKS

Hall, C.M., Roberts, L. and Mitchell, R. (eds) (2003) *New Directions in Rural Tourism*. Aldershot: Ashgate.
Roberts, L. (ed.) (2001) *Rural Tourism and Recreation: Principles to Practice*. Wallingford: CABI.
Roberts, L. (ed.) (2004) *New Directions in Rural Tourism*. Wallingford: CABI.

Self and Other

> *The concept of self and other refers to an individual's own personal identity and how that sense of self is partly shaped by relationship with others. The concept is pertinent to tourism, as many tourism experiences bring the traveller in contact with the other, thus allowing them to redefine their self in relation to the host community or fellow travellers.*

William Shakespeare coined the phrase that the world is a stage and that we are all players on it. Erving Goffmann (1959) in his seminal work, *The Presentation of Self in Everyday Life*, followed Shakespeare's lead and adopted a dramaturgical approach towards society, to explain social identity, social roles, performance, audiences and interaction. Dramaturgical theory suggests that a person's identity is not a stable entity but is constantly re-made as the person interacts with others.

Social identity, or self, is intimately linked to image and power (see **identity** and **sex tourism**). Positive public image (or 'front' as Goffman (1959) calls it) and power are currently considered to be a form of wealth and one that is in short supply. People refer to a partner as their 'significant other', implying by extension that those outside that compact unit are insignificant. Some people have a vital need of 'significant others' in order to reassert themselves. Others satisfy themselves and their needs without requiring other people's evaluations of their actions for reaffirmation.

Most identities are constructed in relation to others and the philosophical basis for this may be found in existential theories of self and other (e.g. Jean Paul Sartre). Edward Said clearly extended this concept in his work on colonial and post-colonial studies. Said's work has greatly influenced tourism studies in its examination of the relationship between the Occident and the Orient and the dominance of European culture and power – 'this dominance, informed by rational and scientific scholarship hence providing adequate justification for the subordination of Orientals, and the oppressive binarism of "us" and "them" or "self" and "Other"' (Smith, 2003: 3).

The concept of self and other, and of **mobility** of identity depending upon physical mobility, change of scene, and confrontation with other cultures and customs, is central to the idea of tourism. To travel is to embark upon a voyage of discovery: self-discovery through contrast and reaffirmation with respect to the other. Just as a tourist resort has a life cycle as it passes through discovery, consolidation, maturity and decline or re-birth (Butler, 2006), so the tourist evolves through different phases of 'otherness', and with different travelling partners, different 'others', according to age and financial circumstances, in 'other' places and spaces or stages.

The 'other' is also central to the projection of tourist image, again depending upon the maturity of the resort, and the type of tourist thus attracted to, or targeted by, the same. The 'other' may be viewed as significant or otherwise, depending upon the geo-political power structures which exist (see **neo-colonialism**) and the degree to which the destination society fits into the Western European's framework of 'civilisation'.

In other concepts (**sex tourism** and **gay tourism**), the 'other' has been explored as the persona adopted by the tourist when abroad and away from familiar surroundings. Tourists temporarily leave behind their everyday identities and move into a transitory world of fantasy. Krippendorf (1987: 33) expressed this concept in the following way:

> Tourists are free of all constraints ... Do as one pleases: dress, eat, spend money, celebrate and feast ... The have-a-good-time ideology and the tomorrow-we-shall-be-gone-again attitude set the tone.

Although 'staged authenticity' is a concept which was coined by MacCannell (1976) to describe tourist resorts which 'play' to the tourists, the term can also be used to describe the tourists who travel to other places not to explore their feelings and go on a voyage of self-discovery, but rather to play to the crowds. 'Distance' as experienced through physical displacement from everyday life (travel) or as lack of cultural similarity (even superiority) causes people to change their habits of social interaction.

In many ways, this is what Cohen describes when he talks about the difference between the 'traveller' and the 'tourist', as summed up in his four typologies of tourists (1972), later expanded upon, and related to tourist destinations, by Plog (1974). These two authors were partly laying the groundwork for what is now known as consumer psychology. Cohen's (1972) 'institutionalised' tourists, so called because they reveal a heavy dependence upon the tourism industry to organise their travel (the individual mass tourist and the organised mass tourist), fall into Plog's (1974) categories of psycho- and mediocentrics, and tend towards established destinations that offer security, familiarity and comfort. These tourists are, to a great extent, responsible for the tourism industry's development of all-inclusive resorts (exclusive of the local public, the 'other') which abound the world over. Cohen's 'non-institutionalised' tourists, the 'drifters' and the 'explorers' (Plog's allocentrics), on the other hand, seek out authentic experiences in unexplored places where they can interact with the locals. For this type of tourist, the human element is essential to the enjoyment of the trip. A typical profile of the 'allocentric' is the **backpacker.**

Just as people tend to backpack and 'rough' it when they are younger, 'footloose and fancy-free', once these 'allocentrics' become parents and have a family, their new social configuration or 'self' as the result of their children and partners, will lead them to be more conservative, more mediocentric, in their tourism tastes. They will return to the places of their earlier travels but the more the destination is visited, the greater will be the local perceived need of 'playing' to the needs of the 'other', the tourist. Consequently, the destination will become more standardised and 'safe' (from the psycho- and mediocentrics' perspective), thus attracting another type of visitor, the 'audience' instead of the 'performer'.

When designing marketing programmes, the experts use consumer tastes or lifestyle profiles and the extent to which the targeted group are 'players' or 'audience' in order to define how to win them over to their product. Tourism destinations are perceived as leaders or followers, with London, New York, Paris, Rome and Berlin having to do little to sell themselves to 'others', whereas less mainstream attractions have to work much harder to develop a tourist industry. Tourism resorts are also influenced by the extent to which a role model is identified with them or not, either favourably or negatively. Thus, the situation of Tibet and

self and other

China (as represented by the person of the Dalai Lama) affected the total 'pull' of the Olympics in 2008. Recent inaugurations of extravagant tourism complexes, such as the Dubai Atlantic Hotel, in times of economic crisis, are the best example of the desire to emulate the 'other' as a motivation for adopting a holiday lifestyle, with Hollywood stars featured sipping Dom Perignon on the terrace to inspire would-be visitors. Marketers use the public projection of the self, as represented by media stars, to convince others to buy their products, a strategy which is used to great effect by the travel trade. This 'identification' with the 'other' is central to marketing and promotion and has been used effectively for centuries in the tourism industry.

See also: identity, neo-colonialism, tourist gaze

FURTHER READING

Highly recommended is the second part of the trilogy by Manuel Castells, *The Power of Identity*. The work of Edward Said on 'the Other', for example his *Orientalism*, has often been applied to tourism.

RECOMMENDED BOOKS AND ARTICLES

Castells, M. (1997) *The Power of Identity*. Oxford: Blackwell.
Cohen, E. (1972) 'Toward a sociology of international tourism', *Social Research*, 39: 164–82.
Krippendorf, J. (1987) *The Holiday Makers*. Oxford: Heinemann.
Said, E.W. (1978) *Orientalism*. London: Routledge & Kegan Paul.

Sex Tourism

Sex tourism is travel with the sole or partial intention of pursuing sexual intercourse with 'others', usually from different social, racial and ethnic backgrounds.

Sex, in its pursuit of escape from the humdrum existence of everyday life, and adoption of a new and exciting identity, is potentially the main motivation behind the leisure industry, from music through to tourism, and in all the forms of the visual arts. Sex sells, particularly in the West and the North, and possibly because we still live in a society where the male perspective is given priority over the female viewpoint, thus emphasising the physical aspect of the love act over the emotional content. It may also be claimed that, because women are adopting male attitudes towards sex tourism, there is no longer a dominant white male perspective but rather a dominant developed-world perspective on the activity. Sex and, more importantly, the trading of sex, involves certain power relationships and value judgements which go far beyond the micro-level of the individual act of prostitution, be it legal or not, mirroring macro-level economic and political attitudes towards regions of the world and their peoples.

Sex tourism, however, has been treated as a peripheral, almost taboo issue in tourism studies until relatively recently. Although the phenomenon has been recognised in academic and especially anthropological circles since the 1970s, it was not until the 1980s that research-based studies started to appear (e.g. Cohen, 1982), and only in the very late 1990s or early 2000s that mainstream textbooks were published (Bauer and McKercher, 2003; Carter and Clift, 2000; Ryan and Hall, 2001). The lack of a clear-cut definition of sex tourism, together with the relative lack of institutional organisation of the activity, contribute to the deficiency of statistics in this sector of tourism, though it is estimated to be a multi-billion-dollar transnational industry. Neverthless, the marketing of sex tourism is becoming more overt, albeit on the internet. Sites like Sly Traveler (http://slyguide.com) provide easily accessible guides to which countries to visit and their main attractions (e.g. red-light districts, clubs and bars, brothels, live sex shows, escort services), plus stories and blogs of other sex tourists. Some of the major sex tourism destinations highlighted are Amsterdam, Bangkok, Rio de Janeiro, Hong Kong, Los Angeles and Tijuana.

The phenomenon of sex tourism is widespread, yet its covert nature often leads to insidious and uncontrollable growth, which is particularly pervasive in developing regions of the world. Although sex tourism can be voluntary or exploitative, commercial or non-commercial (Ryan, 2000), it can be a considerable cause for concern in some developing countries. Local and indigenous women and men are often rendered subservient to the needs of wealthy, powerful Western tourists. As stated by Hall (1992: 74): 'The sexual relationship between prostitute and client is a mirror image of the dependency of South-East Asian nations on the developed world'. Poverty-stricken villagers are sometimes persuaded to sell their young children to the sex tourism industry as a means of ensuring their family's future survival. Sex tourism is arguably part of the same process of 'othering' **(see self and other)**, whereby local people are depicted (and sold) as being exotic/erotic objects of the tourist gaze. Sanchez Taylor (1998) notes the covert racism in the attitudes of some sex tourists who perpetuate the racist stereotype of the exotic and erotic black woman (or man), especially in such destinations as the Caribbean.

Sex tourism usually conjures up the slightly seedy picture of older, out-of-shape men travelling to underdeveloped countries for cheap sexual pleasures, either not available or taboo in their own countries, or outside the moral boundaries or perceived economic possibilities of their everyday persona. Much has been written about the white heterosexual male dominant perspective of tourism, tourism imagery and geography, but there has been little discussion of the changes since the 1960s as a result of a lessening polarisation of the economy, greater female economic independence and homosexuality. The dependency relationship in the context of sex tourism appears these days to be based more on wealth and status than on gender, with sex tourism by heterosexual women or 'Sugar Mummies' becoming more popular, homosexual or pink-dollar tourism of vital importance to the tourism industry, and paedophilia an alarming reality in many Third World countries. However, care must be taken not to equate gay tourism and sex tourism, as they are by no means synonymous. Although some destinations have gained a reputation as being 'safe' gay sex tourism destinations (e.g. Thailand), this does not mean that the seeking of gay-friendly destinations necessarily has a sexual motivation (see **gay tourism**).

It is now becoming more common for Western female tourists to visit destinations such as the Gambia, the Caribbean or India for reasons of sex tourism. However, Sanchez Taylor and O'Connell Davidson (1998) note that adult male prostitutes who cater to demand from female tourists tend to be a lot less vulnerable than women prostitutes who serve a male clientele, as their economic situation is usually less desperate and they are less physically vulnerable. Women also do not typically use the structures of the sex industry such as strip clubs, sex shows and organised tours to meet foreign partners. Women's trips may sometimes be referred to as 'romance tourism' and their temporary partners are named 'escorts' rather than prostitutes. This might be a misrepresentation, but it highlights clearly the social perception that women are not as sexually predatory as men.

Sex tourism is geographically charted according to 'natural values' and 'exoticism' in the South and the East, respectively. The semiotics of 'naturalness' and 'hedonism' implied by the sun and hotter temperatures are built upon consistently by marketing and media worldwide. Avoidance of the everyday stress of First World urban life, including the difficulties of gender relations in their home countries, leads the tourists' fancy towards sex. The East and the exotic 'other', with a different set of moral values and women portrayed as (often willing) sex slaves, are stereotypes which date far back in travel history. The additional required stereotype is that the paid sex is cheap.

The idea of divorce, or liberation from the 'self' of everyday life, is a consistent and constant feature of both male and female hetero- and homosexual justifications of their incursions into sex tourism. Researchers have consistently found that both sexes are seeking an idealised encounter, apparently stemming from their frustrations with gender relations at home. Women and men's sex tourism can, however, be radically different phenomena, with women paying for the attention and devotion that they cannot find in their homes, whereas men are often seeking exciting, 'no strings attached' adventures. Both, however, are clear types of evasion, with each of the genders adopting a totally different persona outside the framework of their everyday existence. The social implications of both male and female adult sex tourism, albeit from different motivations, are equally devastating in their total lack of solidarity with and social responsibility towards the communities visited.

There are serious health implications to sex tourism, with AIDS being pandemic in some countries. There are also significant legal implications, especially with regards to under-age children. Many of the Latin American countries, such as Brazil and Ecuador, have launched strict and rigorously pursued campaigns to crack down on child-sex offenders, indicating the magnitude of the problem. Illegal trafficking, for clandestine rings of prostitution, of women who are often tricked out of their countries and away from their families with the promise of domestic work and official papers in Western Europe, is another major source of risk for women, and is often unchecked, or even connived at by the governments of their home countries (as it represents a major source of remittances). There is a high price in social and cultural terms to be paid by the locals of any destination which makes, or tacitly allows, sex tourism to become its major driver – but it would seem that the West is willing to pay it. The international campaign ECPAT (End Child Prostitution, Pornography and Trafficking, see www.ecpat.net) has done much since the early 1990s to raise awareness to a number of important issues. Such campaigns are needed to protect vulnerable groups, but it is a sad fact of life that sex tourism is as old as time. So long as tourists have money to spend, and local people have something to sell, the sex tourism phenomenon seems unlikely to decline in the foreseeable future.

See also: *neo-colonialism, self and other*

FURTHER READING

There is an increasing number of mainstream textbooks or in-depth studies on sex tourism, for example Carter and Clift's *Tourism and Sex: Culture, Commerce and Coercion*; Ryan and Hall's *Sex Tourism: Marginal People and Liminalities*; and Bauer and McKercher's *Sex and Tourism: Journeys of Romance, Love, and Lust*.

RECOMMENDED BOOKS

Bauer, T.G. and McKercher, B. (2003) *Sex and Tourism: Journeys of Romance, Love, and Lust*. New York: Haworth.

Carter, S. and Clift, S. (eds) (2000) *Tourism and Sex: Culture, Commerce and Coercion*. London: Cassell.

Ryan, C. and Hall, C.M. (2001) *Sex Tourism: Marginal People and Liminalities*. London: Routledge.

Sociology of Tourism

The sociology of tourism is concerned with the relations between tourists as types, and the structuring, function and consequences of the tourist system in general.

The sociology of tourism has been a significant area of academic study for many years. Cohen (1996) suggests that the following domains are of interest within sociological enquiry:

- consequences and impacts of tourism
- the structure and functioning of the tourism system
- relations between tourists and local people
- the tourist.

The sociology of tourism is concerned with the study of tourism as a social phenomenon, including the motivations and behaviour of tourists, and the impacts that this has on destinations and their people. The **anthropology of tourism** focuses on individual experiences in tourism, whereas the sociology of tourism works upon these bases to form generalisations. In the sociology of tourism, therefore, we can talk about tourism in general terms as a modern leisure activity consonant with present consumer trends, together with the commercialisation of hospitality, tourism as democratic travel or modern pilgrimage, tourism as the expression of basic cultural themes (Graburn, 1983), as a process of acculturation or even leisure activities as **neo-colonialism**. The sociology of tourism analyses tourists' motivations, roles and relationships, while studying the impact of institutions and institutionalisation on tourism. The sociology of tourism has to do with types of tourism and tourists, modes of tourism and tourists, the impacts of the leisure activity on the host and guest populations, and the aspirations of both. Whereas the anthropology of tourism focuses on the private aspects of cultural representations and consumption, the sociology of tourism looks at public, generalised notions of cultural representations (stereotypes) and consumption (marketing, general publicity and souvenirs).

Holden (2005) summarises the main traditional pillars of sociological thought and methodology, including structuralism, which analyses the structures of society and how they influence our behaviour. Within this, the main schools of thought are functionalism, where society is viewed as a complex system in which social institutions (including tourism) play an important role in producing stability and solidarity; and conflict theory, which rejects the consensus inherent in functionalism, and instead explores social divisions. Critiques of structuralism tend towards phenomenology, which has emerged as an important alternative sociological paradigm. The focus of phenomenology is on how we as individuals interpret and give meaning to the world around us, and few meanings are fixed or certain. Phenomenology has been criticised for being unscientific and subjective, but, arguably, it better reflects the world as human beings perceive it.

However, this also makes research more complex, especially in the tourism field. Although the economic and environmental dimensions of tourism can be measured quantitatively, the sociological and cultural ones are more qualitative. For example, it is clearly difficult to measure and monitor the socio-cultural impacts of tourism. Culture is dynamic and changes over time, irrespective of tourism development. Firstly, it is difficult to distinguish the impacts of tourism from those of other social or economic developments. Secondly, few reliable tools exist to measure socio-cultural impacts, which are often intangible. However, it should be noted that sociologists (and anthropologists) have been researching the phenomenon of social and cultural change for some time, but it is a complex, time-consuming process.

Early studies of the sociology of tourism focused on the idea that tourism was a form of mindless escapism from the monotony, banality and hardship of everyday life (e.g. Boorstin, 1964). Dann and Cohen (1996) describe how anomie ('meaning a personal state of isolation and anxiety resulting from a lack of social control and regulation') tends to be prevalent in tourism-generating societies, reflecting a general normlessness or meaninglessness, which acts as a major 'push' factor in travel motivation (Dann, 1977). Sharpley (2002) also states how alienation (e.g. from work, community and nature) has become an extrinsic motivating factor in tourism. However, Dann (1977) focuses on the notion that many tourists are also seeking 'ego enhancement', that is, the individual's need for social recognition through the destinations they choose or the wealth they display by travelling.

Later, MacCannell (1976) suggests that some tourists are searching for the **authenticity** which is absent in everyday life. There have been some concerns that tourism can destroy the authenticity of destinations as it commercialises or commodifies culture and lifestyles. However, in some cases, it can also help to protect and revive cultures. Urry's (1990/2002) notion of the **tourist gaze** has also become quite influential within the sociology of tourism and focuses on the tourists' ways of seeing places and people and the way in which the selection of those sights is organised and directed by the tourism industry.

More recent sociological studies have turned their attention to the subject of mobility, including the influence of new technology, communications and media (e.g. Urry, 1990/2002). The (new) sociology of tourism looks at how, in broad terms, patterns of consumption, changes in social hierarchy and visual representations, as projected through the mass media, move consumers towards or away from specific destinations (like Mexico and swine flu in 2009). As consumer tribes and communities have evolved, thanks to revolutions in the mobility of information through TV and the internet, so have brands related to travel and leisure or, more importantly, to consumer lifestyles: Urry (1990/2002: 2) defines these as:

> material transformations that are remaking the 'social', especially those diverse mobilities that, through multiple senses, imaginative travel, movements of images and information, virtuality and physical movement, are materially reconstructing the 'social as society' into the 'social as mobility'.

This is a sociology which is, by definition, cross-cultural, making reference to all the other social semiotic and symbolic representations, public and private, legal, family, gender and religion-related, which structure, qualitatively, our evolution and flow through life, our social 'mobility' (see **mobility**). We know from the sociology of tourism that the North moves towards the South, influenced not only by the climate, but by the perceived family and community values favoured by warm, outdoor (thus, more public) environments, including the perceived relaxation of moral and sexual norms (see **sex tourism**). We are also aware from the sociology of tourism that more men than women travel (due to apportioning of social and family responsibilities) and that tourists tend increasingly to be singles, reflecting solitary life in the modern city, and the lack of real face-to-face communication in the IT age.

We can see then from the sociology of tourism, that consumer trends are no longer dictated simply by nations or local communities in the times of the internet revolution, but have escaped strict geographical and social boundaries. We also know that, thanks to the internet, tourism is no longer supply-led. Consumers now manage more information and can structure their own holiday experiences, to meet up with people with similar likes and dislikes. We also see radical changes in tourist typologies and categorisations, which are now becoming more fluid. The sociology of tourism, in the globalised world, has produced a multiplicity of tourist gazes (Urry, 1990/2002). There are countless mobilities, physical, imaginative and virtual, voluntary and coerced. Therefore, types of tourism experiences and types of tourists become more difficult to define and generalise. The sociology of tourism is influenced more and more by consumer psychology which, in turn, is influenced by mass media.

Some of the most recent sociological research (combined with cultural studies) focuses on social exclusion and marginalisation, which can apply to both the tourist and local residents. This can be based on age, gender, race, sexuality or class. Urry (1995) describes the right to tourism as a form of citizenship which can enhance health and well-being, but there is still a long way to go before this growing leisure activity becomes accessible to all.

See also: anthropology of tourism, authenticity, mobility, tourist gaze

FURTHER READING

The work of Erik Cohen, Dean MacCannell and John Urry are central to the sociology of tourism. It is also worth consulting some of the more general textbooks which provide an overview and summary of the main issues, for example: Apostolopoulos et al.'s *The Sociology of Tourism: Theoretical and Empirical Investigations*; Holden's *Tourism Studies and the Social Sciences*; and Dann and Liebman-Parrinello's *The Sociology of Tourism: European Origins and Development*.

RECOMMENDED BOOKS

Apostolopoulos, Y., Leivadi, S. and Yiannakis, A. (eds) (1996) *The Sociology of Tourism: Theoretical and Empirical Investigations*. London: Routledge.
Dann. G. and Liebman-Parrinello, G. (eds) (2009) *The Sociology of Tourism: European Origins and Development*. Bingley: Emerald Group Publishing.
Holden, A. (2005) *Tourism Studies and the Social Sciences*. London: Routledge.

Special Interest Tourism

Special interest tourism is defined as travelling with the primary motivation of practising or enjoying a special interest. This can include unusual hobbies, activities, themes or destinations, which tend to attract niche markets.

The term 'special interest tourism' has traditionally been used for those forms of tourism which focus on activities which attract a small number of highly dedicated visitors. These may be relatively unusual hobbies or activities which are practised by only a few people. Douglas et al. (2001: 3) describe special interest tourism as an alternative to mass tourism. They suggest that it is 'the provision of customised leisure and recreational experiences driven by the specific expressed interests of individuals and groups.

A special interest tourist chooses to engage with a product or service that satisfies particular interests and needs, so SIT is tourism undertaken for a distinct and specific reason'. They also suggest that special interest tourists are mainly looking for non-exploitative and authentic experiences.

Sometimes the term 'niche tourism' is used instead of special interest tourism (e.g. Novelli, 2005). In his Foreword to the book, Robinson (p. xx) describes niche tourism as:

> an economy of imagination where individual preferences and practices are co-ordinated, packaged and sold. The wants and wishes of the bird watcher, the golfer, the genealogist, the railway enthusiast, can now be purchased; indeed, the fullest stretches of the imagination can now be catered for.

Novelli (2005) suggests that the development of niche products is part of a wider structural process of diversification as the tourism industry seeks to capture new and more profitable markets. Since tourists have become more experienced and demanding, and many take multiple trips per year, there is a growing need for products which are non-standardised and unusual. Unlike mass tourism which takes place in familiar and predictable environments, niche or special interest tourism relies on new destinations or activities to meet the demands of changing markets. The decline in sun-bathing holidays as a result of skin cancer fears means that even the traditional beach holiday tends to include opportunities for special interest activities (watersports, diving) or excursions (to heritage sites or local villages). However, only holidays where a special interest is the *primary* motivation of tourists can be described using this label.

Novelli (2005) suggests that niche tourism can be broken down into a number of macro-niches (e.g. cultural, environmental, rural, urban tourism) and then into further sub-sets or micro-niches. The following table shows the examples given:

Cultural	Environmental	Rural	Urban	Others
Heritage	Nature and	Farm/barns	Business	Photographic
Tribal	wildlife	Camping	Conference	Small cruise
Religious	Ecotourism	Wine/	Exhibition	Volunteer
Educational	Adventure	Gastronomy		
Genealogy	Alpine	Sport	Sport	Dark
	Geotourism	Festivals and	Gallery	Youth
	Coastal	events		
		Arts and	Art	Transport
		crafts		

It is important to make a distinction between macro- and micro-niches, especially for marketing and segmentation purposes. Although special interest or niche tourism often seems to attract a particular type of visitor, there can be very distinctive variations between micro-niches. A good example is **health and wellness tourism** which can be broken down into at least six micro-niches:

Health and Wellness Tourism Micro-Niches	Typical Activities	Typical Visitors
Spa tourism	Healing with medical or mineral waters	Elderly visitors with health problems
Holistic tourism	Body, mind, spirit treatments in a retreat	Middle-aged professionals/ executives
Spiritual tourism	Pilgrimages, ashrams, meditation retreats	Mainly over-30s, some backpackers
Yoga tourism	Asanas and meditation in retreats	Mainly professional women over 40
Medical tourism	Operations, plastic surgery	Westerners, over 40, more likely women
Beauty tourism	Massage, facials, treatments in a spa or hotel	Women, over 25, professionals or executives

Even here, a distinction could or should be made between, for example, historic, medical spas catering for elderly visitors with health problems, and purpose-built recreational spas which attract leisure and beauty tourists. The labels given to special interest or niche tourism need to be carefully considered and the correct markets should be targeted. This means that the numbers for micro-niche or very special interest tourism will be relatively low, but quality and prices tend to be high.

Special interest tourists have some common characteristics, nevertheless. As this type of tourism tends to be relatively expensive (at least twice the cost of a mass package holiday), this can exclude certain markets. Although students, backpackers and low-income tourists may be able to afford some forms of **ecotourism**, **cultural tourism** or **adventure tourism**, such trips may need to be organised independently. Special interest tourists are more likely to be middle-aged and travelling without children (exceptions might be some forms of nature-based or wildlife tourism), as many forms of special interest tourism are not suitable or interesting for children. It is also common for tourists to travel alone. Many special interest tourism holidays are enjoyed by people whose interests are so specific that it can be difficult to find a travelling companion, and so the provision of facilities for single travellers is fundamental to this sector. A singles holiday with a special interest focus might be the ideal way of meeting other like-minded people on holiday.

Special interest tourists may have other specific needs, for example if they are disabled, gay, elderly or in poor health (e.g. medical tourists). Operators may need to organise hotels and transport with disabled access and trained staff on hand to assist visitors. Gay visitors may prefer gay-friendly hotels, spas, cruises or entertainment venues. Elderly visitors may want to visit medical spas but they need to be catered for properly and attended to by qualified staff.

In terms of product characteristics and tourist motivations, special interest tourism could be described as passive (performances, spectator sports), active (adventure sports, diving), experiential (theme parks, space tourism), adventurous (jungle trekking, tribal visits), creative (dance, painting, photography), intellectual (language-learning, **heritage tourism**), or relaxing (**wellness tourism**, birdwatching). Weiler and Hall (1992: 201) described how 'Special interest tourists seem to be much more concerned with seeking both personal and interpersonal rewards and opportunities rather than with escaping personal and interpersonal environments'. This implies that special interest tourism is less about escapism and relaxation, and more about active self-development and gaining new experiences. Although activities may be enjoyable and therapeutic (spas, arts, sports), there is usually either an educational or self-improvement dimension, such as developing a fitter, healthier body or a more creative or lively mind.

As special interest tourism grows and becomes more mainstream, many former niche activities are gaining the characteristics of mass tourism. Good examples include cultural tourism in cities, wildlife safaris or snow sports. As a result, tour operators have to become even more innovative in their product development, packaging or labelling. This may mean that the activities are essentially similar, but a different focus might be given to appeal to different markets. For example, safaris are now being differentiated in some way from each other, e.g.:

- honeymoon or wedding safaris
- photography or painting safaris
- canoeing safaris
- ballooning safaris

- adventure safaris
- bush skills safaris
- golfing safaris
- kids' safaris
- gourmet safaris.

The same is true of cruise tourism, which traditionally tended to be thought of as rather mainstream (i.e. tourism research agencies did not always include cruises as a form of special interest tourism), but now they may offer specific activities (theatre, arts, dance, cookery), special facilities (spas, casinos, gastronomy), catering for special markets (gay and lesbian, disabled, children), or unusual themes (murder mystery, carnival). This shows that the market is becoming more diverse and more receptive to new products.

Douglas et al. (2001) suggest that special interest tourism tends to be more sustainable or ethical than mass tourism. This can be because of the smaller group sizes (typically 10–15 tourists), the fact that visitors are more educated and experienced, or that authentic environmental or cultural experiences are the main focus of the trip (e.g. **ecotourism**, tribal tourism). However, special interest tourism also pushes the boundaries of tourism further and further into new and pristine destinations (even trips into space!), or offers high-impact activities (e.g. adventure sports). There can be considerable risks not only for the locality but also for tourists if, for example, wildlife or adventure tourism is not managed well. **Religious tourism** should be managed in a particularly sensitive way in terms of visitor behaviour, and **dark** or dissonant **heritage tourism** needs to be interpreted carefully. Many special interest tour operators are more aware of the impacts of tourism than mass operators, and most special interest tourists are more receptive to their advice and guidance than mass tourists. However, as special interest tourism grows and more macro- and micro-niches are created, this will mean that even more careful management will be needed.

See also: arts tourism, cultural tourism, dark tourism, ecotourism, gastronomic tourism, health and wellness tourism, heritage tourism, indigenous tourism, religious tourism

FURTHER READING

There are numerous books on the different forms of special interest tourism. These are referred to under the separate sections noted above. However, there have been several books which provide a good overview of the concept of special interest or niche tourism. These include Weiler and Hall's *Special Interest Tourism*; Douglas et al.'s *Special Interest Tourism*; and Novelli's *Niche Tourism: Contemporary Issues, Trends and Cases*. Most mainstream tourism journals also contain articles about different forms of special interest or niche tourism.

RECOMMENDED BOOKS

Douglas, N., Douglas, N. and Derrett, R. (2001) *Special Interest Tourism*. London: John Wiley & Sons.

Novelli, M. (ed.) (2005) *Niche Tourism: Contemporary Issues, Trends and Cases*. Oxford: Butterworth-Heinemann.

Weiler, B. and Hall, C.M. (1992) *Special Interest Tourism*. London: Belhaven Press.

Sports and Adventure Tourism

> *Sports and adventure tourism is defined as the active, passive or nostalgic engagement with sports and sports-related activities while travelling away from one's normal place of residence.*

Sports and adventure tourism appear to be growing as more and more people recognise the health benefits of active holidays. Ritchie (2005) suggests that sport can contribute between 1 and 2 per cent of an industrialised country's GDP, and that 20 per cent of trips in countries such as Britain can be directly related to sports participation. In the case of incidental sports participation (i.e. doing sports activities while on holiday), it can be as much as 50 per cent. Spectator vacations are also growing in popularity as visitors are attracted to sports events such as World Cup football championships or the Olympics. Some destinations (e.g. Melbourne in Australia) have built their reputations as world-famous sporting cities by hosting several successful events.

Standeven and De Knop (1999: 12) define sports tourism as:

> All forms of active and passive involvement in sport, casually or in an orga-
> nized way, for non-commercial or business/commercial reasons, that imply
> travelling away from home and work locally.

Gibson (2002) suggests a further category, which is nostalgia sport tourism. This might involve visiting sport halls of fame and museums, tours to a famous sporting stadium or sport-themed vacations (e.g. cruises, resorts) with sporting professionals. Of course, the three categories of sports tourism – active, passive and nostalgic – can sometimes overlap within one trip.

It is important to note that many sports are practised in some countries but not in others (e.g. football is popular more or less everywhere, but cricket is not; netball is played in Britain, but handball is relatively unknown; certain martial arts are mostly practised in Asia but are not well-known in Europe). This affects tourists' knowledge of sports and their tendency to either participate or spectate.

De Knop (2006) states that there are two types of sport activity holidays: the single-sport activity holiday (e.g. skiing, golf), and the multiple-sport holiday (e.g. in a fitness camp or outdoor adventure setting). Skiing is the most popular of all winter sport activities, accounting for up to 20 per cent of the European holiday market. Golf is also growing in popularity. The number of amateur or semi-professional sportsmen and women may be relatively low, but many travellers have a sports-related hobby where they will happily travel to engage in it. This is sometimes combined with other activities (e.g. business tourism is often packaged with golf; beach tourism is packaged with water sports), but it can also be a primary motivation (e.g. snow sports). Certain sports activities such as swimming, fitness classes or tennis might be undertaken simply because they are available at the destination, and will not serve as a primary motivation for visiting. This constitutes incidental sports tourism.

Large sporting events such as the Olympic Games or World Cup Football Championship can have a major impact on a location, raising its profile as an international destination, bringing about regeneration of the location and raising the profile of sport (the 2002 World Cup final aimed to raise the profile of football in Japan and Korea and Asia more generally). New sports are included in the Olympics every year; in 2008, BMX biking was added and skateboarding may make its debut in London 2012. More emphasis has been placed on the less able-bodied in recent years too, with the increased coverage of the Paralympics (first held in Rome in 1960). The Gay Games were also introduced in San Francisco in 1982, and have since been held in other American cities, Sydney and Amsterdam. Large sporting events can have major positive impacts on a destination and its image, but there can also be problems with legacies of debt and unused facilities. Ritchie (2005) discusses the development of small-scale sporting events as an alternative, as these use existing venues and infrastructure, attract smaller numbers of visitors and are attended by more local participants.

Robinson and Gammon (2004) suggest that there are 'hard' and 'soft' definitions of sports tourists:

Hard Definition – a hard definition of the sport tourist includes those individuals who actively or passively participate at a competitive sporting event. A *hard sport tourist* is someone who specifically travels to and/or stays in places outside their usual environment, for either active or passive involvement in competitive sport. In this case, sport is their prime motivation for travel and would encompass participation at sporting events such as the Olympic Games or the Football World Cup. The competitive nature of these events is the distinguishing factor.

Soft Definition – a soft definition of the sport tourist would be someone who specifically travels to and/or stays in places outside their usual environment for primarily active recreational participation in a chosen sport, for example, skiing and cycling holidays. The active recreational elements are the distinguishing factors here.

Delpy (1998) describes the main motivations for sports tourists as including fun, escapism, relaxation, health and fitness, stress reduction, thrill-seeking, challenge of learning, family cohesion and entertainment.

The market for sports tourism is increasing as people are encouraged to engage in preventive rather than curative healthcare and to become more active in many developed countries today. The rise in everyday activities such as Nordic walking has spread from Scandinavia, and is now included in many holiday and hotel packages. Older people are staying active for longer, and so they are keener to take part in sports. People are also becoming more adventurous and want to try out new and more exciting activities. This has led to a growth in adventure tourism. Types of adventure tourism include the following:

- backpacking
- bushwalking
- cycle-touring
- cross-country skiing
- orienteering
- river kayaking
- rock-climbing
- sailing

- canoeing
- fishing
- hang-gliding
- hot-air ballooning
- hunting
- mountain biking
- mountaineering

- scuba diving
- sea kayaking
- sky-diving
- snowshoeing
- trekking
- whitewater rafting

Shephard and Evans (2005) differentiate between 'hard' and 'soft' adventure tourism. 'Soft' adventure would involve very low risk and could be undertaken by anyone with a reasonable level of fitness, whereas 'hard' adventure would require previous experience, certain levels of competence and the ability and desire to cope with risks and unexpected situations. However, it seems that many of the motivations of all adventure tourists generally involve excitement, stimulation, novelty and risk. Swarbrooke et al. (2003) identify some of the core characteristics of adventure, which include danger and risk, challenge, novelty, excitement and stimulation, escapism, exploration, absorption and emotional contrasts.

However, some 'hard' adventure sports are more risky than others, and can fall under the category of 'extreme sports'. These can include the following:

- off-piste skiing/snowboarding
- surfing
- ice climbing
- deep-sea diving
- sky diving
- kite surfing
- extreme motorsport

- bungee jumping
- storm chasing
- ice diving
- white-water rafting
- base jumping
- cliff jumping
- paragliding

Such sports unsurprisingly seem to have a younger than average demographic. Much of the motivation seems to be linked to the enjoyment of an adrenalin rush caused by the sense of danger and excitement. Overall, adventure tourists tend to be younger than some other sports tourists (e.g. 25–40). More men usually participate than women (which is true of most sports tourism), but now the Adventure Travel Society (2008) suggests that a typical adventure traveller is, perhaps surprisingly, a 47–49-year-old woman.

Overall, it seems that sports tourism is growing in popularity as lifestyles change and there is a greater propensity for people to stay active for longer in their lives. There is also a clear interest in pursuing more exciting and adventurous sports, which take people to remote and often beautiful landscapes. This combines the active component of a sports holiday, with the relaxation and peace which comes from holidaying in a natural environment. Those tourists who are not quite so active or adventurous can still enjoy sports, but as spectators to sporting events, or as visitors to 'nostalgic' attractions, which celebrate the importance of sporting traditions in an international or national context.

See also: special interest tourism

FURTHER READING

There are many books which focus on sports tourism, and some of these include adventure tourism, for example Hudson's *Sport and Adventure Tourism*. Some books focus mainly on sports tourism, such as Hinch and Higham's *Sport Tourism Development*, and Ritchie and Adair's *Sport Tourism: Interrelationships, Impacts and Issues*.

RECOMMENDED BOOKS

Hinch, T. and Higham, J. (2003) *Sport Tourism Development*. Clevedon: Channel View.
Hudson, S. (2008) *Sport and Adventure Tourism*. New York: Haworth Press.
Ritchie, B. and Adair, D. (eds) (2004) *Sport Tourism: Interrelationships, Impacts and Issues*. Clevedon: Channel View.

Sustainable Tourism

Sustainable tourism applies the concept of sustainable development to the tourism industry and strives towards tourism that has the least possible impact on host communities and the environment, while maintaining economic viability.

Over the last two decades, the increasing awareness of the impacts that tourism brings to the environments, economies and cultures of destinations has led to the development of sustainable tourism as both a theory and practice within the management of tourism. Sustainable tourism is concerned with the adverse effects of tourism and is therefore strongly connected to **ethical tourism** and **ecotourism**.

The idea of sustainable tourism is derived from the wider concept of sustainable development, which reflects growing concern about human impact on the environment. Sustainability as a concept has two opposing perspectives – the anthropocentric viewpoint and the ecocentric viewpoint. The anthropocentric position sees humans as the dominant force on the planet, with nature being harnessed for human gain. Conversely, the ecocentric view sees that the quality of the natural environment is more important than the progress of the human race. Viewpoints then range on a continuum between these polar opposites, so that it is possible to have a very weak, weak, strong and very strong position on sustainability (Turner et al., 1994).

International interest in sustainable development first came to the fore in the 1960s when concerns about the balance between economic development and social development began to be articulated. By the mid-1980s, a number of international conferences had been held to debate the issues, and in 1984 the United Nations appointed a World Commission on Environment and Development which produced a publication entitled *Our Common Future* (1987). In this publication can be found the most widely quoted definition of sustainable development, outlined as 'development which meets the needs of the present without compromising the needs of future generations' (UNWCED, 1987). Sustainable development therefore accepts that economies can continue to be developed but they must do so while conserving resources. Further international events were significant in promoting global action: the 1992 United Nations Earth Summit in Rio de Janeiro produced an international blueprint for sustainable development entitled *Agenda 21*, which was signed by 182 heads of state and put into practice at a national and local level (UNCED, 1992). Although tourism was not featured as a key element of Agenda 21, many regional and local governments have successfully applied the principles to their tourism development and operations.

It may seem obvious to us today that tourism, as an industry that uses natural, cultural and human resources, should become part of the global striving towards sustainable development but this approach to tourism has emerged slowly since the post Second World War evolution of international tourism. Jafari (2001) describes this evolution as four sequential platforms or perspectives on the tourism industry: the advocacy platform, the cautionary platform, the adaptancy platform and the knowledge-based platform. These can be summarized as follows, based on the work of Jafari (2001) and Weaver (2006):

The Advocacy Platform
This platform reflects the optimism and confidence with which the evolving tourism industry was regarded in the 1950s and 1960s. Tourism was seen as a creator of revenue and jobs, a force to stimulate regional development, as well as to promote cross-cultural understanding and conservation.

The Cautionary Platform
By the late 1960s and early 1970s, a more cautious approach was beginning to emerge. Unregulated tourism development was causing problems, the seasonality and low pay that characterise many tourism jobs was acknowledged and cultural commodification and conflict were beginning to become apparent.

The Adaptancy Platform
While the Cautionary Platform identified the negative impacts of tourism, it was only in the 1970s and early 1980s, the era of the Adaptancy Platform, that solutions began to be discussed. Alternatives to mass tourism were recommended and it was proposed that these alternative tourism forms be adapted to their local socio-cultural and environmental context.

The Knowledge-based Platform
By the late 1980s and 1990s, it became obvious that alternative forms of tourism were only a partial solution and that a more rigorous and scientific approach to managing the industry was essential. More tourism research was funded, tourism studies were introduced at university level and academic journals on tourism proliferated.

As can be seen from the four platforms or perspectives above, a growing awareness of the negative impacts of tourism has evolved since the 1960s. A wide range of terms has been introduced to describe alternative approaches to tourism and its development – 'green tourism', 'soft tourism', 'responsible tourism', '**ecotourism**' and, of course, 'sustainable tourism'. These terms are still used interchangeably in the literature of tourism management. Along with this varied terminology has come a large and confusing range of definitions of sustainable tourism and there is still no universally accepted definition. However, in 2004, the World Tourism Organisation did establish a set of underlying principles that recognise the economic, environmental and socio-cultural aspects of tourism. These propose that sustainable tourism should:

- make optimal use of environmental resources
- respect the socio-cultural authenticity of host communities
- ensure viable, long-term economic operations, providing socio-economic benefits to all stakeholders. (WTO, 2004a)

These are useful guidelines for the industry and it is important to note that the WTO gives equal prominence to socio-cultural and economic sustainability as these are often seen to come second to the more widely discussed environmental issues (Swarbrooke, 1999). While it is now generally accepted that tourism must become more sustainable if the resources upon which the industry depends are to remain for the future, there are many challenges in trying to implement sustainable tourism strategies (see also **ethical tourism**). These challenges arise from the complexity of the tourism industry with its wide range of stakeholders and the lack of consensus on what sustainable tourism actually is and how it can be monitored (Weaver, 2006). The complex nature of the tourism industry means that in order for sustainable tourism to become a reality, all stakeholders must be involved. This includes the public sector, the industry, host communities, the voluntary sector and tourists themselves. Clearly, the priorities of these groups will differ and in many cases will compete, and their understanding of the concept of sustainability may also be widely divergent.

The lack of consensus on the definition, measurement and monitoring of sustainable tourism also means that it is difficult to put into practice, although a number of measures and tools have been introduced to promote sustainability in destinations and within individual operations in all sectors of the tourism industry, as can be seen below:

Environmental Impact Assessment (EIA) is used in most developed nations to assess the positive and negative impacts of specific developments, both in the planning stages and at the post-development stage. EIAs are useful in making decisions about the appropriateness of new developments but they are applied only to large-scale projects and their implementation is sporadic globally.

Carrying Capacity and Limits of Acceptable Change (LAC) are both measures that limit tourism activity in a destination. Carrying capacity stipulates the amount of tourist activity that an area can absorb before adverse effects are experienced in the destination. Carrying capacity can be seen in terms of a destination's social, ecological and economic capacity. Limits of acceptable change build on the concept of carrying capacity but instead of having fixed limits, the LAC is more flexible, defining the amount and type of change effected by tourism that is acceptable in a destination.

Visitor Management and Zoning are measures which aim to promote sustainability by managing the visitor and their potential impacts on a site. Visitor management aims to control the volume of visitors, modify their behaviour and to adapt the destination to make it more resilient. Zoning contributes to visitor management by addressing potential conflict between users of a site. Creating designated zones for recreation and conservation uses allows the needs of visitors to be reconciled with the needs of the environment.

Along with these approaches to sustainability within the destination, many businesses in the tourism industry have developed strategies, policies and initiatives to demonstrate their green credentials as the following three examples demonstrate:

British Airways have published their annual Social and Environmental Report since 1990. BA works to reduce carbon dioxide emissions, noise pollution and water consumption and funds conservation work around the world.

Grecotel is a chain of 16 luxurious hotels and resorts based in the Aegean Islands. Since the company was founded in 1981, they have pioneered many environmental initiatives to reduce waste and water consumption, design hotels in vernacular styles, source produce locally and fund conservation projects.

The Tour Operators' Initiative for Sustainable Tourism Development was launched in 2000 to encourage greater sustainability in the sector. Members of the scheme must demonstrate a corporate commitment to sustainability and the TOI has developed a set of indicators against which to measure members' operations.

Commentators are cautious about the possibilities for a truly sustainable tourism industry, but welcome any moves within the industry towards a more responsible approach. For sustainable tourism to become a reality, it should not be seen as a particular type of tourism product or business practice but as an ethos informing all stakeholders within the industry.

See also: ecotourism, ethical tourism, indigenous tourism

FURTHER READING

David Weaver's 2006 text *Sustainable Tourism: Theory and Practice* is a useful introduction to the field of study as is David Edgell's (2006) *Managing Sustainable Tourism: A Legacy for the Future*. Readers will also find the *Journal of Sustainable Tourism* an invaluable source of relevant articles.

RECOMMENDED BOOKS

Edgell, D. (2006) *Managing Sustainable Tourism: A Legacy for the Future*. New York: Haworth.
Swarbrooke, J. (1999) *Sustainable Tourism Management*. Wallingford: CABI.
Weaver, D. (2006) *Sustainable Tourism: Theory and Practice*. Oxford: Butterworth-Heinemann.

Tourist Gaze

> The tourist gaze refers to the idea that tourists' ways of seeing places and people and the selection of those sights is directed and organised by the tourism industry.

In 1990, sociologist John Urry published a book entitled *The Tourist Gaze* which has subsequently become a highly influential text within the study of tourism. Urry took the concept of 'the gaze', which was developed by French theorists Jacques Lacan and Michel Foucault in the 1960s, and applied it to the field of tourism. In his work, he emphasises the visual nature of tourism – the way in which tourists seek out and consume visual images and the means by which the tourism industry organises and directs this consumption. At a basic level, tourism's visual characteristics will come as no surprise to readers. Tourists take photographs and buy picture postcards of the places they visit, book window seats on trains, ascend high buildings to appreciate views – indeed, 'sightseeing' is synonymous with tourism and has been since its earliest days. What is interesting about Urry's concept of the tourist gaze is not simply the revelation that tourists like to look at sights, but that the sights they consume are selected, constructed, stage-managed and directed by an increasingly influential tourism industry. Examples of the various equipment and structures created specifically to direct the tourist gaze include pleasure piers and promenades in seaside resorts, hotel balconies and terraces, scenic viewpoints in national parks and the extensive tourism media incorporating guidebooks, postcards, websites and travel programmes.

The construction of the tourist gaze is not a new phenomenon, as Urry explains. When scholastic or scientific travel gave way to the tourism of the Picturesque in the eighteenth century, early European tourists were keen to experience and collect the views described in illustrated guidebooks and many captured these sights for themselves in sketchbooks. The Picturesque way of seeing was to view the world as a series of framed pictures, as if the viewer was in a gallery. The Picturesque gaze prefigured our contemporary tourist gaze, organised around constructed images found in holiday brochures, television programmes and on websites. These images inform visitors about what to look at and, importantly, what to avoid. As Urry says, the tourist gaze does not often include images of 'waste, disease, dead animals, poverty, sewage and despoilation' (Urry, 1990/2002: 129). The sights deemed suitable for the tourist gaze are endlessly reproduced through the tourists' own photographs, which are then recirculated among the tourists' family and friends. Urry acknowledges the importance of photography to the construction of the tourist gaze and indeed to the development of tourism itself – photography and tourism 'each derives from and enhances the other' (1990/2002: 129).

Urry sets out the basic conditions that produce a distinctive 'tourist gaze'. In order for someone to gaze upon something with the regard of a tourist, there must first be a distinction between what is considered an ordinary everyday experience and that which is extraordinary. Potential objects of the tourist gaze must be different from those experiences at home. These objects may be:

- unique objects (such as the Eiffel Tower, or the Grand Canyon)
- particular tourism 'signs' such as a typical English village or a quintessential French chateau

- unfamiliar aspects of that which is familiar (such as museum settings of the lives of historical communities)
- ordinary aspects of life seen in unusual contexts (tourists gazing on locals carrying out domestic tasks under political regimes different from their own)
- familiar tasks (shopping, eating, swimming) undertaken against unusual visual backgrounds
- signs that indicate that a seemingly everyday object is in fact extraordinary (for example, an interpretation board that indicates that an ordinary looking field may have been the site of a decisive battle or event).

As can be seen from the above, people can be an object of the gaze as much as can the natural or built environment, but they too must embody a sense of the 'other' to merit attention. This quality of being 'other' to the tourist might derive from a perceived **authenticity** or exoticism – for example, the tourist may wish to gaze upon local people wearing colourful national costume or carrying out traditional rituals.

The tourist gaze can be experienced within different social contexts appropriate to the nature of the objects viewed. Urry terms the individual, solitary view the 'romantic gaze', where a proper appreciation of a work of art or a lonely mountain scene can only take place if one is alone in contemplation. On the other hand, what Urry calls the 'collective gaze' is levelled at sights and events where crowds of fellow-gazers add to the experience, for example, at a theme park or an event such as the Notting Hill Carnival in London.

As tourism becomes increasingly globalised, the range of objects of the gaze widens; for example, **dark tourism** sites, remote landscapes and adventurous destinations have all become popular in recent years. As more parts of the world become tourism destinations, so the tourism industry develops 'systematic, regularized and evaluative procedures that enable each place to monitor, modify and maximize their location within the turbulent global order' (Urry, 1990/2002: 142). Moreover, the nature of the gazer diversifies as economic and political change opens up travel for more of the world's population. In his second edition of *The Tourist Gaze*, published in 2002, Urry acknowledges these global changes and also addresses some of the criticisms that his 1990 edition prompted. The bulk of these critiques revolve around the notion that in privileging the visual, the other four senses, so important to tourism, have been denied. Tourism, it is argued, is as much about bodily performance, smelling, hearing, touching and tasting as it is about the simple visual appropriation of place. Urry counters the argument that a single tourist gaze is too simplistic to convey the experience of contemporary global tourism by re-asserting the 'awesome dominance of the visual' (1990/2002: 149). However, he does concede that as we become increasingly mobile, experiencing more of the world through sight, sound, touch, smell and taste, the tourist gaze becomes increasingly embodied and omnipresent. Perhaps the prevalence of the tourist gaze in every aspect of our lives means that 'there can be no effective study of "tourism" *per se* as the tourist gaze is simply everywhere and in a kind of way nowhere in particular'(1990/2002: 145).

Despite the critiques outlined above, Urry's *The Tourist Gaze* remains a compelling and influential work as can be seen from the following recent tourism journal articles that utilise and further develop the concept of the gaze.

'The Beach, the gaze and film tourism' (L. Law, T. Bunnell and C. Ong (2007) *Tourist Studies*)

Using the film *The Beach* (based on Alex Garland's book of the same title), this article explores the role of the tourist gaze in **film tourism** and examines how such a gaze can impact on tourist practices in the destination itself as film-viewers seek out their own beach.

'The family gaze' (M. Haldrup and J. Larsen (2003) *Tourist Studies*)

This article takes the concept of the tourist gaze and applies it to tourists' photography practice. The authors argue that although photography allows the visual consumption of places, it also has an important role in producing social relations as many photographs record the performing family rather than the material world.

'The mutual gaze' (D. Maoz (2006) *Annals of Tourism Research*)

This explores the ideas that tourists gaze upon locals but that this is a mutual gaze, as the native population hold their own stereotypical ideas about tourists which shape the way they look upon them.

'Gazing the hood: hip-hop as tourism attraction' (P. Xie, H. Osumare and A. Ibrahim (2007) *Tourism Management*)

Exploring the emerging phenomenon of hip-hop tourism in the USA, this article suggests that hip-hop can be viewed through a sequence of three tourist gazes – the *initial gaze* (relating to curiosity and voyeurism), the *mass gaze* (as the cultural form becomes commodified and globalised) and finally the *authentic gaze* (hip-hop sought out as special interest tourism).

See also: authenticity, post-tourism

FURTHER READING

Clearly, the 1990 and 2002 editions of *The Tourist Gaze* are to be recommended to readers, who may also be interested in following some of the ensuing debate on Urry's work, for example in MacCannell's 'Tourist agency' in *Tourist Studies* and in Franklin's 'The Tourist Gaze and beyond: an interview with John Urry', also in *Tourist Studies*.

RECOMMENDED BOOKS AND ARTICLES

Franklin, A. (2001) 'The Tourist Gaze and beyond: an interview with John Urry', *Tourist Studies*, 1 (2): 115–31.
MacCannell, D. (2001) 'Tourist Agency', *Tourist Studies*, 1: 2–37.
Urry, J. (1990/2002) *The Tourist Gaze: Leisure and Travel in Contemporary Societies*. London: Sage.

Urban Tourism

> *Urban tourism refers to visiting cities and towns with the purpose of sightseeing, shopping, doing business or enjoying the entertainment facilities.*

Urban tourism was one of the earliest forms of tourism, but there was a major shift away from this kind of tourism to coastal, rural or mountain destinations from the 1950s or so until the 1980s. It is not therefore a new form of tourism, but one which is re-emerging. Although urban areas have always attracted visitors, it has only been in recent years that tourism has been recognised as a major contributor to the urban economy. Greg Ashworth was one of the first authors to identify urban areas as specific locations for tourist activities (Ashworth and Tunbridge, 1990). Hoffman et al. (2003) suggest that almost every city recognises tourism possibilities, and has taken steps to encourage it. Most cities and towns offer a range of activities, which visitors may take advantage of (for example, business tourists might undertake cultural tours; cultural tourists might go shopping). Urban tourism is one of the biggest and most important forms of tourism, and is also one of the most complex to manage. Yet more and more towns and cities want to attract tourism. Even former industrial cities are being regenerated and repositioned as tourist destinations.

Urban tourism can include the following activities:

- sightseeing (e.g. historic monuments, archaeology, architecture)
- visiting museums and galleries
- attending theatres, concerts and dance
- visiting for educational reasons
- shopping
- festivals and events
- conferences and business meetings
- eating out, or attending coffee houses, bars and nightclubs
- visiting friends and relatives.

Judd and Fainstein (1999) describe how many cities aim to attract visitors by creating planned tourist zones, which Judd (1999) also describes as 'tourist bubbles', and Hannigan (1998) calls 'urban entertainment districts'. These contain a series of typical and often predictable attractions such as arts venues and museums, bars and restaurants, cinemas and casinos, leisure shopping and entertainment zones. Hallyar et al. (2008) suggest that most cities have areas where a number of similar attractions and activities aggregate alongside tourism-related services, and these areas tend to take on certain spatial, social, cultural and economic identities – they call these areas 'tourism precincts'. These refer to business districts, historic quarters or shopping areas. Increasingly, authors also write of cultural or creative quarters in cities (Law, 2002; Montgomery, 2003, 2004), where there is a high concentration of facilities and services for visitors. Many of these may relate to local heritage and the arts, but more often they are focused on eating, drinking and entertainment. They may also be related to the everyday life and experiences of inhabitants. For example, Shaw (2007) notes that many visitors are attracted to so-called 'ethnoscapes' or areas where immigrants tend to cluster, such as Chinatown, Greektown, Little Italy, Quartier Latin, etc. There can, however, be criticisms of appropriation, commercialisation and voyeurism associated with the consumption of peoples' cultures in this way. However, Maitland (2007) suggests that urban visitors are increasingly seeking activities which fall *outside* traditional tourist areas in order to experience what is distinctive, local and organic to a city, rather than what is developed specifically and often artificially for tourists. This may or may not be a welcome development for local residents.

Despite the difficulties of separating tourists' motivations for visiting cities and towns, urban tourism destinations have certain characteristics which they tend to use as 'unique selling propositions' to give them competitive advantage over other cities. Below is a suggested typology of urban tourism destinations:

- global/world cities (e.g. London, New York)
- national capitals (e.g. Ankara, Bucharest)
- cultural capitals (e.g. Budapest, Prague, Vienna)
- heritage cities (e.g. Venice, Oxford, Cracow)
- art cities (e.g. Florence, Madrid)
- creative cities (e.g. Helsinki, Barcelona)
- industrial cities (e.g. Glasgow, Bilbao)
- sport cities (e.g. Melbourne, Cardiff)
- festival cities (e.g. Rio, New Orleans)
- futuristic cities (e.g. Dubai, Tokyo).

Global/world cities

World cities often correspond to what theorists such as Soja (2000) call a 'postmetropolis', which is economically, politically and culturally heterogeneous, and whose boundaries seem almost limitless. It is a composite landscape, where different built forms are superimposed, one on top of the other over time. New modes of contemporary life are juxtaposed with deeply historic ones. Flusty (2004: 127) describes such cities as 'the place on earth where all places are … '. They cite in particular the example of Los Angeles.

National capitals

Recently, research projects are focusing on the significance of national capital status for many cities (Maitland and Ritchie, 2009). Capital cities play a particularly important role in tourism as they combine political, economic, administrative, cultural and symbolic functions. Tourism research is particularly interesting for those cities whose capital status is relatively unknown or overshadowed by another national city in terms of tourist awareness and visitation, e.g. Madrid and Barcelona; Canberra and Sydney; Ankara and Istanbul.

Cultural capitals

Cultural capitals are those capital cities which have high concentrations of heritage and arts attractions, and tend to be aesthetically pleasing or beautiful. However, they also tend to be the most popular with visitors and can therefore become overcrowded.

Heritage cities

The concept of the tourist-historic city, first developed by Ashworth and Tunbridge (1990), has subsequently been applied and adapted globally. Heritage cities usually have a heavily visited historic centre (e.g. Venice, Cracow). Graham et al. (2000) note that in the second phase of a heritage city's development, there is likely to be an old centre and a newer periphery.

Art cities

Art cities are usually those with a high concentration of galleries, museums and arts venues. For example, Vienna has its 'Museums Quartier' and Berlin has its 'Museum Insel'. Many cities are also famous for their historic collections of art, such as Florence and Rome, and others have important international collections, as in New York, or national collections as in Paris.

Creative cities

Following the work of Richard Florida (2002), many cities have become what might be described as 'creative cities'. This is not necessarily related to the arts and culture, but might reflect the number of innovative features or the attraction of high-tech businesses. They should possess the 'Three Ts – Tolerance, Talent and Technology'. Many creative class workers will live there, and the city should score highly on the 'Bohemian Index' and the 'Gay Index' (e.g. in the USA, San Francisco and New York are ranked highly).

Industrial cities

Many industrial cities have become tourism destinations in recent years because of a series of successful regeneration initiatives. European cities like Bilbao, Glasgow, Liverpool and Rotterdam have built incrementally on a series of initiatives, usually starting with one major catalyst or 'flagship' project, such as the Olympic Games, a major museum, gallery or conference centre that puts it on the map. Much emphasis is also placed on the importance of the European Cultural Capital event, which has had the effect of transforming the image and reputation of many relatively unknown cities.

Sport cities

Sport cities tend to develop as a result of hosting a number of important sporting events (Olympic Games, World Cup Football), or having permanent sporting venues and regular events. For example, Melbourne has become the world's unofficial 'ultimate sports city' because of its hosting of many large successful sporting events and its calendar of all-year-round activities.

Festival cities

Festival cities have world-famous events which usually happen annually, for example the Rio Carnival in Brazil or the Edinburgh Festival in Scotland.

Futuristic cities

Futuristic cities are developing new and high-tech features all the time. This may include innovative architecture or unique attractions. For example, at present Kuwait is trying to compete with Dubai to become the destination of the future. Tourists are attracted by the fantastical nature of the developments.

Whereas some of the capital, cultural, historic and arts cities mentioned above were traditionally on the Grand Tour route of the seventeenth and eighteenth centuries, there are also many new and emergent destinations which are using special events, conferences, shopping, nightlife or contemporary 'flagships' (e.g. modern art galleries, regenerated waterfronts) to attract tourists. It is a competitive market, but still some destinations are becoming saturated and have actively practised de-marketing in recent years (e.g. Cambridge, Dublin, Venice). As budget airline routes increase, the numbers of long-weekend tourists have multiplied, but research has started to indicate that this is not likely to be a sustainable form of tourism, as repeat visitation is unlikely. In some cases, this may be a blessing, as in the case of 'stag and hen' parties (or pre-marriage trips for groups of boys or girls). Many cities in Europe are currently trying to discourage stag and hen groups, as they tend to drink too much and disrespect the local environment and its people. Central and Eastern European and Baltic Cities such as Cracow, Prague, Budapest and Tallinn have been victims of this, as they were considered cheap destinations in which to drink.

There are other management problems which are specific to urban areas, regardless of typology:

Main Management Problems for Urban Tourism Environments

- Problems of over-crowding
- Conservation and environmental protection
- Transport issues (e.g. parking, pedestrianisation, pollution)
- Need for centrally located, accessible accommodation
- Managing local resident and tourist needs simultaneously
- Visitor management and flows
- Need for a lively evening economy to encourage overnight stays
- Retaining character or creating a sense of place
- Marketing and promotion (i.e. creating USPs in a highly competitive marketplace).

Overall, it seems that urban tourism is one of the most diverse forms of tourism, and also one of the most complex to manage. Visitors to towns and cities have a range of different motivations, and many cities can become very congested at certain times of the year (in peak season or during a major festival or event). The rise of budget airlines has increased the number of long-weekend trips to cities, especially in Europe. This has meant the further concentration of tourism, often in small historic centres. On the other hand, the growth of urban tourism is good news for former industrial cities which are trying to transform themselves through **regeneration** and present a new image to the world.

See also: arts tourism, cultural tourism, heritage tourism, regeneration

FURTHER READING

The city has been a source of great fascination to academics and writers for many centuries, and there are many interesting books about urban studies and urban planning. However, those which focus specifically on urban tourism include Hoffman et al.'s *Cities and Visitors*; and Hallyar et al.'s *City Spaces – Tourist Places: Urban Tourism Precincts*.

RECOMMENDED BOOKS

Hallyar, B., Griffin, T. and Edwards, D. (eds) (2008) *City Spaces – Tourist Places: Urban Tourism Precincts*. Oxford: Butterworth-Heinemann.

Hoffman, L.M., Fainstein, S.S. and Judd, D.R. (eds) (2003) *Cities and Visitors*. Oxford: Blackwell.

Law, C.M. (2002) *Urban Tourism: The Visitor Economy and the Growth of Large Cities*. London: Continuum Books.

Maitland, R. and Newman, P. (eds) (2008) *World Tourism Cities*. London: Routledge.

Maitland, R. and Ritchie, B. (2009) *City Tourism: National Capital Perspectives*. Wallingford: CABI.

references

Adams, R. (1986) *A Book of British Music Festivals*. London: Robert Royce.

Adventure Travel Society (2008) http://siteresources.worldbank.org/INTCEERD/Resources/CBT_adventure_tourism_Mallet.pdf [accessed 7 November 2008].

Agarwal, S. (2002) 'Restructuring seaside tourism: the resort lifecycle', *Annals of Tourism Research*, 29 (1): 25–55.

Aitchison, C., MacLeod, N.E. and Shaw, S.J. (2000) *Leisure and Tourism Landscapes: Social and Cultural Geographies*. London: Routledge.

Aktas, G. and Gunlu, E.A. (2005) 'Crisis management in tourist destinations', in W.F. Theobald (ed.), *Global Tourism*. Oxford: Butterworth-Heinemann. pp. 440–57.

Ali–Knight, J., Robertson, M., Fyall, A. and Ladkin, A. (2008) *International Perspectives of Festivals and Events: Paradigms of Analysis*. Oxford: Butterworth-Heinemann.

Allen, J., McDonnell, I., O'Toole, W. and Harris, R. (2008) *Festival and Special Event Management*. Chichester: John Wiley & Sons.

Alleyne-Dettmers, P.T. (1996) *Carnival: The Historical Legacy*. London: Arts Council of England.

AlSayyad, N. (2001) 'Global norms and urban forms in the age of tourism: manufacturing heritage, consuming tradition', in N. AlSayyad (ed.), *Consuming Tradition, Manufacturing Heritage: Global Norms and Urban Forms in the Age of Tourism*. London: Routledge. pp. 1–33.

Apostolopoulos, Y. Leivadi, S. and Yiannakis, A. (eds) (1996) *The Sociology of Tourism: Theoretical and Empirical Investigations*. London: Routledge.

Ashworth, G.J. and Tunbridge, J.E. (1990) *The Tourist-Historic City*. London: Belhaven.

ATLAS (2007) ATLAS Cultural Tourism Survey: Summary Report 2007. Available online at www.tram–research.com/atlas [accessed 12 January 2009].

Bakhtin, M. (1965) *Rabelais and His World*. Cambridge, MA: MIT Press.

Barber, B. (1995) *Jihad vs McWorld*. New York: Times Books.

Bauer, T. G. and McKercher, B. (2003) *Sex and Tourism: Journeys of Romance, Love, and Lust*. New York: Haworth.

Bauman, Z. (1998) *Globalization: The Human Consequences*. Oxford: Blackwell.

Beeton, S. (2005) *Film-induced Tourism*. Clevedon: Channel View.

Bennett, T. (1995) *The Birth of the Museum: History, Theory, Politics*. London: Routledge.

Boniface, P. (2003) *Tasting Tourism: Travelling for Food and Drink*. Aldershot: Ashgate Publishing Limited.

Boniface, B. and Cooper, C. (2004) *Worldwide Destinations: The Geography of Travel and Tourism*. Oxford: Butterworth-Heinemann.

Boorstin, D. (1964) *The Image: A Guide to Pseudo Events in America*. New York: Harper & Row.

Boswijk, A., Thijssen, T. and Peelen, E. (2007) *The Experience Economy: A New Perspective*. Harlow: Pearson Education.

Boyd, S. and Timothy, D. (2002) *Heritage Tourism*. Harlow: Prentice-Hall.

Brown, M.F. (2003) 'Safeguarding the Intangible', *Cultural Commons*, November. Available online at www.culturalpolicy.org/commons/comment–print.cfm?ID=12 [accessed 3 February 2009].

Buhalis, D. (1998) 'Strategic use of information technologies in the tourism industry', *Tourism Management*, 19 (5): 409–23.

Buhalis, D. (2003) *eTourism*. Harlow: Prentice-Hall.

Buhalis, D. (2005) 'Information technology in tourism', in C. Cooper, J. Fletcher, A. Fyall, D. Gilbert and S. Wanhill (eds), *Tourism Principles and Practice*, 3rd edn (1st edn, 1993). Harlow: Prentice-Hall. pp. 702–36.

Buhalis, D. and Licata, M.C. (2002) 'The future eTourism intermediaries', *Tourism Management*, 23 (3): 207–20.

Bull, A.O. (2001) *Re-planning Seaside Tourism in 'Old' Destinations: The North Sea Experience*. Dublin: ATLAS Conference Proceedings.

Burns, P.M. (1999) *An Introduction to Tourism and Anthropology*. London: Routledge.

Burns, P. (2004) 'Tourism planning: a third way?', *Annals of Tourism Research*, 31 (1): 24–43.

Burns, P.M. (2005) 'Social identities, globalisation, and the cultural politics of tourism', in W.F. Theobald (ed.), *Global Tourism*. Oxford: Butterworth-Heinemann. pp. 391–405.

Burns, P.M. and Novelli, M. (2006) *Tourism and Social Identities*. Oxford: Elsevier.

Busby, G. and Klug, J. (2001) 'Movie-induced tourism: the challenge of measurement and other issues', *Journal of Vacation Marketing*, 7 (4): 316–32.

Business Tourism Partnership (2005) 'Business tourism leads the way', www.business tourismpartnership.com/pubs/ToNewYork%20Rogers.pdf [accessed 29 October 2008].

Butler, R. (1980) 'The concept of a tourism area cycle of evolution', *Canadian Geographer*, 24: 5–12.

Butler, R. (2006) 'Tourism development on islands: the continued relevance of the tourism life cycle model', *El Espacio Litoral: Turismos Insulares*. Las Palmas de Gran Canaria: DACT, ULPGC.

Butler, R. and Hinch, T. (eds) (2007) *Tourism and Indigenous Peoples: Issues and Implications*. Oxford: Butterworth-Heinemann.

Buzard, J. (1993) *The Beaten Track: European Tourism, Literature and the Ways to Culture 1800–1918*. New York: Oxford University Press.

Carnegie, E. and Smith, M.K. (2006) 'Mobility, diaspora and the hybridisation of festivity: the case of the Edinburgh Mela', in D. Picard and M. Robinson (eds), *Festivals, Tourism and Social Change: Remaking Worlds*. Clevedon: Channel View. pp. 255–68.

Carrasco, D. (1996) *Those Who Go on a Sacred Journey: The Shapes and Diversity of Pilgrimages*. London: SCM Press Ltd.

Carter, S. and Clift, S. (eds) (2000) *Tourism and Sex: Culture, Commerce and Coercion*. London: Cassell.

Castells, M. (1997) *The Power of Identity*. Oxford: Blackwell.

Cho, S. (2002) 'Comparative analysis of mature travelers on the basis of Internet use', MSc Thesis, Virginia Polytechnic Institute and State University.

Cleaver, M. and Muller, T. (2002) 'The socially aware baby boomer: gaining a lifestyle-based understanding of the new wave of ecotourists', *Journal of Sustainable Tourism*, 10 (3): 173–90.

Cleaver, M., Muller, T.E., Ruys, H.F.M and Wei, S. (1999) 'Tourism product development for the senior market, based on travel-motive research', *Tourism Recreation Research*, 24 (1): 5–11.

Clift, S., Luongo, M. and Callister, C. (2002) *Gay Tourism*. London: Thomson Learning.

Cohen, C. (1988) 'Authenticity and commoditisation in tourism', *Annals of Tourism Research*, 15: 371–86.

Cohen, E. (1972) 'Toward a sociology of international tourism', *Social Research*, 39: 164–82.

Cohen, E. (1982) 'Thai girls and Farang men: the edge of ambiguity', *Annals of Tourism Research*, 9: 403–28.

Cohen, E. (1996) 'A phenomenology of tourist experiences', in Y. Apostopoulos, S. Leivadi and A. Yiannakis (eds), *The Sociology of Tourism: Theoretical and Empirical Investigations*. London: Routledge. pp. 90–111.

Cohen, E. (2003) 'Backpacking, diversity and change', *Journal of Tourism and Cultural Change*, 1 (2): 95–110.

Cohen, E. (2008) 'Death of a backpacker: incidental but not random', *Journal of Tourism and Cultural Change*, 6 (3): 202–28.

Connell, J. (2004) 'Toddlers, tourism and Tobermoroy: destination marketing issues and television–induced tourism', *Tourism Management*, 26: 763–76.

Connell, J. (2005) 'What's the story in *Balamory*?: the impacts of a children's TV programme on small tourism enterprises on the Isle of Mull, Scotland', *Journal of Sustainable Tourism*, 13 (3): 228–55.

Countryside Agency/ETC (2001) *Working for the Countryside – a Strategy for Rural Tourism in England 2001–2005*. London: ETB.

Craik, J. (1994) 'Peripheral pleasures: the peculiarities of post-colonial tourism', *Culture and Policy*, 6 (1): 153–82.

Daniel, Y.P. (1996) 'Tourism dance performances: authenticity and creativity', *Annals of Tourism Research*, 23 (1): 780–97.

Dann, G. (1977) 'Anomie, eco-enhancement and tourism', *Annals of Tourism Research*, 4: 184–194.

Dann, G.M.S. (2001) 'Senior tourism and quality of life', *Journal of Hospitality and Leisure Marketing*, 9 (1/2): 5–19.

Dann, G. and Cohen, E. (1996) 'Sociology and tourism', in Y. Apostopoulos, S. Leivadi and A. Yiannakis (eds), *The Sociology of Tourism: Theoretical and Empirical Investigations*. London: Routledge. pp. 301–14.

Dann, G. and Liebman-Parrinello, G. (eds) (2009) *The Sociology of Tourism: European Origins and Development*. Bingley: Emerald Group Publishing.

Dark Tourism Forum (2008) Online at www.dark-tourism.org [accessed 10 January 2008].

Davidson, R. and Cope, B. (2002) *Business Travel: Conferences, Incentive Travel, Exhibitions, Corporate Hospitality and Corporate Travel*. Englewood Cliffs, NJ: Prentice Hall.

Davidson, R. and Maitland, R. (1997) *Tourism Destinations*. London: Hodder & Stoughton.

Davie, G. (1994) *Religion in Britain since 1945: Believing without Belonging*. Oxford: Blackwell.

DCMS (Department for Culture, Media and Sport) (2004) *Culture at the Heart of Regeneration*, June. London: DCMS.

De Knop, P. (2006) 'Sports and event tourism', in D. Buhalis and C. Costa (eds), *New Tourism Consumers, Products and Industry: Present and Future Issues*. Oxford: Butterworth-Heinemann. pp. 118–26.

Delpy, L. (1998) 'An overview of sport tourism: building towards a dimensional framework', *Journal of Vacation Marketing*, 4: 23–38.

Devereux, C. and Carnegie, E. (2006) 'Pilgrimage: journeying beyond self', *Journal of Tourism Recreation Research*, 31 (1): 47–56.

Douglas, N., Douglas, N. and Derrett, R. (2001) *Special Interest Tourism*. London: John Wiley & Sons.

Eade, J. and Sallnow, M.J. (eds) (1991) *Contesting the Sacred: The Anthropology of Christian Pilgrimage*. London: Routledge.

Economist Intelligence Unit (EIU) (2004) *Business Trip Index*, www.economist.com/media/pdf/BUSINESS_TRIP_INDEX.pdf [accessed 15 November 2006].

Ecotourism Australia. Online at www.ecotourism.org.au/eco_certification.asp [accessed 14 November 2008].

Edgell, D. (2006) *Managing Sustainable Tourism: A Legacy for the Future*. New York: Haworth.

Edgell, D. (2007) *Tourism Policy and Planning: Yesterday, Today and Tomorrow*. Oxford: Butterworth-Heinemann.

EIBTM (2004) *Economic Trends Report 2004*, www.eibtm.com/images/100427/Docs/EIBTMEconomicTrendsReport.pdf [accessed 15 November 2006].

Enteleca Research & Consultancy Ltd (2000) Tourists' attitudes towards regional and local foods. Surrey: Enteleca Research & Consultancy, MAFF & Countryside Agency.

Evans, G. (2001) *Cultural Planning: An Urban Renaissance?* London: Routledge.

Faulkner, B. (2001) 'Towards a framework for tourism disaster management', *Tourism Management*, 22 (2): 135–47.

Fawcett, C. and Cormack, P. (2001) 'Guarding authenticity at literary tourism sites', *Annals of Tourism Research*, 28 (3): 686–704.

Feifer, M. (1985) *Going Places: The Ways of the Tourist from Imperial Rome to the Present Day*. London: Macmillan.

Fennell, D. (2001) 'A content analysis of ecotourism definitions', *Current Issues in Tourism*, 4 (5): 403–21.

Fennell, D. (2003) *Ecotourism: An Introduction*, 2nd edn (1st edn. 1999). London: Routledge.

Fennell, D. (2006) *Tourism Ethics*. Clevedon: Channel View.

Fernandes, C., McGettigan, F. and Edwards, J. (2003) *Religious Tourism and Pilgrimage*. Tilburg: ATLAS.

Florida, R. (2002) *The Rise of the Creative Class*. New York: Basic Books.

Flusty, S. (2004) *De-Coca-Colonization: Making the Globe from the Inside Out*. London: Routledge.

Font, X. and Buckley, R. (eds) (2001) *Tourism Ecolabelling: Certification and Promotion of Sustainable Tourism*. Wallingford: CABI.

Franklin, A. (2001) 'The tourist gaze and beyond: an interview with John Urry', *Tourist Studies*, 1 (2): 115–31.

Frost, W. (2004) 'Braveheart-ed Ned Kelly: historic films, heritage tourism and destination image', *Tourism Management*, 27: 247–54.

Gibson, H. (2002) 'Sport tourism at a crossroad? Considerations for the future', in S. Gammon, and J. Kurtzmann (eds), *Sports Tourism: Principles and Practice*. Eastbourne: Leisure Studies Association. pp. 111–28.

Glaesser, D. (2006) *Crisis Management in the Tourism Industry*. Oxford: Butterworth-Heinemann.

Goffman, E. (1959) *The Presentation of Self in Everyday Life*. New York: Doubleday.

Goodwin, H. and Francis, J. (2003) 'Ethical and responsible tourism: consumer trends in the UK', *Journal of Vacation Marketing*, 9(3): 271–84.

Graburn, N.H.H. (1977) 'Tourism: the sacred journey', in V.L. Smith (ed.), *Hosts and Guests: The Anthropology of Tourism*. Philadelphia: University of Pennsylvania Press. pp. 33–47.

Graburn, N.H.H. (1983) 'The anthropology of tourism', *Annals of Tourism Research*, 10 (1): 9–33.

Graham, B., Ashworth, G.J. and Tunbridge, J.E. (2000) *A Geography of Heritage: Power, Culture and Economy*. London: Arnold.

Guaracino, J. (2007) *Gay and Lesbian Tourism: The Essential Guide for Marketing*. Oxford: Butterworth-Heinemann.

Gunn, C. and Var, T. (eds) (2002) *Tourism Planning: Basics, Concepts, Cases*. London: Routledge.

Haldrup, M. and Larsen, J. (2003) 'The family gaze', *Tourist Sudies*, 3 (1): 23–45.

Hall, C.M. (1992) 'Sex tourism in South-East Asia', in D. Harrison (ed.), *Tourism in the Less Developed Countries*. London: John Wiley & Sons. pp. 64–74.

Hall, C.M. (1994) *Tourism and Politics: Policy, Power and Place*. Chichester: John Wiley & Sons.

Hall, C.M., Sharples, L., Cambourne, B. and Macionis, N. (2000) *Wine Tourism Around the World: Development, Management and Markets*. Oxford: Butterworth-Heinemann.

Hall, C.M. (2005) *Tourism: Rethinking the Social Science of Mobility*. Harlow: Pearson.

Hall, C.M. and Mitchell, R. (2005a) 'Gastronomic tourism: comparing food and wine tourism experiences', in M. Novelli (ed.), *Niche Tourism: Contemporary Issues, Trends and Cases*. Oxford: Butterworth-Heinemann. pp. 73–88.

Hall, C.M. and Mitchell, R. (2005b) 'Gastronomy, food and wine tourism', in D. Buhalis and C. Costa (eds), *Tourism Business Frontiers: Consumers, Products and Industry*. Oxford: Butterworth-Heinemann. pp. 137–47.

Hall, C.M and Page, S.I. (2005) *The Geography of Tourism and Recreation: Environment, Place and Space*, 3rd edn. London: Routledge.

Hall, C.M. and Tucker, H. (eds) (2004) *Tourism and Postcolonialism*. London: Routledge.

189

Hall, C.M., Roberts, L. and Mitchell, R. (eds) (2003) *New Directions in Rural Tourism*. Aldershot: Ashgate.

Hallyar, B., Griffin, T. and Edwards, D. (eds) (2008) *City Spaces – Tourist Places: Urban Tourism Precincts*. Oxford: Butterworth-Heinemann.

Hannaford, J. (2001) 'Two Australian pilgrimages', M. Phil. Thesis, Melbourne: Australian Catholic University.

Hannam, K. and Ateljevic, I. (eds) (2007) *Backpacker Tourism: Concepts and Profiles*. Clevedon: Channel View.

Hannigan, J. (1998) *Fantasy City: Pleasure and Profit in the Post-Modern Metropolis*. London: Routledge.

Hart Robertson, M. (2005) 'Marginal re-presentations: boundaries on identity', *Journal of Mediterranean Studies*, 15 (2): 359–78.

Hart Robertson, M. (2006) 'The difficulties of interpreting Mediterranean voices: exhibiting intangibles using new technologies', *International Journal of Intangible Heritage*, 1: 25–35.

Hayes, D. and MacLeod, N. (2007) 'Packaging places: designing heritage trails using an experience economy perspective to maximize visitor engagement', *Journal of Vacation Marketing*, 13 (1): 45–58.

Heelas, P. and Woodhead, L. (2005) *The Spiritual Revolution*. Oxford: Blackwell.

Herbert, D. (2001) 'Literary places, tourism and the heritage experience', *Annals of Tourism Research*, 28 (2): 312–33.

Herbert, D.T. (1996) 'Artistic and literary places in France as tourist attractions', *Tourism Management*, 17 (2): 77–85.

Hewison, R. (1987) *The Heritage Industry – Britain in a Climate of Decline*. London: Methuen.

Higham, J. (2007) *Critical Issues in Ecotourism: Understanding a Complex Tourism Phenomenon*. Oxford: Butterworth-Heinemann.

Hinch, T. and Higham, J. (2003) *Sport Tourism Development*. Clevedon: Channel View.

Hjalager, A. and Richards, G. (2002) *Tourism and Gastronomy*. London: Routledge.

Hobsbawm, E. and Ranger, T. (eds) (1983) *The Invention of Tradition*. Cambridge: Cambridge University Press.

Hoffman, L.M., Fainstein, S.S. and Judd, D.R. (eds) (2003) *Cities and Visitors*. Oxford: Blackwell.

Holden, A. (2005) *Tourism Studies and the Social Sciences*. London: Routledge.

Hollinshead, K. (1997) 'Heritage tourism under post-modernity: truth and past', in C. Ryan (ed.), *The Tourist Experience: A New Introduction*. London: Cassell. pp. 170–93.

Honey, M. (2005) 'Consumer demand and operator support for socially and environmentally responsible tourism', CESD/TIES Working Paper, No. 104, Washington, DC: TIES.

Horneman, L., Carter, R.W., Wei, S. and Ruys, H. (2002) 'Profiling the senior traveller: an Australian perspective', *Journal of Travel Research*, 41: 23–37.

Hose, T.A. (2005) 'Geotourism: appreciating the deep time of landscapes', in M. Novelli (ed.), *Niche Tourism: Contemporary Issues, Trends and Cases*. Oxford: Butterworth-Heinemann.

Hudson, S. (2008) *Sport and Adventure Tourism*. New York: Haworth Press.

Hughes, G. (1995) 'Authenticity in tourism', *Annals of Tourism Research*, 22 (4): 781–803.

Hughes, H. (1996) 'Redefining cultural tourism', *Annals of Tourism Research*, 23 (3): 707–9.

Hughes, H. (1998) 'Theatre in London and the inter-relationship with tourism', *Tourism Management*, 19 (5): 445–52.

Hughes, H. (2000) *Arts, Entertainment and Tourism*. Oxford: Butterworth-Heinemann.

Hughes, H.L. (2006) *Pink Tourism: Holidays of Gay Men and Lesbians*. Wallingford: CABI.

ICCA (International Congress and Convention Association) (2007) 'Country and city rankings 2007 for number of meetings organised', www.iccaworld.com [accessed 25 November 2008].

IMEX (The Worldwide Exhibition For Meetings and Incentive Travel) (2006) 'ICCA data statistics', www.iccaworld.com/aeps/aeitem.cfm?aeid=107 [accessed 15 November 2008].

Inskeep, E. (1991) *Tourism Planning: An Integrated and Sustainable Development Approach*. New York: Van Nostrand Reinhold.

Inskeep, E. (1994) *National and Regional Planning: Methodologies and Case Studies*. London: Routledge.

Jackson, R.H. and Hudman, L.E. (2002) *Geography of Travel and Tourism*. New York: Delmar Learning.

Jafari, J. (2001) 'The scientification of tourism', in V.L. Smith and M. Brent (eds), *Hosts and Guests Revisited: Tourism Issues of the 21st Century*. New York: Cognizant. pp. 28–41.

Jafari, J., Bushell, R. and Sheldon, P. (eds) (2008) *Wellness and Tourism: Mind, Body, Spirit, Place*. New York: Cognizant.

Jamal, T. and Hill, S. (2002) 'The home and the world: (post)touristic spaces of (in)authenticity', in G. Dann (ed.), *The Tourist as Metaphor of the Social World*. Wallingford: CABI. pp. 77–107.

Judd, D. (1999) 'Constructing the tourist bubble', in D. Judd and S. S. Fainstein (eds), *The Tourist City*. New Haven and London: Yale University Press. pp. 35–53.

Judd, D. and Fainstein, S.S. (eds) (1999) *The Tourist City*. New Haven and London: Yale University Press:

Kim, S.S., Agrusa, J., Lee, H. and Chon, K. (2007) 'Effects of Korean television dramas on the flow of Japanese tourists', *Tourism Management*, 28: 1340–53.

Kirschenblatt-Gimblett, B. (1998) *Destination Culture: Tourism, Museums and Heritage*. Berkeley, CA: University of California Press.

Krippendorf, J. (1987) *The Holiday Makers*. Oxford: Heinemann.

Ladkin, A. (2006) 'Conference tourism – MICE market and business tourism', in D. Buhalis and C. Costa (eds), *Tourism Business Frontiers: Consumers, Products, Industry*. Oxford: Butterworth-Heinemann. pp. 56–66.

Lanfant, M., Allcock, J.B. and Bruner, E.M. (1995) *International Tourism: Identity and Change*. London: Sage.

Larkham, P.J. (1995) 'Heritage as planned and conserved', in D.T. Herbert (ed.), *Heritage, Tourism and Society*. London: Mansell Publishing. pp. 85–116.

Law, C.M. (2002) *Urban Tourism: The Visitor Economy and the Growth of Large Cities.* London: Continuum.

Law, L., Bunnell, T. and Ong, C. (2007) 'The Beach, the gaze and film tourism', *Tourist Studies,* 17 (2): 141–64.

Laws, E., Prideaux, B. and Chon, K. (eds) (2006) *Crisis Management in Tourism.* Wallingford: CABI.

Leask, A. and Fyall, A. (eds) (2006) *Managing World Heritage Sites.* Oxford: Butterworth-Heinemann.

Lennon, J. and Foley, M. (2000) *Dark Tourism: The Attraction of Death and Disaster.* London: Thomson.

Leslie, D. and Sigala, M. (eds) (2005) *International Cultural Tourism: Management, Implications and Cases.* Oxford: Butterworth-Heinemann.

Lofgren, O. (2003) 'The new economy: a cultural history', *Global Networks,* 3 (3): 239–54.

London Bridge Experience (2008) Online at www.thelondonbridgeexperience.com/index.asp [accessed 28 November 2008].

MacCannell, D. (1976) *The Tourist: A New Theory of the Leisure Class.* London: Macmillan.

MacCannell, D. (2001) 'Tourist agency', *Tourist Studies,* 1: 2–37.

Macdonald, S. and Fyfe, G. (eds) (1996) *Theorizing Museums.* Oxford: Blackwell.

MacLeod, N., Hayes, D. and Slater, A. (2009) 'Reading the landscape: the development of a typology of literary trails to inform experience design', *Journal of Hospitality Marketing and Management,* 18: 154–72.

Magyar, R. (2008) 'Hosszú az út a lélekt l a lélekig' ('The road is long from soul to soul'), *Turizmus Trend,* 3: 24–5.

Maitland, R. (2007) 'Culture city users and the creation of new tourism areas in cities', in M.K. Smith (ed.) *Tourism, Culture and Regeneration.* Wallingford: CABI. pp. 25–34.

Maitland, R. and Newman, P. (eds) (2008) *World Tourism Cities.* London: Routledge.

Maitland, R. and Ritchie, B. (2009) *City Tourism: National Capital Perspectives.* Wallingford: CABI.

Malloy, D.C. and Fennell, D.A. (1998) 'Codes of ethics and tourism: an exploratory content analysis', *Tourism Management,* 19 (5): 453–61.

Maoz, D. (2006) 'The mutual gaze', *Annals of Tourism Research,* 33 (1): 221–39.

Mason, P. (2003) *Tourism Impacts, Planning and Management.* Oxford: Butterworth-Heinemann.

Mathieson, A. and Wall, G. (1992) *Tourism: Economic, Physical and Social Impacts.* Harlow: Longman.

McKercher, B. and du Cros, H. (2002) *Cultural Tourism: The Partnership between Tourism and Cultural Heritage Management.* New York: Haworth Press.

Miles, M. (1997) *Arts, Space and the City: Public Arts and Urban Futures.* London: Routledge.

Mintel (2005) *Ethical Holidays – UK.* London: Mintel International Group Ltd.

Mintel (2007) *Holiday Lifestyles – Responsible Tourism.* London: Mintel International Group Ltd.

Mintel (2008) *Travel Agents – UK.* London: Mintel International Group Ltd.

Montgomery, J. (2003) 'Cultural quarters as mechanisms for urban regeneration. Part 1. Conceptualising cultural quarters', *Planning Practice and Research*, 18 (4): 293–306.

Montgomery, J. (2004) 'Cultural quarters as mechanisms for urban regeneration. Part 2. A review of four cultural quarters in the UK, Ireland and Australia', *Planning Practice and Research*, 19 (1): 3–31.

Moore, P. (2007) 'Travel industry veteran taps into faith-based niche', *Denver Business Journal*, 16 February.

Morinis, A. (ed.) (1992) *Sacred Journeys: The Anthropology of Pilgrimage*. New York: Greenwood Press.

Moscardo, G. (2006) 'Third-age tourism', in D. Buhalis and C. Costa (eds), *New Tourism Consumers, Products and Industry: Present and Future Issues*. Oxford: Butterworth-Heinemann. pp. 30–9.

Movie Locations online at www.movie-locations.com [accessed 12 November 2007].

Mowforth, M. and Munt, I. (1998) *Tourism and Sustainability: New Tourism in the Third World*. London: Routledge.

MPI (Meeting Professionals International) (2006) 'FUTURE WATCH 2006: a comparative outlook on the global business of meetings', www.mpiweb.org/CMS/uploadedFiles/Research_and_Whitepapers/futurewatch2006.pdf [accessed 15 November 2008].

Myers, J.E., Sweeney, T.J. and Witmer, M. (2000) A Holistic Model of Wellness, www.mindgarden.com/products/wells.htm [accessed 20 September 2005].

Nash, D. (1977) 'Tourism as a form of imperialism', in V. Smith (ed.) *Hosts and Guests: The Anthropology of Tourism*. Oxford: Blackwell. pp. 33–47.

Nash, D. (1989) 'Tourism as a form of imperialism', in V. Smith (ed.), *Hosts and Guests: The Anthropology of Tourism*. Philadelphia: University of Pennsylvania Press. pp. 37–52.

Nash, D. (1996) *Anthropology of Tourism*. Oxford: Pergamon.

Nash, D. (2006) *The Study of Tourism: Anthropological and Sociological Beginnings*. Oxford: Elsevier.

National Geographic (2008) 'Geotourism', www.nationalgeographic.com/travel/sustainable/about_geotourism.html [accessed 15 October 2008].

National Statistics (2009a) 'Internet access', www.statistics.gov.uk/CCI/nugget.asp?10=8andPos=6andColRank=2andRank=224 [accessed 12 February 2009].

National Statistics (2009b) 'eBusiness' Online at www.statistics.gov.uk/cci/nugget.asp?id=1713 [accessed 12 February 2009].

National Wellness Institute (2007) Online at www.nationalwellness.org [accessed 29 November 2008].

Nolan, M. and Nolan, S. (1989) *Christian Pilgrimage in Modern Western Europe*. Chapel Hill, NC: University of North Carolina Press.

Novelli, M. (ed.) (2005) *Niche Tourism: Contemporary Issues, Trends and Cases*. Oxford: Butterworth-Heinemann.

Nuñez, T. (1963) 'Tourism, tradition, and acculturation: weekendismo in a Mexican village', *Ethnology*, 2: 347–52.

Olsen, D.H. and Timothy, D.J. (eds) (2006) *Tourism, Religion and Spiritual Journeys*. London: Routledge.

Ooi, C. (2002) *Cultural Tourism and Tourism Cultures*. Copenhagen: Copenhagen Business School Press.

Page, S.J. and Connell, J. (2006) *Tourism: A Modern Synthesis*, 2nd edn (1st edn, 2001). London: Thomson International.

Page, S.J. and Dowling, R.K. (2002) *Ecotourism*. London: Prentice-Hall.

Page, S.J., Brunt, P., Busby, G. and Connell, J. (2001) *Tourism: A Modern Synthesis*. London: Thomson Learning.

Papatheodorou, A. (ed.) (2007) *Managing Tourism Destinations*. Cheltenham: Edward Elgar.

PATA (Pacific Asia Travel Association) (2003) 'Crisis – it won't happen to us!' Online at: www.pata.org/patasite/fileadmin/docs/general/CrisisJune07.pdf [accessed 28 October 2008].

Patullo, P. and Minnelli, O. (2006) *The Ethical Travel Guide*. London: Earthscan.

Picard, D. and Robinson, M. (eds) (2006) *Festivals, Tourism and Social Change: Remaking Worlds*. Clevedon: Channel View.

Pike, S. (2008) *Destination Marketing*. London: Butterworth-Heinemann.

Pine, B.J. and Gilmore, J.H. (1998) 'Welcome to the experience economy', *Harvard Business Review*, 76 (4): 97–105.

Pine, B.J. and Gilmore, J.H. (1999) *The Experience Economy*. Cambridge, MA: Harvard University Press.

Pitchford, S. (2007) *Identity Tourism: Imaging and Imagining the Nation*. Oxford: Elsevier.

Plog, S.C. (1974) 'Why destination areas rise and fall in popularity', *Cornell Hotel and Restaurant Quarterly*, 14 (4): 55–8.

Prentice, R. (2001) 'Experiential cultural tourism: museums and the marketing of the new romanticism of evoked authenticity', *Museum Management and Curatorship*, 19 (1): 5–26.

Proff, C. and Hosie, P. (eds) (2009) *Crisis Management in the Tourism Industry: Beating the Odds?* Aldershot: Ashgate.

Prospect Tours (2009) Online at www.prospecttours.com [accessed 12 January 2009].

Puczkó, L. and Rátz, T. (2002) *The Impacts of Tourism: An Introduction*. Hämeenlinna: Häme Polytechnic.

Quinn, B. (2005) 'Arts festivals and the city', *Urban Studies*, 42 (5/6): 927–44.

Raj, R. and Morpeth, N.D. (eds) (2007) *Religious Tourism and Pilgrimage Management: An International Perspective*. Wallingford: CABI.

Reeve, T. (2003) *The Worldwide Guide to Movie Locations*. London: Titan Books Ltd.

Responsible Travel (2008) Online at www.responsibletravel.com [accessed 14 September 2008].

Richards, G. (1996) *Cultural Tourism in Europe*. Wallingford: CABI.

Richards, G. (2001a) 'The development of cultural tourism in Europe', in G. Richards (ed.), *Cultural Attractions and European Tourism*. Wallingford: CABI. pp. 3–29.

Richards, G. (2001b) 'The experience industry and the creation of attractions', in G. Richards (ed.), *Cultural Attractions and European Tourism*. Wallingford: CABI. pp. 55–69.

Richards, G. (ed.) (2007) *Cultural Tourism: Global and Local Perspectives*. New York: Haworth.

Richards, G. and Wilson, J. (eds) (2004) *The Global Nomad: Backpacker Travel in Theory and Practice.* Clevedon: Channel View.

Richards, G. and Wilson, J. (2006) 'Youth and adventure tourism', in D. Buhalis and C. Costa (eds), *Tourism Business Frontiers.* Oxford: Butterworth-Heinemann. pp. 40–7.

Richards, R. and Wilson, J. (2007) 'The creative turn in regeneration: creative spaces, spectacles and tourism in cities', in M.K. Smith (ed.), *Tourism, Culture and Regeneration.* Wallingford: CABI. pp. 12–24.

Riley, R., Baker, D. and Van Doren, C. (1998) 'Movie induced tourism', *Annals of Tourism Research,* 25 (4): 919–35.

Ritchie, B. (2005) 'Sport tourism – small-scale sport event tourism: the changing dynamics of the New Zealand Masters games', in M. Novelli (ed.), *Niche Tourism: Contemporary Issues, Trends and Cases.* Oxford: Butterworth-Heinemann. pp. 157–70.

Ritchie, B. and Adair, D. (eds) (2004) *Sport Tourism: Interrelationships, Impacts and Issues.* Clevedon: Channel View.

Ritchie, J.R.B. and Crouch, G.I. (2003) *The Competitive Destination.* Wallingford: CABI.

Roberts, L. (ed.) (2001) *Rural Tourism and Recreation: Principles to Practice.* Wallingford: CABI.

Robinson, M. and Andersen, H. (eds) (2004) *Literature and Tourism: Essays in the Reading and Writing of Tourism.* London: Thomson International.

Robinson, T. and Gammon, S. (2004) 'A question of primary and secondary motives: revisiting and applying the sport tourism framework', *Journal of Sport Tourism,* 9 (3): 221–33.

Rogers, T. (2003) *Conferences and Conventions: A Global Industry.* Oxford: Butterworth-Heinemann.

Rojek, C. (1993) *Ways of Escape: Modern Transformations in Leisure and Travel.* London: Macmillan.

Rojek, C. (1997) 'Indexing, dragging and the social construction of tourist sights', in C. Rojek and J. Urry (eds), *Touring Cultures: Transformations of Travel and Theory.* London: Routledge. pp. 52–74.

Rolfe, H. (1992) *Arts Festivals in the UK.* London: Policy Studies Institute.

Ryan, C. (2000) 'Sex tourism: paradigms of confusion', in S. Carter and S. Clift Carter (eds), *Tourism and Sex: Culture, Commerce and Coercion.* London: Cassell. pp. 35–71.

Ryan, C. and Hall, C.M. (2001) *Sex Tourism: Marginal People and Liminalities.* London: Routledge.

Said, E.W. (1978) *Orientalism.* London: Routledge & Kegan Paul.

Samuel, R. (1994) *Theatres of Memory.* London: Verso.

Sanchez Taylor, J. (1998) 'Embodied commodities', in *Embodied Commodities: Sex and Tourism,* Tourism Concern, *In Focus,* 30 (winter): 9–11.

Sanchez Taylor, J. and O'Connell Davidson, J. (1998) 'Doing the hustle', in *Embodied Commodities: Sex and Tourism,* Tourism Concern, *In Focus,* 30 (winter): 7–8, 17.

Sarup, M. (1996) *Identity, Culture and the Postmodern World.* Edinburgh: Edinburgh University Press.

Schneiders, S. (1989) 'Spirituality in the Academy', *Theological Studies,* 50 (4): 676–97.

Schouten, F.F.J. (1995) 'Heritage as historical reality', in D. Herbert (ed.), *Heritage, Tourism and Society.* London: Mansell Publishing. pp. 21–31.

Schultz, P. (2003) *1,000 Places to See Before You Die: A Traveler's Life List*. New York: Workman Publishing Company.

Seaton, A.V. (1996) 'Guided by the dark: from thanatopsis to thanatourism', *International Journal of Heritage Studies*, 2 (4): 234–44.

Selwyn, T. (ed.) (1996) *The Tourist Image: Myths and Myth–making in Tourism*. Chichester: John Wiley & Sons.

Shackley, M. (1996) *Wildlife Tourism*. London: International Thompson Business Press.

Shackley, M. (2004) 'Visitor management', in A. Leask and I. Yeoman (eds), *Heritage Visitor Attractions*, 2nd edn (1st edn, 1999). London: Thomson Learning. pp. 69–82.

Sharpley, R. (ed.) (2002) *The Tourism Business: An Introduction*. Sunderland: Business Education Publishers Ltd.

Shaw, S. (2007) 'Ethnoscapes as cultural attractions in Canadian "world cities"', in M.K. Smith (ed.), *Tourism, Culture and Regeneration*. Wallingford: CABI. pp. 49–58.

Sheller, M. and Urry, J. (2004) *Tourism Mobilities: Places to Play, Places in Play*. London: Routledge.

Shephard, G. and Evans, S. (2005) 'Adventure tourism – hard decisions, soft options and home for tea: adventures on the hoof', in M. Novelli (ed.), *Niche Tourism: Contemporary Issues, Trends and Cases*. Oxford: Butterworth-Heinemann. pp. 201–9.

Slow Food Movement (2008) Available at: www.slowfood.com, [accessed 18 October 2008].

Smith, M.K. (2003) *Issues in Cultural Tourism Studies*. London: Routledge.

Smith, M.K. (2005) 'New leisure tourism: fantasy futures', in D. Buhalis and C. Costa (eds), *New Tourism Consumers, Products and Industry: Present and Future Issues*. Oxford: Butterworth-Heinemann. pp. 220–7.

Smith, M.K. (ed.) (2007) *Tourism, Culture and Regeneration*. Wallingford: CABI.

Smith, M.K. (2009) *Issues in Global Cultural Tourism*. London: Routledge.

Smith, M.K., and Puczkó, L. (2008) *Health and Wellness Tourism*. Oxford: Butterworth-Heinemann.

Smith, M.K. and Robinson, M. (eds) (2006) *Cultural Tourism in a Changing World: Politics, Participation and (Re)presentation*. Clevedon: Channel View.

Smith, S.L.J. (1995) *Tourism Analysis: A Handbook*. 2nd edn (1st edn, 1991). Harlow: Longman.

Smith, V.L. (ed.) (1977/1989) *Hosts and Guests: The Anthropology of Tourism*. Oxford: Blackwell.

Soja, E.W. (2000) *Postmetropolis: Critical Studies of Cities and Regions*. Malden: Blackwell.

Standeven, J. and De Knop, P. (1999) *Sport Tourism*. Champaign, IL: Human Kinetics.

Stone, P.R. (2006) 'A dark tourism spectrum: towards a typology of death and macabre related tourist sites, attractions and exhibitions', *Tourism*, 54 (2): 145–60.

Strange, C. and Kempa, M. (2003) 'Shades of dark tourism: Alcatraz and Robben Island', *Annals of Tourism Research*, 30 (2): 386–405.

Swarbrooke, J. (1999) *Sustainable Tourism Management*. Wallingford: CABI.

Swarbrooke, J. (2000) 'Museums: theme parks of the third millennium?', in M. Robinson, N. Evans, P. Long, R. Sharpley and J. Swarbrooke (eds), *Tourism and Heritage Relationships: Global, National and Local Perspectives*. Sunderland: Business Education Publishers. pp. 417–31.

Swarbrooke, J. and Horner, S. (2001) *Business Travel and Tourism*. Oxford: Butterworth-Heinemann.

Swarbrooke, J., Beard, C., Leckie, S. and Pomfret, G. (2003) *Adventure Tourism: The New Frontier*. Oxford: Butterworth-Heinemann.

Tetley, S. and Bramwell, B. (2002) 'Tourists and the cultural construction of Haworth's literary landscape', in M. Robinson and H.C. Andersen (eds), *Literature and Tourism: Essays in the Reading and Writing of Tourism*. London: Thomson International. pp. 155–70.

TIES (2006) The International Ecotourism Society: Global Ecotourism Factsheet. Online at www.ecotourism.org/webmodules/webarticlesnet/templates/eco_template. aspx?articleid=15andzoneid=2 [accessed 14 November 2008].

Tilden, F. (1977) *Interpreting Our Heritage*. Chapel Hill: University of North Carolina Press.

Tourism Concern online at www.tourismconcern.org.uk [accessed 14 September 2008].

Tourism Queensland (2002) 'Grey tourism (seniors)', www.tq.com.au/fms/tq_corporate/research/fact_sheets/grey_tourism.pdf [accessed 5 March 2009].

Towner, J. (2002) 'Literature, tourism and the Grand Tour', in M. Robinson and H.C. Andersen (eds), *Literature and Tourism: Essays in the Reading and Writing of Tourism*. London: Thomson International. pp. 226–38.

Travel Industry Association of America (2002) Online at: www.tia.org/pubs/GeotourismPhaseFinal.PDF [accessed 15 October 2008].

Tresidder, R. (1999) 'Tourism and sacred landscapes', in D. Crouch (ed.), *Leisure/Tourism Geographies: Practices and Geographical Knowledge*. London: Routledge. pp. 137–48.

Tribe, J. (2005) *The Economics of Recreation, Leisure and Tourism*. 3rd edn (1st edn, 1996). Oxford: Butterworth-Heinemann.

Trilling, L. (1972) *Sincerity and Authenticity*. Oxford: Oxford University Press.

Tunbridge, J.E. and Ashworth, G.J. (1996) *Dissonant Heritage: The Management of the Past as a Resource in Conflict*. London: John Wiley & Sons.

Turner, L. and Ash, J. (1975) *The Golden Hordes*. London: Constable.

Turner, R.K., Pearce, D. and Bateman, I. (1994) *Environmental Economics: An Elementary Introduction*. New York: Harvester Wheatsheaf.

Turner, V. (1969) *The Ritual Process*. Chicago: Aldine.

Turner, V. (1978) *Images and Pilgrimages*. New York: Columbia University Press.

Turner, V. (1987) *The Anthropology of Performance*. New York: PAJ Publications.

Tyrell, B. and Mai, R. (2001) *Leisure 2010 – Experience Tomorrow*. Henley: Jones Lang LaSalle.

UNCED (1992) *Agenda 21, United Nations Conference on Environment and Development – 'The Earth Summit'*. Rio de Janeiro: UNCED.

UNESCO (2006) *Discussion Report of the Planning Meeting for 2008 International Conference on Creative Tourism*, Santa Fe, New Mexico, 25–27 October.

UNESCO (2009) 'Intangible cultural heritage', www.unesco.org/culture/ich/index. php?pg=00002 [accessed 6 February 2009].

United Nations (2002) 'The ageing of the world's population', www.un.org/ageing/popageing.html [accessed 10 February 2009].

UNWCED (1987) *Our Common Future* (Brundtland Report). New York: UNWCED

Urry, J. (1990/2002) *The Tourist Gaze: Leisure and Travel in Contemporary Societies*. London: Sage.

Urry, J. (1995) *Consuming Places*. London: Routledge.

USA Today (2006) 'U.S. business tourism suffers on travel restrictions', www.usatoday. com/travel/news/2006–11–06–report–us–tourism_x.htm [accessed 15 November].

Var, T. and Gunn, C. (eds) (2002) *Tourism Planning: Basics, Concepts, Cases*. London: Routledge.

VisitBritain (2008) 'Visitor attraction trends in England 2007: final report', www. tourismtrade.org.uk/MarketIntelligenceResearch/DomesticTourismStatistics/Visito rAttractions/default.asp [accessed 12 January 2009].

VisitEngland (2004) *The Enjoy England Brand Essence*. London: VisitEngland.

Waitt, G. and Markwell, K. (2006) *Gay Tourism: Culture and Context*. New York: Haworth Press.

Walsh, K. (1992) *The Representation of the Past: Museums and Heritage in the Post-modern World*. London: Routledge.

Walton, J.K. (2000) *The British Seaside: Holidays and Resorts in the Twentieth Century*. Manchester: Manchester University Press.

Wang, N. (1999) 'Rethinking authenticity in tourism experience', *Annals of Tourism Research*, 26 (2): 349–70.

Weaver, D. (2006) *Sustainable Tourism: Theory and Practice*. Oxford: Butterworth-Heinemann.

Weiler, B. and Hall, C.M. (1992) *Special Interest Tourism*. London: Belhaven Press.

Wheeller, B. (1993) 'Sustaining the ego', *Journal of Sustainable Tourism*, 1 (2): 121–9.

Wheeller, B. (1994) 'Egotourism, sustainable tourism and the environment: a symbi-otic, symbolic or shambolic relationship?', in A.V. Seaton (ed.), *Tourism: The State of the Art*. Chichester: John Wiley. pp. 647–54.

Williams, R. (1976) *Keywords*. London: Fontana.

Winter, T. (2002) 'Angkor meets *Tomb Raider*: setting the scene', *International Journal of Heritage Studies*, 8 (4): 323–36.

Wolf, E. (2008) 'Food tourism is on the boil', London: Travelpress, www.airhighways. com/food_tourism.htm [accessed 15 May 2008].

WHO (World Health Organisation) (1948) Online at www.who.int/about/en [accessed 2 November 2008].

WTO (World Tourism Organisation) (2001) Online at www.unwto.org/ethics/back ground/en/background.php?subop=1 [accessed 17 September 2008].

WTO (2004a) *World Tourism Organisation Survey of Destination Management Organisations*. Madrid: UNWTO.

WTO (2004b) 'World Tourism Organisation sustainable development of tourism: concepts and definitions', www.worldtourism.org/frameset/frame_sustainable.html [accessed 16 October 2008].

WTTC (World Travel and Tourism Council) (2008a) 'Tourism satellite accounting', www.wttc.org/eng/Tourism_Research/Tourism_Satellite_Accounting [accessed 15 October 2008].

WTTC (World Travel and Tourism Council) (2008b) 'Simulated satellite accounting research: methodology and documentation', March, www.wttc.org/bin/pdf/ original_pdf_file/2008_methodology.pdf [accessed 15 October 2008].

Xie, P., Osumare, H. and Ibrahim, A. (2007) 'Gazing the hood: hip-hop as tourism attraction', *Tourism Management*, 28 (2): 452–60.

Zeppel, H. (2006) *Indigenous Ecotourism: Sustainable Development and Management*. Wallingford: CABI.

Zeppel, H. and Hall, C.M. (1992) 'Arts and heritage tourism', in B. Weiler and C.M. Hall (eds), *Special Interest Tourism*. London: Belhaven Press. pp. 47–65.

index

index

index

index

207